TOWARD A CIVIL DISCOURSE

Pittsburgh Series in Composition, Literacy, and Culture

David Bartholomae and Jean Ferguson Carr, Editors

TOWARD A CIVIL DISCOURSE

RHETORIC AND FUNDAMENTALISM

SHARON CROWLEY

UNIVERSITY OF PITTSBURGH PRESS

Published by the University of Pittsburgh Press, Pittsburgh PA 15260

Copyright © 2006, University of Pittsburgh Press

Manufactured in the United States of America

Printed on acid-free paper

10 9 8 7 6 5 4 3 2 1

Library of Congress Cataloging-in-Publication Data

Crowley, Sharon, 1943-

   Toward a civil discourse : rhetoric and fundamentalism /
Sharon Crowley.

      p.   cm. — (Pittsburgh series in composition, literacy, and
culture)

   Includes bibliographical references and index.

   ISBN 0-8229-5923-2 (pbk. : alk. paper)

   1. Civil society.   2. Communication—Political aspects.
3. Religion and politics.   I. Title.   II. Series.

   JC337.C76 2006

   320.973014—dc22   2005034015

In Memory of Bryan Collier Short

Without Whom

CONTENTS

PREFACE

While writing this book I was repeatedly reminded of what the postmodern concept of difference actually means in practice. I cannot accept either the principles or the specific teachings of apocalyptist discourse, and the more I study apocalyptism, the more intense becomes my desire not only to dissent from it but to warn others of the ideological dangers it poses to democracy. I raise this point here because my status as an outsider to conservative religious thought brings to the fore the central issues raised in this book: How can outsiders discuss insiders' beliefs with anything like fairness and accuracy? How can believers converse with unbelievers? And finally, is it possible to persuade people who subscribe to intensely resonant belief systems to adopt different positions?

Fundamentalist Christianity is a serious scholarly endeavor—lay believers and ministers study the Bible daily, while seminarians and theologians are steeped in doctrinal and church history. However, fundamentalist scholarship differs greatly in both substance and approach from that practiced in the academy, which term in this context refers to nonfundamentalist universities and colleges. I am indebted in several chapters of this book to masterful studies of American Protestantism and the Christian Right written by scholars in religious studies and the social sciences. But fundamentalist intellectuals regard academic scholarship on religious belief as inaccurate or unfair (Noll). Tim LaHaye, a prolific Christian author, calls scholars who are connected with the academy "secular humanists." Despite his sweeping representation of academic scholarship, however, not all those who work in universities can rightly be called "secular." Some of the scholars cited here in fact profess religious belief, and at least one is a theologian.

I see few ways around the divide erected by conflicting belief systems, short of conversion, for an outsider who would analyze the discourse of believers. As a result I worry that in many places in this book I am simply returning the favor of misrepresentation. One can mitigate the difficulty posed by difference, perhaps, by relying on ethical scholarly standards. Barbara Herrnstein Smith articulates one such set of standards as follows: "accurate citation, representative quotation, nontendentious summary, and forbearance from name-calling and motive-mongering" (*Belief* xix). I tried to adhere to these standards when reading apocalyptist discourse, but frankly I had difficulty with the last requirement, for reasons I outline later. My seeming inability to bridge these intellectual differences is an extremely frustrating state of affairs, because my professional affiliation, as a rhetorician, commits me to finding the available means of persuasion in any given case. I wrote this book in order to determine whether there is any way in to the intellectual, religious, and political differences studied here. I found a few paths, some well worn and others choked with rabbit brush. But paths there are.

ACKNOWLEDGMENTS

I owe much to the rhetorical theorists cited in the text. Thanks in particular to Janet Atwill, Barb Biesecker, and Deb Hawhee for their example and for their scholarship. I also owe much that is not explicit in the text to Victor Villanueva for those conversations about racism that I never could get over, and to Victor Vitanza for showing me what is possible in rhetorical theory. I am indebted as well to the students who participated in a seminar on the rhetoric of liberalism offered long ago at the University of Iowa and to Fred Antczak, who team-taught it with me. Steve Mailloux was once again asked to read a prospectus I had written, and he recklessly recommended to the publishers that they consider it. I am grateful to him and to other, anonymous reviewers of the manuscript for their useful comments. Of course the usual disclaimer applies: none of my factual errors or misguided opinions can be attributed to anyone else.

Nancy Gutierrez negotiated a year's leave of absence from my teaching duties in 2003. Thanks, Nancy. I also thank the editors at the University of Pittsburgh Press for the courteous way in which they do business.

I am indebted, as always, to my sisters, Kay Conway Bridenbaugh and Pat Conway Allen, for their exemplary strength. The composition of this book also owes much to my neighbors, Betty and Marv Ruckman, who are always there when they are needed by the reclusive academic who lives next door. I owe a particular debt to Katherine Heenan and Jan Norton, who read draft after draft of this stuff and offered sobering advice (the only sobriety to be had on some occasions). Michael Stancliff talked me through the early chapters while we were supposed to be working on something else. Katherine, Jan, and Colleen O'Neill gave unstinting support during

Spooky's long last days. Colleen is my best source for how politics are playing out on the ground, as well as a lively participant in phone conversations that imagine the farthest possible reaches of global conspiracy. Thank you all. Margaret Fuller has once again slept through a lengthy process of composition, and as always I am grateful for her substantial presence close by my elbow.

This book is dedicated to the memory of a savvy man and a dear friend who carved out a safe space for invention within the walls of an unimaginative and unforgiving institution. Although Bryan was a critic of presence, he personified it. The space created by his absence can never be filled with quite the same verve and style.

Tilly Warnock once remarked that writers need to let the lawn die. So all writers should be so lucky as to live in the desert. This book was written in the purple shadow of the Superstition Mountains. Arizona is my *topos,* a place where you can invent with the windows open.

1

ON (NOT) ARGUING ABOUT
RELIGION AND POLITICS

In the spring of 2003, during the American invasion of Iraq, my friend Michael attended a peace vigil. As he stood quietly on a street corner with other participants, a young man leaped very close to his face and screamed: "Traitor! Why don't you go to Iraq and suck Saddam's dick?" Michael was taken aback by the vehemence with which the insult was delivered as much as by its indelicacy. Why, he asked, does disagreement make some people so angry?

This is and is not a rhetorical question. That is to say, it is a question about rhetoric, and the question requires an answer. In *A Rhetoric of Motives* Kenneth Burke asserts that "we need never deny the presence of strife, enmity, faction as a characteristic motive of rhetorical expression" (20). But in America we tend to overlook the "presence of strife, envy, faction" in our daily intercourse. "Argument" has a negative valence in ordinary conversation, as when people say "I don't want to argue with you," as though to argue generates discord rather than resolution. In times of crisis Americans are expected to accept national policy without demur. Indeed, to dissent is to risk being thought unpatriotic.

Inability or unwillingness to disagree openly can pose a problem for the maintenance of democracy. Chantal Mouffe points out that "a well-functioning democracy calls for a vibrant clash of democratic political positions. If this is missing there is the danger that this democratic con-

The Boondocks © 2003 Aaron McGruder. Dist. By Universal Press Syndicate. Reprinted with permission. All rights reserved.

frontation will be replaced by a confrontation among other forms of collective identification" (*Democratic* 104). When citizens fear that dissenting opinions cannot be heard, they may lose their desire to participate in democratic practices, or, to put this in terms congenial to Mouffe's analysis, they may replace their allegiance to democracy with other sorts of collective identifications that blur or obscure their responsibilities as citizens.

Something like this seems to have happened in America. Members of a state legislature flee the state's borders in order to avoid voting on a bill that will gerrymander them out of office. Other legislatures are unable to cooperate well enough even to settle on a method of deliberation. Authorized public demonstrations are haunted by the possibility of violence. Media pundits tell us that "the nation" is "polarized." Citizens do not debate issues of public concern with family, friends, or colleagues for fear relationships will be irreparably strained in the process. Joan Didion suspects that we refrain from discussing current events because "so few of us are willing to see our evenings turn toxic" (23). Didion writes that some issues, such as America's relations with Israel, are seen as "unraisable, potentially lethal, the conversational equivalent of an unclaimed bag on a bus. We take cover. We wait for the entire subject to be defused, safely insulated behind baffles of invective and counterinvective. Many opinions are expressed. Few are allowed to develop. Even fewer change" (24). Clearly this state of affairs threatens the practice of democracy, which requires at minimum a discursive climate in which dissenting positions can be heard.

Discussion of civic issues stalls repeatedly at this moment in American history because it takes place in a discursive climate dominated by two powerful discourses: liberalism and Christian fundamentalism.[1] These two discourses paint very different pictures of America and of its citizens' responsibilities toward their country. Liberalism is the default discourse of American politics because the country's founding documents, and hence its system of jurisprudence, are saturated with liberal values. The vocabulary of liberalism includes commonplaces concerning individual rights, equality before the law, and personal freedom. Because of its emphasis on the last-named value, liberalism has little or nothing to say about beliefs or practices deemed to reside outside of the so-called public sphere. Indeed, in the last fifty years American courts have imagined a "zone of privacy" within which citizens may conduct themselves however they wish, within certain limits (Gorney 135–39). Fundamentalist Christians, on the other hand, aim to "restore" biblical values to the center of American life and politics. If they have their way, Americans will conduct themselves, publicly and privately, according to a set of beliefs derived from a fundamentalist reading of the Judeo-Christian religious tradition. One might say, then, that the central point of contention between adherents of these discourses involves the place of religious and moral values in civic affairs: should such convictions be set aside when matters of state policy are discussed, or should these values actually govern the discussion?

Because most Americans subscribe at the very least to the liberal value of individual freedom, the increasing popularity and influence of Christian fundamentalist belief has created debate, often acrimonious, on many issues of current public concern: abortion rights, prayer in school, same-sex unions, and censorship, as well as more explicitly political practices such as taxation, the appointment of judges, and the conduct of foreign policy. And even though the variety of fundamentalist Christianity I will here call "apocalyptist" is professed by a minority of religious believers in America, its adherents' vocabulary and positions have indeed begun to influence policy developed in civic spheres (see chapter 5). Furthermore, terms and beliefs invented within this discourse ("family values," "partial-birth abortion," "judicial activism") have entered common parlance—the discursive realm from which rhetorical premises are drawn.

I forward the ancient art of rhetoric as a possible anodyne to this situation, in the hope that rhetorical invention may be able to negotiate the deliberative impasse that seems to have locked American public discourse into repetition and vituperation. I hope to demonstrate that the tactics typically used in liberal argument—empirically based reason and factual evidence—are not highly valued by Christian apocalyptists, who rely instead on revelation, faith, and biblical interpretation to ground claims. We thus need a more comprehensive approach to argument if Americans are to engage in civil civic discussion. Rhetorical argumentation, I believe, is superior to the theory of argument inherent in liberalism because rhetoric does not depend solely on appeals to reason and evidence for its persuasive efficacy. Since antiquity rhetorical theorists have understood the centrality of desires and values to the maintenance of beliefs. Hence rhetorical invention is better positioned than liberal means of argument to intervene successfully in disagreements where the primary motivation of adherents is moral or passionate commitment. Susan Jacoby provides a compelling description of the role played by passion in the maintenance of belief and of the difference it makes in terms of persuasiveness: "In August 2003, when federal courts ordered the removal of a hefty Ten Commandments monument from the Alabama State Supreme Court building, thousands of Christian demonstrators converged on Montgomery. . . . They were not only outraged but visibly grief-stricken when the monument was moved out of sight. It was, one demonstrator said with tears in his eyes, like a death in the family. Secularist civil libertarians who had brought the lawsuit, by contrast, spoke in measured objective tones about the importance of the First Amendment's separation of church and state" (364). I hope to establish that deeply held beliefs are so tightly bound up with the very bodies of believers that liberals' relatively bloodless and cerebral approach to argument is simply not persuasive to people who do not accept liberalism or whose commitment to liberalism is less important to them than are other sorts of convictions.

I need to say up front, however, that rhetoric is not a magic bullet. A rhetorician can make no promises when it comes to changing minds, particularly those of people who are invested in densely articulated belief systems. Usually people invest in such a system because it is all they know, or because their friends, family, and important authority figures are similarly invested, or because their identity is in some respects constructed by the beliefs inherent in the system. Rejection of such a belief system ordinarily requires rejection of community and reconstruction of one's identity as well. Hence the claim I make in this book for the efficacy of rhetoric is limited: it will work better in the present climate than liberal argumentation because it offers a more comprehensive range of appeals, many of which are considered inappropriate in liberal thought. In order to be of use in a postmodern setting, however, the conceptual vocabulary of rhetoric must be rethought. If this can be accomplished, rhetoric can become a productive means of working through issues that concern citizens.

American Liberalism and the Second Coming

Mouffe and Ernst Laclau define hegemony as "the achievement of a moral, intellectual and political leadership through the expansion of a discourse that partially fixes meaning around nodal points. Hegemony . . . involves the expansion of a particular discourse of norms, values, views and perceptions through persuasive redescriptions of the world" (qtd. in Torfing 302).[2] A discourse that achieves hegemony in a given community is so pervasive there that its descriptions of the world become thoroughly naturalized. Furthermore, its conceptual vocabulary literally "goes without saying"—that is, its major terms are seldom subjected to criticism. Liberalism has enjoyed hegemonic status in American discourse since the early nineteenth century. Apocalyptism has an even longer history in America, but it has never achieved the hegemonic status enjoyed by liberalism or by mainstream Christianity, for that matter. I will argue that at this moment in history, however, a version of Christian fundamentalism, driven by apocalyptism, is in hegemonic contention with liberalism because it motivates the political activism of the Christian Right. The considerable political and ideological successes of this faction have rendered the terms and conjectures of liberalism available for examination and possible redescription. In democracies a serious challenge to a hegemonic discourse is likely to create uneasiness and rancor because ownership of the master terms of political discourse, and hence of political and cultural power, is at stake.

Liberalism emerged as a set of political beliefs and practices in company with capitalism during the seventeenth and eighteenth centuries.[3] According to Anthony Arblaster, the fundamental values of political liberalism are freedom, tolerance, privacy, reason, and the rule of law (55). In an American context equality should be added to this list. There are many varieties of liberalism, among them the classical liberalism of Mary Wollstonecraft; the utilitarian liberalism of John Stuart Mill; the welfare-state liberalism of Franklin Roosevelt; and the contemporary merger of liberalism with free-market capitalism in the ideology called "neoliberalism," exemplified by the centrist politics of Bill Clinton (Lind). Welfare-state liberalism is no longer influential in American politics; Senator Ted Kennedy, who supports subsidized health care for all Americans, is a lonely avatar on the national level. Nonetheless, surveys establish that most Americans still support welfare-state liberal programs such as Social Security and Medicare. More important from a rhetorician's point of view, America's founding documents are saturated with liberal principles. Hence children and adults who apply for citizenship are exposed to liberal beliefs while becoming acquainted with America's civic lore. Not the least notable assertion in that lore is that "all [citizens] are created equal." The necessity of placing brackets in this famous line points up the fact that exclusions were endemic to Enlightenment liberalism. Despite this, the liberal values of equality and liberty are the most inclusive political values ever incorporated into a polity, and they have been used repeatedly since the nation's founding to extend civic and civil rights to previously excluded groups (Condit and Lucaites). Liberal beliefs permeate our judicial system, as well as our daily talk about "freedom," "equality," "privacy," and "rights." That is to say, bits and pieces of liberal ideology still circulate widely in public discourse in the form of commonplaces, and it is on the level of common sense that liberalism (still?) enjoys hegemonic status.

I am aware of course that liberalism is ordinarily contrasted to conservatism. However, nonreligious conservatism is a minority discourse in America, as is illustrated by the cases of neoconservatism and libertarianism. Our national politics has moved to the right since the 1970s because of a powerful alliance forged during that decade between conservative political activists and apocalyptist Christians (Diamond, *Spiritual* 56–60). The social agenda that motivates the religious Right is of little interest to economic conservatives, but their acquiescence to it was required in order to amalgamate a voter base that was sufficiently extensive to elect conservatives to office. While this collaboration has not been entirely free of ideological strife, it has achieved astonishing results in elections at all levels. Moreover, some of its slogans and typical patterns of thought have now become commonplace. An example can be found in the morphing of the term *liberal* itself; the term used to refer to someone who espoused welfare-state political positions and/or who believed that moral and social behavior was a matter for individuals to decide. But *liberal* can now be wielded as a term of opprobrium, meaning something like "free-thinking, immoral elitist."

Like liberalism, Christianity is a hegemonic discourse in America, as is demonstrated by the fact that it is difficult for non-Christians to remain unaware of Christian belief and practice. Church bells ring in nearly every American neighborhood on Sunday mornings, and during periods of Christian celebration, such as Christmas and Easter, every mall and many homes are decked out with images and symbols evoking these commemorations. In a study undertaken in 2001 more than three-quarters of the Americans surveyed identified themselves as Christians.[4] Of course there are many varieties of Christian belief. In America most Christians are Protestants, although a significant minority (25 percent) of those who identify themselves as Christian are Roman Catholic. The variety of Christian belief in which I am interested here typically flourishes among conservative Protestants called "evangelicals" or "fundamentalists," although apocalyptist beliefs may be held by mainstream Protestants and Roman Catholics as well.[5] As we shall see, scholars and pundits do not agree about how many people can accurately be called "conservative Christians." Here I accept Christian Smith's careful estimate: about 29 percent of the American population so identify themselves (*Christian* 16). Here the term *apocalyptism* signifies belief in a literal Second Coming of Jesus Christ, an event that is to be accompanied by the ascent of those who are saved into heaven.[6] Apocalyptists believe that this ascent, called the "Rapture," will occur either prior to or during the tribulation, a period of worldwide devastation and suffering. Finally, at the last judgment, evil will be overcome and unbelievers will be condemned to eternal punishment. I argue that this theological scenario founds a political ideology, a set of political beliefs subscribed to by millions of Americans who may or may not accept as literal truth the end-time prophecies announced in the Christian Bible. Domestically this politics favors the infusion of biblical values into American law and maintenance of the patriarchal nuclear family. Its foreign policy is aggressively nationalist.

The phrase "liberal Christian" is not an oxymoron. Many of America's founders were practicing Christians, and yet they based the Constitution of the United States on the Enlightenment principle of natural human rights. In his study of America in the early nineteenth century Alexis de Toqueville claimed that Christianity actually reinforced the liberal values that inform America's founding documents, noting that Christianity held "the greatest power over men's souls, and nothing better demonstrates how useful and natural it is to man, since the country where it now has widest sway is both the most enlightened and freest" (1: 290–91). However, Randall Balmer argues, against de Toqueville, that there is no "mystical connection" between religion and politics in America. In his opinion the disestablishment clause of the First Amendment, barring the institution of a state religion, has in fact insured maintenance of political stability. Balmer writes that a "cornucopia of religious options" has "contributed to America's political stability by providing an alternative to political dissent" (*Blessed* 39). In other words, potent beliefs that could threaten liberal democracy regularly drain off into religious enthusiasm. Balmer's example is the emergence of the Jesus movement out of the political turbulence of the 1960s.

The relation of apocalyptism to conservative Christian political activism is complex. On its face apocalyptism would seem to obviate an interest in politics. Someone who believes that she is at any moment about to be snatched up into heaven is unlikely to be interested in earthly matters. Charles Strozier remarks, for example, that "democracy is not well grounded in the lives of . . . Americans . . . who believe in the Rapture" (120). Nevertheless, public figures who are associated with Christian political activism, such as Pat Robertson and Jerry Falwell, do hold apocalyptist beliefs, and apparently they do not find it difficult to reconcile the two. Such reconciliation became easier during the 1980s, when interpreters of biblical prophecy modified the apocalyptic narrative in order to suggest that political involvement was necessary in order to hasten the advent of the end time (see chapter 4). Nor does subscription to conservative Christian beliefs necessarily entail either conservative politics or political activism. Based on his survey of evangelical opinion, Christian Smith concludes:

Evangelicals are often stereotyped as imperious, intolerant, fanatical meddlers. Certainly there are some evangelicals who exemplify this stereotype. But the vast majority, when listened to on their own terms, prove to hold a civil, tolerant, and noncoercive view of the world around them. . . . The strategies for influence of evangelical political activists and those of ordinary evangelicals are obviously worlds apart. The former can be alarmist, pretentious, and exclusivist. The latter emphasize love, respect, mutual dialogue, taking responsibility for oneself, aversion to force and confrontation, voluntaristic ground rules of engagement, and tolerance for a diversity of views. Clearly, many of the evangelical political activists who are in the public spotlight do not accurately represent the views and intentions of their supposed constituency. (The fact that they are largely self-appointed, not elected, with little accountability to the grassroots majority may help to explain this.) Yet many outsiders make little distinction between the two, and the masses of ordinary evangelicals around the country remain misunderstood, their views thought of as no different from those of Randall Terry, James Kennedy, Pat Buchanan, and other evangelical leaders of similar persuasion. (*Christian* 48)

In fact some fundamentalist Christians still adhere to the policy of withdrawal from worldly matters that was widely adopted after the Scopes trial in 1925 (Carpenter). Nancy Ammerman points out that prior to the 1980s "pastoring churches and establishing schools had long been the more likely strategies of people who called themselves fundamentalists. Not all saw politics and social change as their mission, and many had discounted such activities as useless, even counterproductive" ("North American" 1). Ammerman also notes that "the name 'fundamentalist' is not necessarily synonymous with 'conservative,' because it is possible to accept fundamentalist Christian beliefs, such as the Virgin Birth or the Resurrection, while seeking naturalistic rather than supernatural explanations for them" ("North American" 2). Some fundamentalist and evangelical Christians in fact hold liberal political beliefs. Spokespersons for this position, such as those who write for Sojourners.com, regularly express dismay about the agenda and tactics of the Christian Right. In addition, subscription to the political agenda forwarded by the Christian Right can be justified on nontheological grounds. That is to say, conservative Christian voters who support this agenda may do so for reasons that have little direct correlation with apocalyptism: they may wish to protect their families from what they see as a decline in moral values, for example.

Despite this long list of qualifications, it remains true, as Sara Diamond points out, that "the evangelical subculture . . . is like a big ocean in which the Christian Right's activist fish swim—and spawn" (*Not by Politics* 11). Diamond, who has studied the Christian Right since its origin during the 1970s, claims that apocalyptism is one of the "ideas" by means of which the movement "sustains its fervor" (*Not by Politics* 197). That is to say, apocalyptism does ideological work by offering intellectual sustenance to political activists. I will argue that apocalyptism does more than this: it actually connects political activity to Christian duty. The apocalyptic flavor of dominion theology—the belief that Christians can hasten the Second Coming by creating a Christian kingdom here on earth—motivates Christian activists to convert unbelievers (Detwiler 105–11). But it also motivates them to alter the ideological underpinnings of American democracy, and for a radical few, apocalyptism rationalizes a desire to overturn the U.S. Constitution and its associated body of law as well. Concerned Women for America, a Christian organization that claims to have over five hundred thousand members, states its mission as follows: "to protect and promote Biblical values among all citizens—first through prayer, then education, and finally by influencing our society—thereby reversing the decline in moral values in our nation" (http://cwfa.org). The desire to convert all citizens to "biblical values" could hardly be made more explicit. Beverly LaHaye, the founder and former chair of this organization, is an apocalyptist. Her group's determination to "influence society" and "reverse the decline in moral values" is a direct challenge to liberalism and, arguably, to liberal democracy itself. Frederick Clarkson writes that "such views are the rule, rather than the exception in Christian Right circles. Patricia Hoffman, who is a leader of both the Christian Coalition and Concerned Women for America . . . has written that 'separation of church and state is a bogus phrase. Our country was founded on Biblical principles and we need to turn back to God and His precepts'" (17). And a small group of Christian intellectuals—called reconstructionists—has articulated an explicit plan for replacing liberal democracy with theocracy (Clarkson; Martin). They hope to pave the way for this possibility by the pursuit of theonomy, the replacement of American law with biblical law. George W. Bush's proposal in 2004 to add an amendment to the Constitution forbidding same-sex marriage is an example of the will to theonomize, however cynical its politics. Apocalyptism rationalizes all of these desires by reassuring Christian activists that their work will be rewarded when they are raptured. Their assurance that dissenters will suffer horribly during the tribulation may be equally attractive to believers.

In his study of "Christian anti-liberalism" Jason Bivins claims that "self-consciously Christian protests" against the state's perceived "lack of moral authority have been proliferating since the 1960s" (2). Bivins defines "political religion" as "action conducted in political spaces or contexts for explicitly religious reasons" (6). In his view liberalism presents several difficulties to politically committed Christians insofar as it "is associated with representative democracy, has tended to privilege individual over collective rights, favors negative liberty (freedom from coercion) over positive liberty (freedom to participate in politics in active, constructive ways), and seeks to protect moral and religious pluralism by separating public from private realms of society, keeping the public free from contentious moral or religious beliefs that are regarded as threats to political stability. . . . By divesting public life of moral and religious participation, liberal political order in the United States lacks a moral orientation" (3).

The category "Christian anti-liberal" includes Catholic activists Daniel and Phillip Berrigan, whose pacifist agenda must be anathema to apocalyptists. Nonetheless, conservative Christian activists take up all of the specific complaints against liberalism listed by Bivins. One of these is liberalism's elevation of individual rights over the good of the group. "Family values" is of course an important commonplace within the preferred politics of conservative Christianity, and this "focus on the family," to borrow a phrase from James Dobson, posits a superior moral status for the nuclear family.

The hierarchical privilege awarded to the family trumps any individual rights to which husbands, wives, or children might lay claim. Adherents to this ideology are antifeminist, and they reject as well legal and social practices they define as endorsing the rights of individuals over those of the family unit—divorce, sex education, and abortion, for example. Another complaint against liberalism centers on its negative view of liberty. Tim LaHaye, husband of Beverly LaHaye and coauthor of the popular *Left Behind* novels about the end time, claims that freedom from coercion by church or state produces citizens who are committed to nothing but the pursuit of their own happiness (LaHaye, *Battle;* LaHaye and Noebel, *Mind Siege*). And Christian reconstructionists argue that positive liberty can only be achieved through acknowledgment of the primacy of God's will (Barkun, *Religion* 200–209). A third complaint involves the liberal distinction between public and private spheres, which confines religious belief and practice to the latter realm. This distinction frustrates citizens who wish to participate in politics for religious reasons or to lend a religious cast to public proceedings or venues. Resistance to the distinction emerges in arguments over prayer in school or display of the Ten Commandments in civic settings.

I realize that my concern about esoteric theological matters may seem overblown and that I may seem to overestimate the power and abilities of a small group of intellectuals and a somewhat larger group of activists who are committed to an ideology that seems bizarre when measured by the standards of secular politics. However, the Christian Right is currently packing the judiciary and legislative bodies at all levels with like-minded believers in an effort to establish God's kingdom on earth, an eventuality that some among them believe will hasten the advent of the apocalypse. Since the 1970s religiously conservative Christians have mobilized at the grassroots, often working through established churches in order to elect politicians who are sympathetic to their positions on family values and other social issues. Their work has achieved stunning results. In 1994 conservative Christians awarded the Republican party a majority in Congress for the first time in many years. In 2000 Republicans gained the presidency and held majorities in both houses of Congress as well, something that had not happened since 1952. Kevin Phillips estimates that in the 2000 election "roughly 55 percent of the people who voted for George W. Bush were Armageddon believers" (242). ("Armageddon" refers to the prophesied battle between Christ and Antichrist that is to occur on the plain of Megiddo during the end time.) Phillips wonders if Bush's support among apocalyptists was as pervasive as it seemed: "could 75 to 80 percent of the believers in Armageddon have voted for Bush? So it appears" (242). Phillips's conjecture seems confirmed by the election of 2004, in which Bush won 79 percent of the evangelical vote.[7] Once again, not all evangelicals are apocalyptists. But even allowing for this distinction, it seems that activists who believe in the imminence of the end time can exert considerable political muscle.

The Ethics of Fundamentalisms

Hegemonic discourses construct and inform community experience to such an extent that their assumptions seem natural, "just the way things are." The very inarticulateness of hegemonic belief is a source of its power. In *What's the Matter with Kansas?* Thomas Franks argues that belief in capitalism runs so deep among populist conservatives that they literally cannot see how it damages their lives. Franks's representative Kansans blame "the government" or "liberals" for falling wages and rising prices, all the while electing politicians who regularly betray their economic interests in favor of policies favored by corporations and wealthy citizens. One such citizen is Rupert Murdoch, whose Fox entertainment empire dispenses the news programs that conservatives watch, as well as the quasi-pornographic entertainment that the Christians among them claim is offensive. Contradictions like this are apparent to unbelievers like Franks, who can subject them to criticism because he is no longer informed by the ideologies that give rise to them. But believers have little incentive to examine their beliefs unless they encounter critical discourse that they can both hear and grasp. Indeed, adherents' response to criticism indicates the degree to which the belief systems to which they subscribe can be characterized as fundamentalist.

William Connolly defines fundamentalism as "a general imperative to assert an absolute, singular ground of authority; to ground your own identity and allegiances in this unquestionable source; to define political issues in a vocabulary of God, morality, or nature that invokes such a certain, authoritative source" in which believers ground their "identity and allegiances" (*Ethos* 105). Connolly points out that any belief system, including liberalism, can be adhered to with fundamentalist intensity. This can occur when the fundamental ideals motivating a system of beliefs (God, nature, reason) are protected by "a set of political strategies" that define "every carrier of critique or destabilization as an enemy marked by exactly those defects, weaknesses, corruption and naivetes" that believers feel they are "under an absolute imperative to eliminate" (*Ethos* 105–6). In other words, fundamentalist adherents of ideologies project vices defined by their preferred system of belief onto those who adhere to other systems. True believers in American super-patriotism, for example, characterize dissenters as traitors to the ideals they value most: nationalism and capitalism.[8] Hence the aptness of McGruder's cartoon: dissenters are "French-lovin' commie scum."

Fundamentalism is of course a kind of foundationalism. By pointing this out I do not mean to resurrect the foundationalist/antifoundationalist argument that troubled scholars in many disciplines during the 1980s (Fish, *Doing*). But I do not want to lose sight of an important point that was made during that debate. Ideological foundations are exclusive only if they are taken to be noncontingent—that is, if they are taken to apply noncontextually or universally. This holds no matter whether foundations are called "transcendental signifieds" (Jacques Derrida), a "metaphysical dream" (Richard Weaver), "rational man" (the Enlightenment), or "first principles" (Aristotle). Theoretically every belief system depends from some principles, values, experiences, desires, or habits of knowing. To that extent every belief system is foundational, and hence antifoundationalism is not coherent unless it is read as a critique of belief systems that posit universal or noncontingent foundations.

Elizabeth Minnich argues that belief systems that take a given starting point as universal must also assume that any being whose subjectivity is not legitimated by that starting point is of secondary or lesser worth. In patriarchy, for example, the identification of subjectivity with masculinity effectively marginalizes women. When a metaphysics informs a politics, those who are marginalized by its foundational ideal or ideals can be constructed by policy as invisible or worse, as worthy of subjugation and defeat (58–59). Minnich treats antifoundationalism as a rational position, but I think it is, finally, an ethical preference. Those who espouse it obviously value contingency and inclusion over certainty and exclusion.[9] And anyone who wants to mount an offense against a fundamentalism must do so by evaluating the status and treatment of its ideals within the system of beliefs those ideals create and validate. To attack a fundamentalism on the ground that it is not rational is to apply a standard that is valued in some belief systems and not in others; to treat rationality as universally binding is, willy-nilly, to fall into yet another fundamentalism. In the present intellectual climate, informed as it is by scientific and liberal rationalisms, it is unfashionable to argue that the maintenance of belief depends upon evaluation. But as a rhetorician I am not loathe to argue from value.

When foundations are held to be primary, noncontingent, and nonnegotiable, then systems of belief stemming from them become fundamentalisms. All ideologies are held by their subscribers to be preferable to the available alternatives—there is not much point in being a liberal if you don't think that freedom and equality are better values than whatever else is out there. Environmentalism remains a foundationalism even when its central ideal—preservation of Earth's natural systems, say—is taken to trump all other ideals (freedom to travel how and where one likes, for instance). For environmentalist belief to become fundamentalist, preservation of Earth's systems must be treated as preferable everywhere and for all time. A fundamentalist environmentalist might argue, for example, that Earth's systems were in pristine condition prior to the evolution of humankind and that we should therefore strive to return the planet as close to that condition as possible (even in this outlandish example fundamentalism becomes a warrant for mass extinctions). But in any fundamentalism an ideal or ideals must also be considered nonnegotiable. This returns us to Connolly's definition: defenders of fundamentalisms do not evaluate the ideals that drive them; were they to do so, they would risk discovering incoherence and other flaws. Rather, they invest their energy in protecting those ideals from assault by unbelievers. In the present political context, then, the term *fundamentalist* delineates a particular strategy (and tone) that permeates defenses of political and religious belief systems: a desire to preserve one's own founding beliefs from threat at any cost. Typically this is accomplished either by rendering opposing claims unworthy of consideration and/or by excoriating the character of people who disagree with one's founding claims. Fundamentalist liberals tend to employ the first option, while fundamentalist conservatives tend to take the second route—although both groups can, and do, resort to either tactic.[10]

The Goals and Strategies of Christian Fundamentalism and Liberalism

The minimal religious goal of Christian fundamentalism is the achievement of personal salvation. Apocalyptist Christians who believe that salvation can result from human effort also accept the conversion of unbelievers as a moral and sacred duty, and those who are politically inclined want to bring American legal and political practices into line with their religious beliefs. And as I note above, radically conservative Christians accept and proselytize theonomy—the belief that biblical law should become the law of the land. As Connolly's analysis suggests, apocalyptists depict those who dissent from these programs as opponents. In more extreme versions of this ideology dissenters are characterized as evil.

Today few rhetors speaking for the political Right will openly admit that exclusivity drives conservative ideology just as surely as it marks right-ist political practice. A cleavage between "us" and "them" motivates con-temporary conservative rhetoric, a cleavage starkly articulated in Chris-tian fundamentalism as an absolute difference between the saved and the unsaved. This difference is meant literally within fundamentalism, but it circulates as a figure in conservative discourse where, it must be admitted, much more is made of postulated differences between men and women, whites and blacks, straights and gays, than in other contemporary politi-cal discourses. Contemporary Christian rightist discourse relies upon and fosters a hypersensitivity to the hierarchic dichotomies it characterizes as absolute, and its more extreme varieties pose significant danger to those whom it caricatures as inhabiting the reductive identities it assigns, such as "Jew" or "homosexual" (Barkun, *Religion;* Cohn, *Warrant;* Herman). Many rightists now speak and write as though they accept a firmly marked dichotomy between good and evil, although they may be ignorant of the apocalyptic cosmology from which the distinction derives. For example, the title of a book by conservative commentator Sean Hannity is *Deliver Us from Evil: Defeating Terrorism, Despotism, and Liberalism,* as though each of these practices were equivalent to the others, and as though all were evil.

For their part liberals want to preserve the brand of liberal democracy developed in America during the Enlightenment. They hope to achieve this by creating consensus about contested issues, and they forward reason and tolerance as means of securing agreement. The elevation of empiri-cally based reason as a preferred source of argumentative premises deval-ues appeals to tradition, authority, or desire, exactly as was intended by early liberal thinkers who were anxious to end the epistemological domi-nance of religious belief. Bruce Lincoln notes that Enlightenment thinkers "struggled to replace a well-established regime of truth with one of their own creation, whose methods, standards of expertise, problematics, au-thority structures, and institutional centers were still emergent. The older hegemon has 'faith' and 'revelation' as its epistemological watchwords, theology and doctrine as its prime discourse, orthodoxy and salvation as its goals, the church as its chief institution. Against this, the philosophes made 'reason' their rallying slogan and 'enlightenment' their goal, while polemically redescribing their adversaries' concerns as 'idle superstition'" (57). When liberals tout their version of reason as the only authentic source of argument, clearly they face the ethical risk of excluding the arguments of those who prefer to legitimate claims in other ways.

Liberals sometimes feel that religious fundamentalists are intolerant because the latter refuse to adopt their preferred, rational approach to negotiation and adjudication of disagreements. But liberals can be equally intolerant when they refuse to negotiate their demand that argument be rational in their sense of that term (see chapter 2). And while tolerance ordinarily restrains liberals from characterizing those who oppose them as enemies, their acceptance of reason as a primary mode of argument nonetheless devalues any appeal to divine authority. Hence liberal argumentative strategy discounts the very grounds from which Christian fundamentalists mount claims and proofs. Christian fundamentalists are irritated in turn not only by rejection of their primary authority but by liberals' refusal to prioritize arguments according to their quality, or, more precisely, to measure the worth of arguments against a standard. They are of course aware that liberal values saturate American political and judicial discourse, and their experience with the legal system has repeatedly demonstrated that the values they are asked to adopt while deliberating public issues are part and parcel of the very ideology they reject. Stanley Fish discusses a lawsuit brought by born-again Christians against a public school reading program, the aims of which were to expose children to a variety of points of view. Fish notes: "It was the contention of Mrs. Frost and the other parents who joined in her suit that the free-exercise rights of their children were infringed when they were required to study views that contradicted and undermined their most cherished convictions" (*Trouble* 156). In other words, these parents resisted the liberal desire to instill tolerance in children. Ironically they based this claim on an appeal to yet another liberal principle—the free exercise of religion enshrined in the First Amendment. The case was decided against them, according to Fish, because the judges involved failed "to understand . . . that the distinction between exposure and indoctrination is an artifact of the very liberalism Vicki Frost rejects" (*Trouble* 157). For the petitioners seeing is believing; if children are "exposed" to non-Christian values, their beliefs will perforce be contaminated by those values.[11] In this case, then, the petitioners appealed to a principled intolerance of difference, a value that is not easily grasped within commonsense liberalism, where tolerance is often thought of as "the way things are."

Clearly the preferred argumentative strategies, as well as the ultimate goals, of liberalism and apocalyptism are wildly incompatible. Would-be theonomists or theocrats cannot possibly succeed in realizing their goals without severely altering the American Constitution and its attendant body of law. Like liberals, I too wish to preserve democracy, and hence I am not in sympathy with the goals of a theology-driven fundamentalism whose proponents desire to abrogate religious and other freedoms embedded in the Constitution. Despite its failings, liberalism may be the best politics we are likely to get in the near term. The liberal values of freedom and equality are responsible, historically, for the inclusion of groups whose members were once not admitted to citizenship. In my opinion liberalism is superior to other currently available political discourses that legitimate exclusion by means of rigidly policed hierarchical dichotomies, if only because history shows that liberalism allows rectification of its typical exclusions. However, this should not stop us from trying to adapt liberalism toward a political model that enables disagreement without necessarily incurring incivility, intimidation, or violence.

The Blurring of Public and Private Domains

In *The Politics* Aristotle claims that in a democracy the relations obtaining among members of an *oikos,* or household, are dictated by nature (I.2). The Greek *oikos* was constituted by a citizen's family, slaves, and estates. In Aristotle's Athens, that most misogynist of cultures, women were quite literally confined within the relative privacy of the household. Slaves, that is, those who were deemed unable to "foresee things needed" and who were thus considered unfit to rule, were also deemed "by nature" to belong within that sphere (I.2; Neel). According to Hannah Arendt, ancient Greek thinkers argued that the *oikos* was quite different from the *polis* insofar as nature dictated establishment of the former; specifically nature decreed that humans band together in common shelters for protection, nutrition, and communion. Hence true freedom could be had only through participation in the affairs of the *polis,* which "knew only equals, whereas the household was the center of the strictest inequality. To be free meant both not to be subject to the necessity of life or the command of another *and* not to be in command oneself. It meant neither to rule nor to be ruled" (Arendt 30).

In *On Rhetoric* Aristotle delineates three sorts of issues that are appropriate for consideration by citizens acting within a democratic *polis*: what the community should do (deliberative rhetoric), what has been done in the past (judicial or forensic rhetoric), and what actions deserve communal praise or blame (epideictic rhetoric) (I.3.1358a–b). Some issues raised in the deliberative arenas delineated by Aristotle are economic in the modern sense insofar as they concern the allocation of revenues to acts such as making war (I.4.1359b). But the deliberative discussions carried on by citizens were not confined to economic questions alone. They also reflected on issues having to do with maintenance of the community—as Aristotle puts it, citizens deliberate about "war and peace, national defense, imports and exports, and the framing of laws" (*Rhetoric* I.4.1359b).

In the modern period the ancient distinction between public and private was reinscribed to locate deliberation about the economy—as newly defined by capitalism—wholly within the so-called public sphere.[12] Eighteenth-century liberal accounts of the public/private distinction retained Aristotle's gender politics but rewrote the class of slaves so that it included those whose labor produced profit without their achieving access to capital—that is, workers. Issues concerning capitalists were available for public discussion, but issues that interested women, slaves, and the poor were excluded from civic arenas by the operative definition of "citizen" as "white male property owner." And in another departure from classical political thought, a second liberal gesture relocated epideictic—argument about values—within the purview of private individuals, effectively rendering ethical discourse off-limits to civic discussion (see chapter 2). Today disagreements about values reach an impasse in part because liberals consider values to be private matters. Hence they are reluctant to discuss moral issues in civic settings, preferring to debate only those issues that are supposedly amenable to reason and that are thus, by definition, suitable for public discussion. Conservative Christian activists, on the other hand, unabashedly appeal to moral and religious values no matter the site in which their arguments are made.

Aristotle configured the *agora*, the site where citizens assembled to discuss issues, as the sole civic arena. Liberalism has followed suit by imagining that civic debate occurs in institutions sponsored by the state—legislatures and courtrooms—and in the press. But civic debate has always occurred elsewhere—around hearths and kitchen tables, for example. And in recent years issues formerly considered to be private—such as the appropriate configuration of families—have emerged as topics suitable for discussion by legislators and judges, thanks to the political efforts of the Christian Right (Berlant). In other words, the liberal distinction between public and private is difficult to maintain (Warner, *Publics*). In this book, then, the term *civic arenas* is meant to include dinner tables, street corners, break rooms, classrooms, church basements, pubs, women's clinics, dentists' offices—wherever people debate issues of state policy and civic conduct.

Toward Political Agonism

Chantal Mouffe asserts that democracy must be preserved despite the failings of liberalism. Even as she credits liberalism as the belief system that made modern European and American democracies possible, she is concerned that its goal of consensus is both unrealizable and dangerous˙ to the preservation of democratic practices. Mouffe points out that this goal actually reduces or hides altogether the realm she calls "the political": "To envisage politics as a rational process of negotiation among individuals is to obliterate the whole dimension of power and antagonism . . . and thereby completely miss its nature. It is also to neglect the predominant role of passions as moving forces of human conduct. Furthermore, in the field of politics, it is groups and collective identities that we encounter, not isolated individuals, and its dynamics cannot be apprehended by reducing it to individual calculations" (*Return* 140). That is to say, the political is about power: its acquisition, generation, and maintenance. Because of this we must not discount the role played by desire and other passionate commitments in political activity. In this arena powerful individuals do emerge and act, but their actions are governed by beliefs and desires that are communal, that are generated by and within the political.

The political is not the same thing as politics, which Mouffe defines as "the attempt to domesticate the political, to keep at bay the forces of destruction and to establish order" (*Return* 141). Politics has to do with making decisions that entail choices between two or more possibilities, decisions that cover over the antagonism between and among positions. In liberal politics this process is called "compromise" or "reaching consensus," terms that valorize the fact of agreement at the same time as they elide the exclusions required to reach it. In a democracy each articulated possibility will be constructed by (and will construct in turn) constituencies of partisans and opponents. A president offers war as a possible solution to a perceived threat; the articulation of this possibility constructs adherents and dissenters. In response to the president's proposal other citizens generate different strategies, such as sanctions, assassination, peacekeeping by a neutral party, and so on; these possibilities construct partisans, dissenters, and yet other possibilities in turn. That is to say, political discourse is generated by means of metonymy—chains of arguments related by difference rather than identity. Perhaps we can find a way out of the current ideological impasse, then, by foregrounding difference. Mouffe in fact uses Jacques Derrida's concept of difference to argue that the primary relation of the political is antagonism: "One of Derrida's central ideas is that the constitution of an identity is always based on excluding something and establishing a violent hierarchy between the resultant two poles—form/matter, essence/accident, black/white, man/woman, and so on. This reveals that there is no identity that is self-present to itself and not constructed as difference, and that any social objectivity is constituted through acts of power. It means that any social objectivity is ultimately political and has to show traces of the exclusion which governs its constitution, what we can call its 'constitutive outside'" (*Return* 141). The "constitutive outside" of a polity such as the United States, obviously, is all other states. "The French," "the Israelis," "the Iraqi people" in part construct American citizen-identity insofar as they are "outside-us." But clearly "insides" and "outsides" can be constructed within states as well, among groups whose beliefs, goals, and tactics differ. James Morone points out that "the boundary separating a privileged us from a less reliable them" appeared very early in American history, and it "would not evaporate" despite liberal egalitarian hopes: "That line got constructed not simply out of birth and rank but out of convictions about grace, about moral superiority" (47). In other words, one line of distinction between "us" and "them" commonly used in America has always had a religious coloring.

Mouffe's concern is that the "violent hierarchy" inherent in the political may become constructed as a friend/enemy relation: "in the domain of collective identifications, where what is in question is the creation of a 'we' by the delimitation of a 'them,' the possibility always exists that this we/them relation will turn into a relation of the friend/enemy type. . . . This can happen when the other, who was until then considered only under the mode of difference, begins to be perceived as negating our identity" (*Return* 2–3). The super-patriotism generated by the events of September 11, 2001, constructed America as a nation of like-minded patriots, a tightly knit "we" whose identity was threatened by an enemy whose actual location in the world shifts alarmingly from Afghanistan to Iraq, from Iran to

Palestine to Syria, to North Korea and back again. The "enemy," the negating opposite of "us," can reside within our midst as well, in the persons of Arab Americans and war protestors.

Liberalism forgets or erases the we/they relation that necessarily informs the political. Liberal rhetorical theory assumes that all members of a democratic polity will be willing to examine and weigh contending positions in a rational fashion, aiming for compromise where this is possible and settling for tolerance where it is not. Clearly, apocalyptism is a direct challenge to this belief. Mouffe points out that political legitimacy is not any longer grounded on rationality in contemporary democracies (as if it ever was); rather, hegemonic discourses become so because someone in power takes or once took them to be legitimate (*Democratic* 100). This link between legitimacy and power remains in place only as long as a hegemonic discourse successfully fends off contenders. The limits of any hegemony, then, are defined by sufficiently powerful antagonistic beliefs that contest its primacy (Laclau and Mouffe 122–27). Put another way, the borders of a hegemonic discourse are defined by the limits of its power to interpellate adherents, to police their desire to accept or defect. That its critics on both the Left and the Right are now able to see that liberalism is an ideology rather than a fact of nature suggests that its hegemony faces a significant challenge.

Given the antagonisms that exist at the borders of hegemonic discourse, Mouffe calls for discursive strategies that can rewrite the friend/enemy relation so that those who differ are conceptualized as adversaries rather than enemies: they are "no longer perceived as an enemy to be destroyed, but as . . . somebody whose ideas we combat but whose right to defend those ideas we do not put into question" (*Democratic* 102). The effect of such a reconceptualization, she hopes, would be to "legitimate opponents," that is, always to keep in mind that their claims are legitimate within the borders of the hegemonies to which they subscribe and that their antagonism toward "us" and our ideals is such that it can never be resolved solely by rational means. To treat opponents as adversaries—as people who maintain agendas that compel them as forcefully as our own compels us—is not easy: it requires that participants "undergo a radical change in political identity. It is more a sort of conversion than a process of rational persuasion" (Mouffe, *Democratic* 102). Mouffe uses *conversion* here in the sense given it by Thomas Kuhn, who argues that "adherence to a new scientific paradigm is a conversion" (Mouffe, *Democratic* 102). However, the religious overtones carried by this term cannot be lost on her.

Acceptance of one's opponents as legitimate adversaries requires a change in subjectivity, a change in orientation toward antagonistic discourses, and an attitudinal change toward those with whom one disagrees. The difference between this model of politics, which Mouffe calls "agonistic pluralism," and liberal democracy is that in the former "the prime task of democratic politics is not to eliminate passions from the sphere of the public . . . but to mobilize those passions towards democratic designs" (*Democratic* 103). The mobilization of passions, I submit, is a task for rhetoric. Indeed, Mouffe herself appeals to "the great tradition of rhetoric" as a means of accomplishing this task, citing the work of Chaim Perelman and Lucie Olbrechts-Tyteca as exemplary (*Return* 130).

I want to complicate Mouffe's discussion of political agonism by reading it alongside an ethical stance toward the political derived by Janet Atwill from her study of preclassical rhetoric. According to Atwill, the Older Sophist Protagoras argued that the political art "consists of two qualities," *aidos* and *dike,* generally translated "respect" and "justice" (210). As is typical of archaic Greek thought, these concepts indicate reflexive relationships among members of a polity: Atwill notes that "respect toward others is inextricably tied to the respect one can expect for oneself" (211). What this means is that politics (and rhetoric) must turn on respectful relationships wherein everyone is willing to address, and be addressed by, an other (Lyotard). Respect requires justice because, as Atwill puts it, "good faith efforts are difficult when the stakes and resources of each party are unequal" (212). Just relations between and among opponents are also difficult to establish when the argumentative goal is consensus, when everyone begins with the knowledge that the positions taken by some or all must be eroded or even forgotten if deliberation is to succeed. Indeed, the achievement of consensus can simply mean that the most powerful interests managed to silence all other parties. On the other hand, one of the great achievements of liberal argument is that it does acknowledge the necessity of respectful address to others, unlike authoritarian (and unjust) discourses that refuse to do even this much. According to Atwill, "because purely authoritarian discourse is concerned solely with strengthening an already rigid position, it is an almost ceremonial rejection of a relationship" (212). What is missing from America's civic discourse at this moment, then, it seems to me, is a willingness to acknowledge difference while remaining open to the necessity of respectful address to others and to their positions. This does not mean that any party to an argument must ever or always "cave," as my students might say. Rather, all parties must understand that an unwilling caving in of any party to an argument diminishes all other parties.

The accounts of the political I have briefly reviewed here are idealist. They carve out difficult paths to walk, particularly in a time and place where citizens' discursive responses to events are generally manufactured for them by government and the media. But ideals show us what is possible. One of the functions of rhetoric since ancient times has been to envision the available argumentative possibilities (Aristotle, *Rhetoric* II.19. i–xiv). Since most of the major disagreements that currently circulate in American political discourse arise from conflicts between liberal and apocalyptist approaches to argument, it seems imperative that some means be found that can address their differences. I appeal to rhetoric at this juncture not because I think it is another foundationalism that can solve all disagreements whatsoever. Far from it. But as I have said repeatedly, rhetoric does have a major advantage over liberal strategies of argument insofar as it is able to address ideological and emotional claims as well as rational ones. I hope to show that well-prepared rhetors can find openings within situations where disagreement occurs, openings that can help participants to conceive of themselves and their relation to events in new ways. To my mind this is at the very least an improvement over the current ideological impasse, to which Americans typically respond with anger or silence.

2

SPEAKING OF RHETORIC

Rhetoric is a very old art. Conceivably its practice began when human beings learned to talk, and surely when they discovered differences of opinion. Theories of rhetoric developed in the West as early as the sixth century BCE, and rhetoric was studied in Western schools from ancient times through the Renaissance. Throughout this long period it was taught to men (and on rare occasions women) who were positioned to become leaders in their communities. Rhetoric is useful to communities because those who practice it—here called "rhetors"—can find ways to alleviate disagreement; those who study it—here called "rhetoricians"—try to understand why disagreement occurs so they may help rhetors figure out how to alleviate it. Granted, rhetors sometimes deliberately obfuscate or mislead, and sometimes they foment or intensify disagreement. This fact does not undermine the usefulness of rhetoric itself, however. In *On Rhetoric* Aristotle notes that all good and useful things, such as "strength, health, wealth, and military strategy," harbor the potential for harm, "for by using these justly one would do the greatest good and unjustly, the greatest harm" (I.1.1355a). In other words, ethical risk is involved in the use of any powerful art or attribute. The power of rhetoric lies in its discrimination of a conceptual vocabulary and a set of discursive strategies that allow those who are familiar with it to intervene fruitfully in disputes and disagreements. Risk is entailed when access to rhetorical power/knowledge is unevenly distributed within a polity.

Charles Sears Baldwin, an early twentieth-century historian of rhetoric, depicted the Second Sophistic (100–400 CE) as a period during which rhetoric was degraded because Roman emperors allowed no space for political disagreement. After the assassination of Julius Caesar in 44 BCE a series of emperors assumed power over the former republic of Rome. They ruled the vast Empire and the citizens of Rome alike with a mixture of guile, repression, and strategic assassination. The ruthlessness of these regimes had a chilling effect on rhetorical practice. Tacitus remarks in his history of the Imperial period that "the rising tide of flattery had a deterrent effect. . . . The reigns of Tiberius, Gaius, Claudius, and Nero were described during their lifetimes in fictitious terms, for fear of the consequences" (31). Nearly two thousand years later Baldwin summarized what happens to rhetoric when it cannot be tied to civic deliberation: "sophistry is the historic demonstration of what oratory becomes when it is removed from the urgency of subject matter. Seeking some inspiration for public occasions, it revives over and over again a dead past. Thus becoming conventionalized in method, it turns from cogency of movement to the cultivation of style" (15). Today historians of rhetoric might quarrel with Baldwin's negative assessment of sophistry. But his point still holds: rhetoric cannot thrive in polities where open disagreement is discouraged.

During the American colonial and revolutionary periods rhetoric was taught to everyone who entered a school or college; its study and practice were required at Harvard College, for example, from its founding in the early seventeenth century. Samuel Eliot Morison claims that "rhetoric, studied from classical texts, manuals, and collections of *flores*, and practised constantly by declamation in English and Latin, taught [students] how to speak and write with 'clearness, force, and elegance'" (30). However, instruction in rhetoric faded from school curricula in the late nineteenth century and is no longer readily available. It is increasingly hard to find professing rhetoricians in American colleges and universities, where rhetorical studies resides at the margins of communication and English departments. In civic spheres rhetoric is held in such low esteem that it is often taken to be part of the problem rather than its cure. I refer of course to the view that rhetoric is somehow false or unreal, that it gets in the way of meaningful discussion. Today rhetoric, a formidable art of persuasion studied by Aristotle and practiced by Cicero, is identified with "spin." Spin is what people spout when they want to cloud the issue rather than clarify it, or when they have nothing of consequence to impart but are expected to speak nonetheless. Spin interprets facts in a light favorable to the interpreter, and its practice implies that facts may be unintelligible or even dangerous if encountered unspun.

Rhetoric is something else altogether. Ancient rhetoricians conceived of rhetoric as an art of invention.[1] They taught their students how to find and use arguments made available by the cultural contexts that give rise to disagreement, firmly grounding their instruction in issues arising within the arena that Chantal Mouffe calls "the political." When rhetoric-as-invention was widely taught in American schools, impassioned oratory sparked movements such as abolition and women's suffrage. Today fine oratory can still be heard on occasion. Al Sharpton's speech at the 2004 Democratic convention powerfully reminded his audience of the price African Americans have paid for the right to vote: "Mr. President, the reason we are fighting so hard, the reason we took Florida so seriously, is our right to vote wasn't gained because of our age. Our vote was soaked in the blood of martyrs, soaked in the blood of Goodman, Chaney, Schwerner, soaked in the blood of four little girls in Birmingham. This vote is sacred to us. This vote can't be bargained away. This vote can't be given away. Mr. President, in all due respect, Mr. President, read my lips: Our vote is not for sale" (http://americanrhetoric.com). Reporters who interviewed Sharpton after his speech either did not know or did not care about the history he invoked. They worried instead that he had used more than his allotted time. And so they spun Sharpton's artful and moving rhetoric into irrelevance.

I think that the cultural invisibility of rhetoric, conceived as an art of invention, bears a dialectical relation to Americans' current unwillingness to disagree. We dislike disagreement because it seems to invite discord. But discord is inevitable if we don't know how to resolve civic issues with at least a modicum of civility. Because rhetoric is no longer widely studied, Americans may not know that it is possible for anyone to find arguments other than those that rehearse exhausted canards and follow well-worn paths. And if they do suspect that alternative arguments have been drowned out by spin, they still may not know how to find them. If Americans do not know how to invent arguments, if they do not know that they can discover alternatives to the positions defined by powerful people and institutions, democracy is indeed in trouble.

Rhetoric as Invention

Michael Billig notes that attempts to define rhetoric are complicated by the fact that the term is ambiguous, insofar as it is "both the means of inquiry and its object" (*Ideology* 23). But the word *rhetoric* contains yet other ambiguities insofar as it refers to generalizations about rhetoric (what I call "rhetorical theory"), as well as to the body of arguments that are made within a given discursive situation (as in "there was more rhetoric from the White House today"). Because this last usage participates in the degradation of rhetoric as evasive, deceptive, or empty, I use the word *rhetoric* to refer to theory or practice rather than to a body of arguments about a specific issue. I also resist the popular sense of school rhetoric that reduces it to lists of rules governing grammar, usage, sentence composition, and delivery. Rather, I adopt Aristotle's definition of rhetoric as "an ability, in each case, to see the available means of persuasion" (*Rhetoric* I.2.1355a). I prefer this definition because it emphasizes the art of finding or discovering arguments. The definition also ties rhetoric to culture by locating the need for it within disagreements that arise in the course of events and by locating the available arguments themselves within those events. As ancient rhetors such as Gorgias and Cicero argued in theory and personified in practice, any art or practice entitled to be called "rhetoric" must intervene in some way in the beliefs and practices of the community it serves. Hence any rhetorical theory must at minimum formulate an art of invention, as Aristotle did; furthermore, the arguments generated by rhetorical invention must be conceived as produced and circulated within a network of social and civic discourse, practices, images, and events.

Despite the necessity that rhetorical practice be located in specific times and places, it is nonetheless possible to synthesize more general observations about the operation of rhetoric. Aristotle thought this was best done by observing the work of successful rhetors (*Rhetoric* I.i.1354a). In Aristotle's Greek the verb *theorein* literally means to "observe from afar"; it refers to someone sitting in the topmost row of the theater. A theorist is the spectator who is most distant from the scene being enacted on stage and whose body is thus in one sense the least involved in the production but who nonetheless affects and is affected by it. The implication is that while theory lacks the immediacy of practice, its distance from events permits a wider-ranging view. And theory need not be thought of in its modern senses of representation or prediction. Janet Atwill points out that the

Greek term carries overtones of "spectacle," and so "the 'representation' related to *theoria* is more appropriately identified with a situated, temporal performance than with the reproduction of a concept or 'idea'" (79). That is to say, a theory is itself a performance, a doing, or an act that recalls a constructed set of other performances. This is the spirit in which Gorgias may be thought to have produced theory: he instructed his students in the art of rhetoric by repeatedly performing instances of it for them. Another way to put this is to say that theories are rhetorical inventions: depictions or assessments produced by and within specific times and locations as means of opening other ways of believing and acting.

The practice of rhetoric continues apace whether or not scholars or theorists pay any attention to it and whether or not practitioners know that they are, indeed, engaging in rhetoric. However, attention to rhetorical theory can affect the quality of practice insofar as theory articulates and disseminates alternative strategies of invention into the culture at large, particularly if these are taught in school. The attempt made here to demonstrate the importance of a vigorous rhetorical theory to the maintenance of civil society is motivated by my concern about the currently hostile climate toward open, careful discussion of important political and social issues.

Disagreements, Threats, Coercion, and Violence

Currently participants in civic discussions appear reluctant to submit their claims to the risk of argument. Opposing claims are ignored rather than engaged. Take, for example, the long-running refusal of partisans in the disagreement over legalized abortion to debate their opponents' positions (Condit; Hunter). Pro-choice advocates take as their major premise a proposition about the political rights of women; pro-life advocates, on the other hand, conduct a metaphysical or theological argument about the beginning point of life. (This disagreement is of course an instance of the hegemonic struggle between liberalism and fundamentalist Christianity.) Pro-lifers seldom confront the issue of whether women have the right to make decisions about their own reproductive choices. Pro-choicers have proven somewhat more willing to engage the pro-life argument that characterizes life as beginning at conception, usually by arguing that a fetus is not a person until it can survive without its mother. However, many pro-choicers see the issue of when life begins as irrelevant to this disagreement, which they take to be political rather than metaphysical.

An ancient teacher of rhetoric would have realized immediately that this disagreement is not in stasis; that is, its participants do not agree on the point about which they disagree, and hence two different and incompatible arguments are being mounted.[2] Unless stasis is reached, debate about abortion rights cannot become an argument, and until argument begins, no nonviolent resolution can occur. Argument entails the exchange of claims and evidence about a disputed position; minimally it requires an advocate to recognize that an opponent has a position on the issue at hand. Recognition of opponents as people who hold viable positions, whether these are acceptable or not, is entailed in Mouffe's call for political agonism and in Atwill's claim that rhetoric requires willingness to be addressed by an other. That is to say, argument minimally requires an advocate to acknowledge that his or her claim is controversial. Ethically speaking, if participants in a dispute do not formulate the position about which they disagree, the necessary respect for an other may not be in play, and neither the conduct nor the outcome of the argument may be just. Rhetorically speaking, if stasis is not achieved, each side may generate all the evidence in the world to support its claims and yet never engage in argument.

Pro-lifers have occasionally felt sufficiently secure, rhetorically, to refer to themselves as "anti-choice," a formulation that does put the disagreement into stasis because it acknowledges the existence of the chief opposing claim. If they were to engage pro-choicers on this ground, headway toward agreement might be made. In the present discursive climate, however, it is not in their interest to articulate the arguments that follow upon an anti-choice claim—that women, by virtue of their gender, do not have (liberal) rights to privacy and freedom. And so it is unlikely that pro-lifers will move very far past anti-choice sloganeering, at least in public venues. On the other hand, pro-choicers cannot refer to themselves as "anti-life" and win adherents, although their opponents cheerfully characterize them in just that way. In 2003 the debate over legal abortion observed its thirtieth anniversary as a centerpiece of American public discourse, and while its participants' tactics have changed over this period of time, their major premises have not. No doubt this disagreement has failed to achieve stasis because both sides know that counterclaims to the positions they have taken up are extremely unattractive. And while the argument is stalemated, the tactics of pro-life partisans have escalated toward violence, including harassment of patients and the murder of providers (Reiter). The stakes of the disagreement over abortion have become very high indeed, and its continuing failure to achieve stasis can only exacerbate this situation.

There are many reasons why disagreements do not mature into ar-

gument. As I suggest above, partisans may not know that it is possible to
frame propositions in such a way that a disagreement can achieve stasis
and hence open the possibility of exchange. Or perhaps no party is willing
to do the hard intellectual work that is necessary to construct refutations
of the premises put forward by another. My students tell me that they do
not argue about politics or religion because they do not wish to risk losing.
Since they readily associate loss of an argument with the state of character
they call "being a loser," they preserve their integrity by refusing to engage
in argument at all. Another possibility is that participants in a disagreement actually enjoy prolonging it—disagreement engages emotions such as
anger, after all, and indulgence in anger may give pleasure to some people.
In the case of the disagreement over abortion rights, I suspect that activists on all sides of the issue insufficiently respect their opponents. Equally
likely though, people do not enter into argument because they do not wish
to risk having their minds changed. Argument entails this risk because of
its requirement of exchange.

Anyone who supported America's invasion of Iraq in 2003 certainly
had many available means of persuasion ready to hand, arguments helpfully supplied by the Bush administration: we made war in order to free
the Iraqi people from tyranny and to give them a chance to become self-
governing; because Saddam Hussein was stockpiling weapons of mass destruction; because his regime supported terrorists, and so on. At the time
the incident at the peace vigil took place, polls showed that nearly three-
quarters of Americans supported the war, and surely these arguments were
circulating within nearly every community in America (indeed, they continued to circulate long after facts had shown them to be untenable). With
all of these means of persuasion available, then, why would someone who
supported war feel moved to shout insults at people standing quietly on a
street corner as an act of protest against war? Granted, the insult itself contained an argument: the instruction to "suck Saddam's dick" can follow
as a conclusion to an *enthymeme* whose major premise is something like
"Anyone who protests the war supports the enemy."[3] However, the premise
was clearly faulty on empirical grounds available at the time. Polls showed
that most Americans, even those who opposed war, thought that the Iraqi
dictator's regime was intolerable; hence it was unlikely that the protestors sympathized with Saddam Hussein. Moreover, one can oppose war
on grounds that have nothing to do with specific political aims—pacifism,
sorrow over the death and destruction caused by war, fear of reprisals, concern about costs, and so on. But the person who delivered the insult clearly

was not aiming to enter into argument with the vigilants. More likely the intent was to belittle by queering or feminizing them. The vehemence with which the insult was uttered may have been calculated to frighten them into halting their protest altogether.

People sometimes resort to intimidation and harassment, rather than rhetoric, when their beliefs are challenged by their recognition that others hold differing beliefs. The liberal rights to freedom of speech and freedom of assembly are commonplaces in American discourse, no matter how frequently these rights are violated in practice. Their articulation within our common discourse exerts ideological force on all Americans, even on those who would deny these rights to others. If the anger expressed during the encounter at the peace vigil did in fact indicate uneasiness or awareness of contradiction between one belief system and another, rhetoric could, perhaps, still find room to operate in this instance and others like it. On the other hand, people who utter threats and insults may not care about persuading others; they may wish, rather, to force behavior or speech that offends them to disappear, even if this means that those who hold or represent countering positions must be silenced or, in extreme cases, made to disappear along with their dissenting views. In such cases their need for assent or silence overwhelms ordinary standards of civility and ethics. Raphael Ezekiel, author of *The Racist Mind,* talked with neo-Nazis and Klansmen so frequently and listened to them so sympathetically that some members of these groups began to receive his visits warmly. Despite their apparent fondness for him, Ezekiel's informants rudely and repeatedly called him "kike" and "Jewboy" while in conversation with him (12, 22). And the cases of Eric Robert Rudolph and Paul Hill affirm that extremist pro-lifers are willing to use murder to end practices with which they disagree, despite the fact that shooting abortion workers and bombing women's clinics endanger the lives of "the unborn" in whose interest they claim to act (Mason 46).

The coercive goal of violence is deterrence. This makes it very different from rhetoric, where the goal is persuasion. Rhetoric has little chance of curbing the actions of people who are willing to commit murder in order to quell dissent or halt practices of which they disapprove. Violent tactics are used precisely when persuasion cannot be achieved by some other means. Victims of torture are forced by the administration of pain to conform to the torturer's desire, but this does not mean that they have, necessarily, been persuaded to accept that desire.[4] Throughout Western history the relation of torture to truth-telling has been contested (DuBois). And in the wake of the Abu Ghraib prison scandal, FBI interrogators claimed that torture does not achieve the goal of truth-telling because those who are subjected to it will say anything required of them. The achievement of persuasion by means of torture is equally uncertain. A torturer can convince victims to defect or to act in support of a new cause only by means of repeated threats or the enactment of additional violence, and while victims can be forced to cooperate this does not mean they will continue to do so once they are out of danger. Terrible acts of violence may, in fact, stimulate opposition from those who would otherwise remain passive or unaligned. Few Americans knew or cared about Al Qaeda prior to the events of September 11, 2001, but the group has since become the ostensible object of a massive "war on terror."

Rhetoricians have argued for centuries about whether verbal coercion (including the force of law, threats, and harassment) falls within the realm of rhetoric.[5] I suggest that it does not. Even if the arousal of fear or shame or the threat of incarceration or violence succeeds in silencing dissenters, it is hard to grant that persuasion has taken place. If the name-calling and the insults hurled at the peace vigilants actually did silence them or cause them to disperse, for example, there is nonetheless no guarantee (and no evidence) that these tactics moved any vigilant to change his or her position on the war. What I have just written about threats and coercion must be qualified by consideration of the power relations that obtain in a given case, however. A child who eats her broccoli because she has been threatened with early bedtime if she does not do so does indeed comply with a parent's desire; this does not necessarily entail that she has been persuaded that broccoli tastes good or is good for people, or that she ought to do whatever she is told. The child complies because the alternative is worse. In this case she and the parent are not engaged in argument because the parent has not recognized, or better, legitimized, her dissent. When the child is no longer on the downside of family power, if she truly does not like broccoli she will eat it only if some argument has persuaded her to do so, unless of course she is constrained by some other power relation, and assuming as well that she has not gotten into the habit of eating broccoli because of repeated commands to do so (see chapter 3).

Persuasion is often thought in a very narrow sense to mean convincing someone that her position is wrong or that someone else's position is right. Ideally, however, all parties to an argument risk alteration of their positions as argument proceeds, and it is hard to know what winning or losing might mean in such a situation. That is to say, arguments can't be "won" in the way that basketball teams win games, because there are no rules or principles that can determine what "winning" means in argument as there are in basketball. If I succeed in persuading you to change your mind about the injustice of preemptive war, for example, I have not "won" much of anything except your (perhaps temporary and lukewarm) adherence to this position. And by entering into argument with you, I put my own position at risk; during argument you may in fact convince me that in this or that particular case a preemptive war was just, in which case I must qualify my original claim. You can read this as a "win" if our relationship is competitive for some reason, and I suppose in this circumstance "victory" in an argument provides satisfaction similar to that achieved when, for example, the Phoenix Mercury finally wins a game. That is to say, just as we may extrapolate from "My team beat yours" to "My team is better than yours," we may extrapolate from "You accepted my claim" to "I am smarter than you." This is exactly why my students say they do not engage in argument. However, unless participants in arguments are keeping score for some reason involving power relations that may or may not have anything to do with the argument at hand, "winning" an argument is not a permanent achievement. If I convinced you to entertain a new position that somehow requires you to alter your belief system in some more extensive way, you may not retain it. You may also adhere to it for reasons other than those I forwarded during our argument. Or you may see that your new position opens up lines of argument that I had not foreseen. Because of its requirement of exchange and its potential for change, then, argument seldom culminates in a decisive win or loss.

In politics, to be sure, "winning" an argument can be thought of in terms of success in implementing or overturning policy. Currently pro-life advocates are changing policy by electing or appointing believers to legislatures and the judiciary rather than by trying to convince opponents. But this strategy, clever as it is, is limited by the finite number of believers who can be put into policy-making positions. As I write this chapter, a ban on the medical procedure that pro-life advocates refer to as "partial-birth abortion" has just been passed into federal law. Pro-lifers hope that this is a step toward outlawing abortion altogether. However, at the very moment the president signed the legislation, district judges filed injunctions against its enforcement (Entous). This example illustrates that in a democracy there is always more to say about policy as long as all members of the polity remain unpersuaded of its efficacy. In 1973 justices of the Supreme Court were persuaded that women's claim to citizenship entailed their right to reproductive choice, and they overturned bans on abortion that were then in place. Today a majority of legislators and judges have yet to be convinced of the legitimacy or justice of overturning *Roe v. Wade,* although pro-life advocates have managed to outlaw other medical procedures and pharmaceuticals that they define as abortion. More generally, while a majority of Americans are apparently made uncomfortable by the practice of abortion, they remain as yet unconvinced that curtailment of abortion rights is either justified or right. Until a preponderance of legislators accepts some claim that denies reproductive choice to women, then, the available resorts for determined pro-lifers include continued argument, on the one hand, or intimidation and violence on the other.

The Limitations of Liberal Rhetorical Theory

If rhetoric is to be practiced usefully and responsibly, it must be rescued from its current reputation as a strategic art of deception. Ironically rhetoric now needs an agent and better public relations. Its importance and usefulness must be made clear to activists, scholars, and citizens who need it in order to find their way through a thicket of competing claims and to pursue the work of political and social change. My attempt to rehabilitate rhetoric begins with a meditation on its modern history.

Despite its contemporary low profile, for at least two thousand years of Western history rhetoric was consciously deployed by influential political actors to gain sought-after ends, and the art itself was studied by thinkers who are today identified with other fields of study. A list of influential figures who studied or taught rhetoric includes Aspasia, Plato, Diotima, Aristotle, St. Augustine, Catherine of Siena, Erasmus, Francis Bacon, Queen Elizabeth I, Vico, Adam Smith, and Nietzsche, among others. Henri Marrou's description of the relation of rhetorical study to public life during the Hellenistic period applies equally well to educated men and (a few) women through the Renaissance: "The truth is that there was no end to the study of rhetoric. . . . There was no boundary between the schools and the life of letters—a man of letters went on composing declamations . . . all his life, and the transition from school exercise to public lecture took place imperceptibly" (204). Despite its longstanding centrality to Western culture, however, rhetorical theory suffered a series of insurmountable intellectual challenges with the triumph of modernity, so much so that during the late nineteenth century rhetoric virtually ceased to be studied in European and American schools and colleges. Its disappearance at that point marked its first absence from Western curricula since the third century BCE. Marrou explains its disappearance by questioning the intellectual sophistication of modern thought: "for us moderns, rhetoric means artificiality, insincerity, decadence. Perhaps this is simply because we do not understand it and have become barbarians ourselves" (204). Other historians of rhetoric mourn the comparative anemia of modern rhetorical theory. Vincent M. Bevilacqua, for example, laments that "the modern scientific study of rhetoric has proven both vapid and fruitless. . . . Modern . . . rhetoric has in the main delineated the measure of all things while perceiving the meaning and value of nothing" (28). Brian Vickers depicts modern distaste for rhetoric by citing an analogy from Wilhelm Busch: "we like cheese well enough, but we still cover it up" (vii).

History does not always accommodate tradition, particularly a tradition so ancient as the study of rhetoric. Rhetorical study was already five centuries old when Cicero used rhetoric to alert the Roman Senate to Caesar's ambition. Some seventeen hundred years later it did not readily adapt to the sweeping changes ushered in by two of the major intellectual achievements of modernity: liberalism and science. Liberal and scientific thinkers located invention in encounters between individuals and nature rather than in the common language of the polity (Crowley, *Methodical*). In modern rhetoric, then, the quality of invention would depend upon the quality of the mind that produced it rather than on the quality of the arguments made available by language and culture, as ancient rhetoricians had maintained.

Eighteenth-century rhetorical theorists adopted a liberal notion of the subject and installed that subject as the source of rhetorical invention in place of ancient topical strategies. In his hugely popular *Lectures on Rhetoric and Belles-Lettres* (1783), for instance, Hugh Blair advised his students to lay aside their commonplaces, trusting instead to their native genius and study of the empirical world in order to generate arguments (2: 401–2). Commonplaces were a central feature of ancient thought about invention, where it was assumed that rhetors found arguments and proofs in the circulation of language-in-use. Having rejected these tactics as artificial, however, Blair and his contemporaries looked for a new source of authority for invention, and they found the liberal subject—that free and sovereign individual who can think his way through disagreements by resorting to reason and who authorizes the results of his investigation by appeal to his very ability to reason. I use the masculine pronoun here because the liberal subject is coded as masculine (Hirschmann). Despite its exclusiveness, this model of subjectivity is attractive because it depicts rhetors as in control of the production and reception of language, movements, and gestures. Liberal rhetorical theory presumes that rhetorical activity occurs in the following way: a free, knowing, and sovereign agent is moved by circumstances to survey the landscape; develop appropriate arguments concerning it; clothe them in persuasive language; and repeat them to an audience of equally free, knowing, and sovereign subjects who hear/read without impediment or distortion.

Postmodern thought has of course called the liberal subject into question, and it has expressed reservations about the representational capacity of language as well. But liberal rhetorical theory also has inherent shortcomings that severely limit its potential as a means of adjudicating disagreement. First, it takes understanding as its primary goal, and because it privileges understanding it can elide the possibility that audiences who grasp a rhetor's message perfectly well may nevertheless resist it. Second, liberal thought separates values from reason. Alison Jagger characterizes this second move as follows:

For both the Greeks and the medieval philosophers, reason had been linked with value insofar as reason provided access to the objective structure or order of reality, seen as simultaneously natural and morally justified. With the rise of modern science, however, the realms of nature and value were separated: nature was stripped of value and reconceptualized as an inanimate mechanism of no intrinsic worth. Values were relocated in human beings, rooted in human preferences and emotional responses. The separation of supposedly natural fact from human value meant that reason, if it were to provide trustworthy insight into reality, had to be uncontaminated by or abstracted from value. Increasingly, therefore, though never universally, reason was reconceptualized as the ability to make valid inferences from premises established elsewhere, the ability to calculate means but not to determine ends. (130)

In the liberal dispensation values were associated with emotional responses, and both were consigned to the sphere of individual human perception. Reason remained the vehicle of public discussion and debate because it presumably worked in the same way for everyone, or at least for everyone who was presumed eligible to participate in the public sphere.

The gendered quality of the distinction between disembodied public reason and private, passionate evaluation should be apparent. In his history of liberalism Anthony Arblaster argues that the liberal account of reason was worked out as a means of adjudicating competing desires, and in Western thought desire is unfailingly associated with women (35; Butler, *Subjects*). Liberal thinkers tried to eliminate the impact of passion and interest in public debate by rendering empirically based reasoning as the only legitimate means of assembling evidence and drawing conclusions. Such reasoning was conceived as a means of manipulating information, and this process or method was thought to be common to everyone who was defined as having legitimate access to civic discourse (that is, propertied men). In this model the information received from sensation (that is, from experience) did differ from person to person depending on individual life circumstances. Individual experience was in part constituted by emotional response as well, and emotional responses were thought to determine values. The differences in perception and belief stemming from individual personal experience could be mitigated in public debate if each individual subjected his sensory impressions and emotional responses to the operations of reason. That is to say, arguments or claims based on moral and emotional commitment had to be subjected to reason in order to make them legible and hence useful to others.

In liberal epistemology understanding means something like "grasping by means of reason." In the second part of his *Essay Concerning Human Understanding* (1694), "On Ideas," John Locke treats understanding as the combination and recombination of ideas drawn from perception and manipulated by the operations of reason. In the final section of the treatise he defines reason as "the discovery of the certainty or probability of such propositions or truths which the mind arrives at by deduction made from such ideas, which it has got by the use of its natural faculties; viz. by sensation or reflection" (IV.xviii.2). Locke consistently found that nonrational sources of belief, such as faith, were inferior to reason in regard to the level of certainty accruing to each. He defined faith as "the assent to any proposition, not thus made out by the deductions of reason, but upon the credit of the proposer, as coming from God, in some extraordinary way of communication. This way of discovering truths to men, we call revelation" (IV.xviii.2). Locke followed Protestant usage in his discussion of revelation, installing awareness of divine revelation within the individual mind rather than in a tradition of interpretation. In addition, he distinguished an authentic, divine revelation from merely human "enthusiasm," which he characterized as the "ungrounded fancies of a man's own brain" (IV.xix.3). Enthusiastic "impulses" and "conceits" arose from "a warmed or overweening brain" that worked "in concurrence with . . . temper and inclination" so that persons afflicted with enthusiasm insisted that they "cannot be mistaken in what they feel" (IV.xix.7, 8). The danger of enthusi-asm, for Locke, was that revelations fostered by it cannot be warranted by anything other than an individual's intuition of their rightness.

In this model of human understanding, then, thought becomes thor-oughly internalized and individualized. One may be suspicious even of claims based on divine revelation, given that individuals who lay claim to divine authority have no way of distinguishing godly revelation from merely human enthusiasm—aside from their own conviction that they have been so favored. Locke was equally suspicious of the persuasive power of "the passions": "Let ever so much probability hang on one side of a cov-etous man's reasoning, and money on the other; it is easy to foresee which will outweigh. Earthly minds, like mud walls, resist the strongest batteries: and though, perhaps, sometimes the force of a clear argument may make some impression, yet they nevertheless stand firm, and keep out the enemy, truth, that would captivate or disturb them. Tell a man passionately in love that he is jilted; bring a score of witnesses of the falsehood of his mistress, it is ten to one but three kind words of hers shall invalidate all their testimo-nies" (IV.xx.3). In this view emotions can hamper the operations of reason and get in the way of truth.

George Campbell likewise separated reason or understanding from other intellectual processes such as evaluation and commitment. At the outset of *The Philosophy of Rhetoric* (1776) he distinguished understand-ing from persuasion based on their respective appeals to different mental compartments: "All the ends of speaking [that is, of rhetoric] are reducible to four; every speech being intended to enlighten the understanding, to please the imagination, to move the passions, or to influence the will" (1). Campbell assumed, then, that an audience is able to understand or grasp an argument without becoming committed to it or moved to action by its advocacy. His distinction between understanding and conviction was an innovation in rhetorical theory, and his distribution of rhetorical appeals among faculties of mind was a studied departure from ancient rhetorical thought. Ancient rhetoricians had tied the choice of appeal to the situation within which the rhetorical act occurred, taking special care to note the disposition of an audience toward a rhetor's character and the argument. Hostile, weary, indifferent, or confused audiences each bore a quite dif-ferent relation to a rhetor, and hence each required an approach tailored to the occasion—conciliation, dissembling, or humor, for example.[6] In Campbell's model, however, because understanding is theoretically avail-able to all who can reason, rhetors could appeal to the understanding in any circumstances where reasonable people were among the projected audience, no matter their prior opinions on the issue being discussed or their assessment of a rhetor's character.

Campbell's discrimination of a distinct appeal to the understanding was enabled by two assumptions made throughout his treatise: that the processes involved in "natural logic" (that is, reasoning) are universally available because they depend on the natural workings of the mind and that language is perfectly representative (61, 216–17). That is to say, any proposition or proof derived by means of reason and expressed in suitably clear language is presumed to be fully present to the understanding of any auditor or reader who is able to exert his or her own rational capacity on its reception. Mathematicians and formal logicians use models of reasoning that meet these criteria. But since Campbell was concerned with ethical and political arguments, which are not governed by well-formed rules of articulation, he was unable to maintain understanding as a pure category. On the very next page of the *Philosophy,* in fact, he enlarges the scope of understanding to include conviction: "When a speaker addresseth himself to the understanding, he proposes the instruction of his hearers, and that, either by explaining some doctrine unknown, or not distinctly comprehended by them, or by proving some position disbelieved or doubted by them. In other words, he proposes either to dispel ignorance or to vanquish error. In the one, his aim is their information; in the other, their conviction" (2). And so now appeals to understanding actually have two aims. Campbell's choice of "conviction" suggests that appeals to the understanding may be resisted by people who hold beliefs that are "in error." At this point he does not say how error comes about, but presumably it arises when someone mistakenly assesses the workings of nature or suffers a lapse in reason. With some difficulty Campbell maintains this distinction between understanding and conviction throughout the *Philosophy* because it buys him something he wants: an argumentative arena that is free of passion. Since full-blown persuasion requires appeals to all four of the faculties (the understanding, the passions, the imagination, and the will), it can be effected only with the assistance of all the bells and whistles accumulated by the ancient rhetorical tradition. The more staid and sober process of securing conviction, however, requires only an appeal to reason.

Campbell does recognize that the achievement of understanding depends on the dispositions of audiences and that as a result it is not entirely within a rhetor's control. But he devotes only one page of his treatise to a consideration of audiences as consisting of "men in particular," that is, audiences who may not respond to arguments in a wholly or primarily rational fashion: "The difference between one audience and another is very great, not only in intellectual but in moral attainments; that may be clearly intelligible to a House of Commons, which would appear as if spoken in an unknown tongue to a conventicle of enthusiasts. That may kindle fury in the latter, which would create no emotion in the former but laughter and contempt. The most obvious difference that appears in different auditories, results from the different cultivation of the understanding; and the influence which this, and their manner of life, have both upon the imagination and upon the memory" (95). He wisely advises rhetors who are faced with resisting audiences to adjust their appeals to differing "interests," exploiting the passionate commitments of monarchists to "pomp and splendour" and of republicans to "liberty and independence." This passage marks a departure from Campbell's usual insistence that the minds of "men" are universally receptive to rational appeals. He also admits that the "capacity" for rational thought differs among individuals (48). This difference in capacity stems from an audience's "different cultivation of the understanding" or the influence of "their manner of life." In his overtly class-conscious era Campbell readily assumed that life situations might prevent all people from exercising rational understanding in the same ways. But he was careful to separate the role played by "manner of life" in impeding understanding from failures that result from something quite different: a passionate and/or moral reluctance to be persuaded. Lack of understanding requires education; resistance requires a rhetor to pull out all the oratorical stops.

The privilege granted to reason in liberal rhetorical theory serves an important liberal value: tolerance (Arblaster 66–70). Ellen Rooney claims that within liberal rhetorical theory tolerance translates into "an ethic of general persuasion" (58). The possibilities that any rhetor can persuade any auditor, or that any reader is open to persuasion by any text, are articles of faith in this view. As Rooney puts it, liberal rhetoricians "imagine a universal community in which every individual . . . is a potential convert to persuasion" (2). This move constitutes listeners or readers as fundamentally alike at the same time it erases the theoretical possibility that dissent may persist. But of course people do refuse to be persuaded on occasion, and they do so in the House of Commons as well as in conventicles of enthusiasts. Ironically, then, liberal tolerance must be purchased by means of an exclusionary move. To put this in terms congenial to postmodern analysis, tolerance can be achieved only if difference is elided. To put the point bluntly, liberal pluralism harbors the hope that difference can be erased if only everyone will just be reasonable—which means something like "think as we do."

The privilege granted to understanding, as opposed to persuasion, endured into twentieth-century liberal rhetorical theory. I. A. Richards held that rhetoric ought to be a "remedy for misunderstanding," and his own *Philosophy of Rhetoric* (1936) is a compendium of tactics for eliminating roadblocks to perfectly clear communication (3). In *Practical Criticism* (1929) Richards recounts his astonished discovery that students are unable to understand poetry if poems are presented to them without identifying context—who wrote them, when, where, and so on (12). Richards was apparently confident at the outset of his experiment that even very difficult texts would open up to decipherment by any reader. That is to say, Richards had lost sight of Campbell's observation that the quality of one's life circumstances can impede understanding. Holding onto an ethic of general persuasion, he assumed that the ability to read poetry depends on individual capacities for understanding—that is, on native intelligence—rather than on acquaintance with the appropriate contexts, which in this case could have been provided by instruction. Richards's response to his experiment demonstrates that if understanding and reason are posited as universally available, and if language is considered to be a trustworthy representation of "meaning," then failures of persuasion must be theorized as occurring when people do not or cannot use their rational capacities. That is to say, failures of persuasion are due to inadequacies in audiences.

Liberal rhetorical theorists tend to read failures of persuasion across three registers. Such failures may result from what Campbell called "party spirit"—single-minded adherence to a dogma or doctrine whose principles serve as major premises for arguments on any issue. Or an audience may give in to passion, allowing desire to govern reason. This sort of failure occurs when the faculties are wrongly prioritized. A third possible barrier to persuasion may exist in an audience's "manner of life," such as gender, ethnicity, class, or socioeconomic circumstances. Some liberal rhetorical theorists would exclude appeals to life circumstances from the province of argument altogether. Here, for example, is Wayne Booth: "When I reduce your effort to discuss reasons to a mere expression of irrational forces (your id, your class, your upbringing, your inherited language), I make it impossible for you to reply—except, of course, with similar charges. Criticism stops and reductive vilification begins" (*Critical* 259). In this work Booth assumes that arguments made from a rhetor's life situation are not rational, and hence it is unacceptable to appeal to them as a means of resolving disagreement.

To his credit Booth did not remain satisfied with this position. He begins *The Company We Keep* with the admission that he had once been unable to accept an argument made by Paul Moses and Charles Long, his colleagues at Chicago. Moses had claimed that racism so taints Mark Twain's *Huckleberry Finn* that he was unable to teach the novel, even though it was required reading for undergraduates at the time (3). Moses's warrant about *Huckleberry Finn* derived from his personal experience of white racism, experience in which Booth admits he cannot share. Throughout the nearly five hundred pages that constitute *Company* Booth struggles with the issues raised for liberal pluralism by rhetorical encounters with difference, that is, with resistance to persuasion, and he finally admits that his love for *Huckleberry Finn,* coupled with his respect for Twain's artistry, motivated his own earlier conclusions about its worth (477). He also realizes that his own life circumstances, as a male professor whose ethnicity typically goes un(re)marked, allowed him to assume, initially, that rational arguments on any issue hold the same appeal for everybody. And he acknowledges as well that his initial position was both partial and exclusive insofar as he blamed the incapacities of audiences for failures to understand: Moses's position violated academic norms of objectivity; he must have had such a shoddy education that he could not think "properly" about questions relevant to the worth of a novel, and so on (3). Booth concludes by writing that his estimation of *Huckleberry Finn* "has been turned, once and for all, for good or ill, from untroubled admiration to restless questioning" (477–78). He does not say whether he still requires his students to read the novel, or if he does, whether or not he takes them along the same tortuous critical path he trod in order to reach this conclusion.[7]

Liberals who are less thoughtful than Booth may never come to such conclusions, because liberalism assumes that rational people operate with a kind of understanding that is relatively free of motivation by desire, interest, or life situation. This assumption drove the decision in the Frost case cited by Fish: the "exposure" of children to diverse values need not entail their persuasion to such values. The privilege awarded to understanding in liberal thought simply elides the possibility that a person's nationality, gender, sexuality, ethnic affiliation, religious beliefs, and so on might lead her to refuse someone else's readings of his preferred texts, that such circumstances might indeed lead her to refuse to read some texts at all (if she has the power to enact such a refusal). Liberals cannot admit to failures of persuasion on these grounds because liberalism abhors exclusivity even more deeply than it abhors difference. As Samuel Weber aptly observes, liberalism is that "form of exclusion which, whenever possible, denies its own exclusivity" (46).

Today liberal rhetoricians still hope that appeals to understanding can overcome beliefs stemming from passionate commitment or life circumstances. The word *rhetoric* does not appear in the index of *Democracy and Disagreement,* an ambitious work in political theory that attempts a rhetorical project nevertheless: to resolve the problem of "moral conflict" in American politics. Its authors—Amy Guttmann and Dennis Thompson—accept that disagreement is inevitable when moral and political issues are under discussion. In order to alleviate such disagreements, they devise an approach they call "deliberative democracy" that is intended to help citizens talk their way through conflicts. Its central principle is reciprocity, which "asks us to appeal to reasons that are shared or could come to be shared by our fellow citizens" (14). Their faith in reason and shared understandings sounds familiar enough to readers of George Campbell. In Guttmann and Thompson's work lack of understanding implies that disagreement results from a failure of imagination: people disagree because they cannot grasp the suffering of others. Put positively, the implication is that peaceful resolutions of disagreements can occur if citizens become able to understand the circumstances of one another's lives, can grasp the motives and actions of others with clarity and/or achieve empathy with one another. While I do not doubt that the achievement of understanding would greatly assist the resolution of disagreements, I suffer from a failure of imagination regarding its feasibility in the really hard cases of disagreement that Americans face today. I can imagine no amount or quality of rational deliberation that would convince people who kill abortion providers, tie a dying gay man to a fence, or drag an African American man behind a pickup truck to "understand" the situations of their victims so thoroughly that they desist from such practices. Nor can I imagine myself agreeing that such acts are justified on any grounds whatsoever, even though I have a fairly complete understanding of the belief systems that underwrite them because I too was raised with the discourses of sexism, heterosexism, and racism. I assume that on some level all of us who were similarly raised immediately grasp the motives underlying such horrible acts (see chapter 3). And subscription to dominant ideologies is regularly reinforced in our culture lest anyone begin to see beyond their limits. Proselytizers regularly knocked on my door while I was writing this book, offering me Bibles to read or red, white, and blue ribbons to wear in order to reinforce my subscription to Christianity and the super-nationalist hysteria that infected the country after 9/11. (I confess that I was not always able to exercise liberal tolerance on these occasions.)

Like liberal rhetorical theorists, I believe that if democracy is to thrive, citizens must negotiate their disagreements with one another. However, I part from liberal belief in at least two respects. I reject the claim that disagreements can be resolved solely by appeals to empirically based reason. It is unlikely that someone who learned in childhood to hate homosexuals will reject homophobia upon being shown statistical, representative, exemplary, or anecdotal evidence that gay people are in fact productive members of society, that they commit fewer crimes than straights, and so on. Nor is such a person likely to be moved by ethical arguments about the partiality of heterosexism or by demonstrations of the discriminatory practices that ineluctably depend from it. Second, I do not expect that full agreement can ever be reached on any issue that concerns a large group of citizens. The liberal hope is that reasoning through difficult issues will somehow allow a consensus to emerge. But the only way to achieve consensus is to discount or eliminate dissent, that is, to quiet or exclude differing points of view. The fact is that the liberal depiction of tolerant deliberation is itself a belief, part of an ideology that rigorously excludes those who value other sorts of proof, such as gut feelings, or who appeal to various sorts of authority, such as faith or tradition or human nature or God, in order to authenticate their claims. I worry that liberal hope for realization of an argumentative ideal such as "deliberative disagreement" covers over a kind of elitist exclusionism at the same time as it forever postpones adjudication of opposing points of view. Given these difficulties, it seems prudent to search for other grounds from which to think about political argument. With that project in mind, I turn to premodern rhetorical theory as a place from which to begin.

May the Forces Be with You

If liberal rhetorical theorists take the individual mind as their starting point, postmodern theorists emphasize the centrality of language to the construction of human subjectivity. This alteration in focus has been dubbed the "linguistic turn." Postmodern thinkers draw from a surprisingly small list of conceptual vocabularies. Derridean post-structuralism relies on Saussurean linguistics, as does Lacanian psychoanalysis, which draws from Freud as well. Foucault developed his notion of "discourse" out of his historical studies, as well as the work of Nietzsche, Althusser, and Austin. Theorists of ideology such as Raymond Williams, Stuart Hall, Laclau, and Mouffe are of course indebted to Marx and subsequent thinkers in the Marxist tradition, primarily Gramsci and Althusser, although they too draw on Saussure. Aside from scholarship contributed by rhetoricians, however, the list of exploited vocabularies does not include ancient rhetorics. Work produced by Janet Atwill, Debra Hawhee, Susan Jarratt, Steven Mailloux, Jasper Neel, and Victor Vitanza, among others, suggests that postmodern notions are not incommensurate with ancient rhetorical thought.[8] It appears that scholars outside the field of rhetoric are unaware of the conceptual vocabulary of ancient rhetorics, or if they are aware (as Derrida was), they do not exploit this vocabulary. Goran Therborn, for example, expanded Althusser's discussion of interpellation into a taxonomy that bears a striking resemblance to ancient teaching about invention. He posits that ideologies "subject and qualify subjects by telling them, relating them to, and making them recognize" three modes of interpellations: what exists (and what doesn't), what is good and its oppositions, and what is possible and impossible (18). Under the first heading ideologies tell us "who we are, what the world is, what nature, society, men and women are like." Under the second ideologies interpret what is right, just, beautiful, enjoyable, and so on. And under the third ideologies pattern the consequences of change; in this mode they give shape to "our hopes, ambitions, and fears." Students of ancient rhetorics will recognize the ancient topics of conjecture, quality, and possibility in Therborn's taxonomy. Ray McKerrow makes this association of old and new explicit when he suggests that the modes of interpellation are adaptable to contemporary use insofar as they can "function as rhetorical *topoi* for the defense of a given ideology" (200). Topical theories of invention were featured in both major branches of ancient rhetorical thought—sophistic and Aristotelian—and both traditions located invention within language-in-use—that is, within discourse.

Despite its great age, ancient rhetorical theory has much to offer postmodernity. Postmodern thought requires attention to location and awareness of contingency. Similar theoretical habits can be found in what we know of (or can read into) the work of ancient rhetorical theorists as well, particularly that generated by the Older Sophists. The postmodern turn toward language is also compatible with Aristotle's focus on the invention of propositions and arguments in *On Rhetoric*, and it resonates as well with what is known (or assumed) about preclassical rhetorical theory. I will argue that Protagoras and Gorgias—who flourished during the fifth century BCE—can be read to have articulated theories of invention that resonate with the linguistic turn. To the extent that such an argument is viable, it follows that ancient and postmodern rhetorics are more similar to each other than either is to modern rhetoric because of their mutual emphases on discourse as a primary source for the construction of human subjectivity. From the point of view of the history of rhetoric, then, modernity is a discontinuity and postmodernity can be characterized as having made not a "turn" but a "return" to the notion that discourse is an appropriate point of entry for theorizing human inscription (Derrida, *Of Grammatology* 15; Sanchez).

However, the great age of ancient rhetorical thought can pose problems to anyone who would reread it in order to construct a contemporary rhetorical theory. For one thing, ancient rhetorics were generated within cultural regimes that were particularly repressive for women and slaves. Some portions of ancient rhetorical thought need rethinking, then, in order to neutralize, as much as possible, the exclusions embedded in it. For another, the conceptual vocabulary invented by ancient rhetoricians is extremely rich, and as a result it generated a long history of commentary and practices in the West. Because of the scope and flexibility of ancient rhetorical thought, rhetorical theory and pedagogy remained indebted to it for over two thousand years, adapting it by selecting and emphasizing the portions—invention, style, or delivery—that were most useful in a given time and place. However, the very weightiness of this tradition invites reification, and this tendency is exacerbated by an equally long history of reduction and simplification of its major terms for use in elementary instruction. For example, a rich legacy of ancient thought about the subtleties and complexities involved in adapting powerful proofs such as *ethos, logos,* and *pathos* to specific rhetorical situations has transmogrified in the school tradition into a bit of formalist lore about the "points" of "the communication triangle." Confronted with the intellectual richness of the rhetorical tradition, on the one hand, and its association with exclusive social practices, on the other, I resort to *bricolage.* With Derrida I recognize "the necessity of borrowing one's concepts from the text of a heritage which is more or less coherent or ruined" at the same time as I take up "the means at hand," which include appropriate reservations about the fit of that heritage with the requirements of the present (*Writing* 285).

A contemporary theory of rhetoric must do more than revive ancient notions, however; it must adapt old notions to address contemporary rhetorical situations. A substantial part of this project involves rereading modern interpretations of ancient concepts.[9] For example: the Older Sophists referred to commonly held beliefs as *doxa,* which term was habitually rendered as "opinion" by nineteenth-century translators. This translation can mislead modern readers because they read within an epistemological tradition that takes opinions to be held by individuals, who can be thought to invent original or unique opinions. And since modern thought privileges reason, which is theoretically available to all, opinion—its uninformed opposite—takes on the flavor of the particular. As a result, opinion has a bad odor. My dictionary of Greek philosophical terms, published in 1967, insistently contrasts *doxa* to *episteme,* noting that the distinction between opinion—"an inferior grade of cognition"—and *episteme*—"true knowledge"—dates back to the Pre-Socratics (Peters 40). However, if we resist the hierarchic implication (attributed to Plato) that associates *doxa* with "mere appearance," and if we resist as well the liberal assumption that opinions are (only) held by individuals, other ancient senses of *doxa* might perhaps be recovered. The first sense of the term listed in Liddell and Scott's lexicon of ancient Greek is in fact "expectation," which is derived from the very source (Xenophon) cited by F. E. Peters in his lexicon (Liddell 209). "Expectation" lends a temporal cast to *doxa,* implying something previously constructed that can, in an event, be met or thwarted. And the second sense of *doxa* emphasizes its communal cast and lends it an affinity to *ethos* (character): "the opinion which others have of one, estimation, reputation, credit, honour, glory." If indeed ancient thinkers can be read as having forwarded a concept of opinion that is both temporal and communal, we arrive at something that can be quite useful to a postmodern theory of rhetorical invention: *doxa* designates current and local beliefs that circulate communally. Read in this way the very old notion of *doxa* is compatible with the results of current research on belief and memory undertaken by psychologists and neurologists, and it also resonates with Pierre Bourdieu's use of *doxa* to name what he calls "enacted belief" (*Logic* 68). (I return to these matters in chapter 3.)

If rhetorical invention is an art of finding arguments made available by and within a situation, as Aristotle suggests in his definition of rhetoric, then potential arguments are thrown up by the circumstances of communal life. That is to say, rhetorical arguments circulate within *doxa.* In this view rhetorical arguments are always already available; they are simply activated or enlivened within a rhetorical encounter. Jacques Derrida might have said that rhetorical arguments are cited.

This reading aligns with the (supposed) epistemology of Protagoras, who taught that the universe is constituted by the clash of opposing forces (Untersteiner 82). Protagoras believed that these contending forces are made manifest by nature: according to Sextus Empiricus, Protagoras "says that the reasons of all the appearances are present in the matter, so that the matter is capable, as far as lies in its own power, of being everything that appears to everybody" (I.218). The word translated here as "reasons" is *logoi,* which means "words" or "speech" in preclassical Greek (Liddell 477). Contending *logoi* make the world apparent. Protagoras's notorious "man-measure" doctrine makes sense in the context of his epistemology of clashing opposites: human beings perceive and select from among the available multitude of contending *logoi* those that address a particular moment and location. Humans are indeed the "measure" of all things, because it is they who perceive, evaluate, choose, and express from among the plenitude of *logoi* thrown off by things in the world. Sextus Empiricus explains that, according to Protagoras, humans "apprehend different things at different times according to their various dispositions," which can include "differences in age, the question whether one is asleep or awake, and every type of variation in one's condition" (I.218). Janet Atwill argues that because of the plenitude of available *logoi,* Protagoras's "doctrine maintained that subjectivity is contingent on incalculable specificities, encompassing physical perception itself. The dictum challenged static models of both subjectivity and 'reality'" (19). In other words, subjectivities, and our impressions of reality itself, are mobile, various, and contingent on circumstance. The *logoi* that get taken up are also temporal, local, and contingent, although thanks to language (and to writing in particular), upon their articulation humans may begin to treat them as though they continually refer to some stable reality. That is, their rhetoricity, their performativity, can easily be overlooked or forgotten.

The tendency of postmodern thought to reject dualism lends it an additional analytic advantage over modernism, in my opinion. Postmodern thinkers typically recast modernist binaries as reciprocal relations. Where a modern thinker might consider reason to be opposed and superior to emotion, for example, a postmodern thinker is likely to conceptualize reason and emotion as existing in a relation to one another such that they are mutually dependent and mutually constructive. Pierre Bourdieu calls this sort of relation "reflexive" (*Pascalian* 10). Postmodern thinkers have applied this strategy of turning binaries into relations (which can fairly be called "deconstruction") to a number of other hierarchical dichotomies favored in modern thought: man/woman, individual/society, experience/ knowledge, thought/language, theory/practice, and so on. This strategy is ordinarily touted as a guard against exclusion, but I find that it has another advantage as well: it opens up for consideration a range of middle grounds that are rendered invisible by dichotomous thinking—it is possible to conceive of more genders than two; we remember that communities of various sizes and constitutions (family, colleagues, bridge clubs, football fans, political parties) mediate between "the individual" and "society," and so on. When applied to Aristotle's central teaching about invention, this strategy implies that because of the movement of difference the relative availability of the "available means of persuasion in any given case" is contingent and reflexive with regard to circumstances. Arguments are more or less available in given spatial and temporal contexts; that is, their relative availability exists along a range of possibilities opened within a given situation. History, ideology, and power relations dictate that some arguments can be made in a given time and place by some people, while others cannot.[10] A white politician could not make Al Sharpton's arguments about African American voting rights with anything like the same level of effectiveness among audiences who are prepared to hear. Indeed, when whites speak for African Americans on any issue, they risk giving offense. This possibility may or may not have anything to do with a rhetor's personal history or *ethos,* and it is not always at work, either, as Bill Clinton's example demonstrates.

If we conceive the relative availability of arguments as lying along a range or spectrum, its endpoints can designate arguments that can be imagined or desired but that cannot be constructed in a given cultural time and place. A feminist project that would articulate women as subjects can serve as an example of a desired argument that is as yet unavailable. Feminists have on occasion dislodged historic constructions of women as secondary to men in importance and ability, however, although this achievement never quite seems to be permanent. Nearer the center of the spectrum of availability lie arguments that can be generated by a few but not yet widely grasped (new research in mathematics, say). Closer yet to the center lie arguments that can be generated by many but not yet heard by institutions such as the media (such as proposals made by Dennis Kucinich during the 2004 Democratic primaries for free college tuition and

health care for all children). Arguments about widely discussed or controversial issues, such as abortion rights, lie nearer the center of the spectrum
because they are repeatedly articulated. Argumentative canards (what the
ancient rhetoricians called "commonplaces") occupy the center: "liberals
are soft on defense." Kucinich's arguments may move closer to the center
of the spectrum with the passage of time, eventually becoming commonplaces, while current commonplaces may lose not only their currency but
their availability. Formerly powerful commonplaces are still available but
can no longer be readily grasped: "Tippecanoe and Tyler too" is so remote
from the contemporary discursive context that most people need to con-
sult a historical reference to understand its use. To say that availability can
be arrayed along a range or spectrum is not to say that the flow of difference necessarily results in progress; it is only to claim that the relative
availability of arguments changes over time.

   In contrast, modern senses of invention as discovery or creation gloss
over the roles of difference and contingency in making arguments available. Yameng Liu characterizes modern attitudes toward invention as follows: "To 'discover' is to make visible or known something that, though
hidden and unknown previously, has always been 'out there,' something
whose existence prior to its 'discovery' is immediately recognized because
of its fundamental fit with the order of things already familiar to us. To
'create,' on the other hand, suggests bringing into being something that
has never before existed, some strange entity snatched *ex nihilo* which is,
presumably, completely different from whatever has been accepted as part
of the 'reality,' and which, therefore, refuses to conform to our habitual
scheme of conceiving the world" (54). In modern thought discovery happens when a stable world reveals itself to determined investigators. And if
the poet Shelley is to be believed, creation occurs by means of an utterly
mystified process—revelation, perhaps, or the "inspiration" in relation to
which composition is mere stenography. (Locke's name for inspiration was
"enthusiasm.") The difficulty with these definitions of invention from a
postmodern point of view is that they require an inventing subject who
maintains a continuing and coherent relation to a similarly continuing
world that she observes and ruminates upon. In the case of creation the
composer possesses a uniquely organized mind from which something
new can spring. In her discussion of Gorgias's theory of invention Hawhee notes that "the discovery and creation models both depend on active
constructions that presuppose a subject that is better described as the out-

come of the rhetorical situation" (17). If rhetorical subjects are outcomes, invention is located within rather than prior to a rhetorical event. Rhetors participate in such events, but they never simply instigate them. Hawhee argues that a double move occurs within a rhetorical encounter: "the discursive encounter itself forges a different subject . . . and the emergent subject becomes a force in the emerging discourse" (17). That is to say, within a rhetorical encounter rhetors' discourse merges with and emerges from *doxa;* discursive performances entail or produce the very subjectivity we call "rhetor." Hawhee's theory of invention privileges movement, flow, permeability; it is "a simultaneously interruptive and connective hooking-in to circulating discourses" (24). Her appeal to flow and movement invokes the ancient concept of *dunamis,* which was defined in preclassical Greek as "ability," "capacity," or "power" and only later, by Aristotle, as "potential." Hawhee aligns these older senses of power with the Foucauldian notion, an alignment that can be had by translating Foucault's *pouvoir* as Gayatri Spivak does, as "can-do-ness" (Hawhee 29; Spivak 34). This attitude toward power as capability, Hawhee notes, clarifies Foucault's insistence that power is productive.

Spivak derives the sense of power as "can-do-ness" during her attempt to rescue Foucault's treatment of this notion in *La volonte savoir* from "paleonymic" readings (Foucault, *Archaeology* 122; Spivak 31). Spivak argues that "force" has a catachrestic relation to power: "the condition of possibility of power (or power intelligible in its exercise)—'this moving base'—is therefore unmotivated, though not capricious. Its 'origin,' thus heavily framed, is in 'difference,' inequalities in force relations. To read this only as 'our experience of power,' or 'institutional power' (as most people—like Walter J. Ong—read 'writing' as 'systems of graphic marks') is the productive and risky burden of paleonymy that must be persistently resisted as it enables practice. 'Force' is the subindividual name of 'power,' not the place where the 'idea' of power becomes 'hollow' or 'ambiguous'" (31). "Force" is another name for power, a name that highlights its mobility and productivity. Barbara Biesecker explains that Foucauldian power "names not the imposition of a limit that constrains human thought and action but a being-able that is made possible by a grid of intelligibility. Power is a human calculation performed within and inaugurated by the 'lines of making sense' that are operative at a particular historical moment" (356). Like electricity, power travels along the "grid of intelligibility," invoking "lines of making sense," lining up both alongside and crossways, merging and dispersing at connecting points or nodes. Because it has histories, power is differentially distributed along lines and among nodes. In this model of power, then, any rhetorical encounter becomes a lining up alongside or diversion of forces, or, put differently, a recombination or disorientation of already aligned forces. Cultural, discursive, and local-situational contexts generate a huge but nonetheless finite number of "unmotivated, though not capricious" forces.[11] These can include, minimally, a time and place, a disagreement, available arguments, and—once the rhetorical encounter has begun—a rhetor or rhetors. Within such an encounter can-do-ness, capability, *dunamis,* produce rhetorical forces such as conjectures, *enthymemes,* gestures, stances, and movements.

If one sense of power is "can-do-ness," surely it is a defensible leap to the assumption that rhetorical power can be activated by people who are equipped to articulate available openings in discourse, in both senses of "formulating" and "connecting." This is not to imply that the subjectivity of "rhetor" ever inhabits anyone for long periods of time or without competition from other subjectivities. On the other hand, while the movement of difference is incessant, some elements of performances can be repeated. Each instance of a performance will differ from all others, of course, but continuities and similarities (more lines of force) can occur from occasion to occasion; such continuities and similarities, occurring repeatedly over time and place, can be called "style." Gorgias, for example, is famous for his habit of antithesis. Here is a sample from his "Encomium of Helen": "for either by will of Fate and decision of the gods and vote of Necessity did she do what she did, or by force reduced, or by words seduced or by love possessed" (6). This is not mere style in the sense that it is ornament, that the point could have been made plain without it. Greek and Latin terms for stylistic ornament (*turn* and *figure,* respectively) both allude to the human body in motion. Gorgias's "turns" and "figures" are performances that can open other paths in *doxa,* exploit lines of force that can perform other ways of judging Helen's action (Hawhee 23–24). Gorgias apparently wrote no textbook of rhetoric, which is in keeping with his pedagogical preference for teaching by example. He delivered speeches on the same topic over and over but improvised each *toi kairoi,* in accordance with the dictates of time and place (Philostratus I.9.xi). Conceiving rhetorical power as "can-do-ness" aligns it with the Gorgian sense of rhetoric as improvisation, of seizing the *logos* that works in the right place at the right time.

Rhetorical Readiness

Improvisation does not imply unpreparedness—far from it. It is precisely preparedness that enables rhetorical improvisation. I noted earlier that Spivak reads Foucault's power/knowledge as a catachrestic pair: "lines of knowing constituting ways of doing and not doing, the lines themselves irregular clinamens from subindividual atomic systems—fields of force, archives of utterance" (37). One has to do in order to know, but one has also to know in order to do. Athletes and musicians achieve preparedness with practice, but practice can be enhanced by study. My use of "study" here is not meant to invoke only images of musty libraries. Athletes and musicians study by doing exercises, looking at video or listening to tapes, watching others perform or heeding the advice of teachers and coaches. Study is efficient; its advantage is that it allows anticipation of missteps. Put another way, study can reduce the extent of trial and error because students can learn from the mistakes and successes of exemplars and teachers. But study can also mislead because moves that worked in one situation may not be appropriate for the next.

Isocrates declared that mastery of an art such as rhetoric requires three things: aptitude, study, and practice ("Against the Sophists" 17). Atwill points out that aptitude is itself produced by study and practice: "the successful performance of the rhetor who has appropriated both rules and proper timing is often a testimony not to his mastery of an art but, paradoxically, to his 'natural' ability—and even 'natural' virtue. It is when art 'appears to disappear' that it has been most successfully appropriated—or transformed into 'nature'" (59). In this view Michael Jordan and Yo-Yo Ma are committed rather than talented. This analysis may move close to what Isocrates may have meant. He insisted, for example, that his instruction would not change a venal person into a virtuous one ("Antidosis" 275). To do so requires that a student be committed to acquiring virtue, which entails in turn that virtue be studied and practiced—precisely the tactics that repel people who would be vicious. On the other hand, Isocrates was confident that instruction in rhetoric could teach people to invent arguments: "formal training makes [students] more skillful and more resourceful in discovering the possibilities of a subject; for it teaches them to take from a readier source the topics which they otherwise hit upon in haphazard fashion" ("Against the Sophists" 15). The fine points of delivery, obviously, are best acquired by imitation and practice. But the power of invention is usefully enhanced by study, in the sense of "going to the library." That way is efficient, and it is also available when an exemplar may not be readily at hand. People who want to learn ancient Greek today have to work without the example of native speakers, and so the library sense of study is our only option. Study can defy the contingencies of time and place, but only to some extent. No one is certain whether the careful phonetic reconstructions of classical Greek made by modern linguists could actually be understood by Plato. A similar situation would obtain for an aspiring student-rhetor in Isocrates' school. He could read Gorgias's speech on Helen and imitate it, and yet after Gorgias's death he had no standard, aside from the collective memory of those who had heard and seen Gorgias perform, against which to measure the quality or aptness of his imitation. (The limitation on teaching-by-performance has been alleviated to an extent by audio and video recording technology.)

There is another upside to study insofar as knowledge of past performances may actually stimulate useful or memorable realignments of old materials. Acquaintance with the topics of invention is to rhetors as playbooks are to athletes or as chord progressions are to musicians—they are repertoires, available for plunder should a circumstance arise in which they might be used or riffed upon. Knowing when and how to riff comes from study and practice: the need to riff arises during an encounter with other players or with an audience; the knowledge acquired by preparation is in turn shaped by that situation.

The appearance of textbooks is a sure indication that a practice has become codified or institutionalized to such an extent that it can be learned without a model. The Greek term for study and practice was *techne,* usually translated as "art." With the advent of literacy the word *techne* came to designate artifacts, such as manuals of instruction, as well as a body of lore and its associated practices. Aristotle's lost collection of textbooks on rhetoric, for example, is called *Synagoge Technon*. George Kennedy argues that rhetoric was "conceptualized" during the late fifth and fourth centuries BCE, that is, during what is now called the classical period (*Classical* 7). By "conceptualization" Kennedy seems to mean "disciplined" in the sense that practitioners are "able to give a systematic description of [their] method" (*Classical* 7). It can be argued, however, that rhetoric became a *techne*—in an older sense of lore and its associated practices—much earlier. And so while it remains true that the word *rhetorike* first appears in Plato, this event was no doubt preceded (and motivated) by a long history of "making do" argumentatively (Schiappa, "Did Plato"). Pierre Bourdieu posits that arts or "fields" are constructed when practices are no longer repeatedly instantiated "without passing through discourse. . . . Excellence has ceased to exist once people start asking whether it can be taught" (*Outline* 200 n. 20). Ironically such closure occurs because of the incessant movement of difference, when the "confrontation of different styles . . . makes it necessary to say what goes without saying, justify what is taken for granted, make an ought-to-be and an ought-to-do out of what had up to then been regarded as the only way to be and do" (*Outline* 200). In other words, *techne* can emerge when practitioners begin to riff. In her study of Pre-Socratic attitudes toward *techne* Atwill is at pains to distinguish an older sense of study/practice from its later formulation as "skill" or "instrumentality" (as in our "technique" and "technology"). She argues that preclassical thinkers treated *techne* as a way or a path that could be "retraced, modified, adapted, and 'shared.' The purpose of such a path, at least in ancient depictions of invention, is not to find a 'thing.' A *techne* deforms limits into new paths in order to reach—or better yet, to produce—an alternative destination" (69). This preclassical sense of invention retains its sophistic association with practice, temporality, and location, contingency and situatedness.

In sum, then, a rhetor is someone who is committed to the study and practice of invention, who by virtue of that preparation has achieved rhetorical "can-do-ness." She is ready to seize appropriate arguments when they are made available by the movement of contending discursive forces, of *logoi*. The name "rhetor" evokes a subjectivity rather than a person, a subjectivity that may be inhabited momentarily, on occasion, or more or less consistently in the case of a professional speaker, writer, or journalist. Anyone may inhabit that subjectivity, but those who are prepared do so with a higher chance of success at persuading whatever audiences emerge during rhetorical encounters than those who are not prepared. Without preparation in invention would-be rhetors stand about the same chance of success as I have when I pick up a basketball or a cello. Invention suited to specific situations need not be learned in school. It may be absorbed on the street or in the boardroom. However, awareness of invention as a general set of strategies that can be adapted to almost every situation is enhanced by systematic study.

A Postmodern Discursive Ethic

The postmodern sophistic model of rhetorical invention sketched here privileges movement, flexibility, contingency, and difference. A discursive ethic emerges from the primacy awarded to these values. The point of ethical rhetorical exchange is never to shut down argumentative possibilities but to generate all the positions that are available and articulable in a given moment and situation. An ethical rhetor can never foreclose the possibility that an opposing argument will open new lines of rhetorical force. Good rhetoric looks for all available arguments, just as Aristotle insisted. Bad rhetoric, on the other hand, is static and univocal. It favors the status quo and extrapolates predictions from it. It may posit unities that transcend temporal and local contexts. A bad argument shuts down alternatives and hides the proliferation of differences created by its very formulation.

Of course these definitions of good and bad arguments bar fundamentalisms from inclusion in the category of "good rhetoric." They reflect my preferences for inclusion rather than exclusion, profligate over miserly invention, democracy instead of authoritarianism. These are the evaluative foundations from which I work (at this moment). I can do nothing else, and I can't be sure as I name them that I'm telling the truth. Moreover, I realize that in other historical or geographical contexts any of these values can become vices. Barbara Herrnstein Smith argues that values exist in an economy of relations to one another such that the worth of each depends on its relations to others (*Contingencies* 30). That is to say, values are contingent. Her position is postmodern because it recognizes that values function within systems of differing relations to one another. It is also political, but it certainly isn't conservative, and it's not quite liberal either. A preference for contingency does not entail tolerance for all possibilities. It does require awareness that there are other ways of seeing, knowing, and believing, all shaped by temporal and spatial circumstance. Some of these are readily available in a given context, while others are simply glimmers on an epistemological horizon. Some ways of believing have constructive effects, and others are simply destructive. Whether these effects are good or bad, of course, depends.

A crucial difference between liberalism and postmodernism is that the latter provides theoretical space for the making of ethical judgments (Derrida, *Limited* and *Acts;* Lyotard; Lyotard and Thebaud). Such judgments are always limited in scope by the fact of their contingency, but they can and must be made. Some situations throw up so many compelling arguments on all sides that they are in fact undecidable on their so-called merits. The practice of clitoridectomy is a case in point (Walker and Parmar). Given the complex cross-cultural valuations raised by this practice, one simply takes a position on it, realizing its contingency and living with the consequences of having taken that position. If I take up a position on this or any other question, my having done so emphatically does not entail that my "personality" is improved or tainted. A postmodern rhetorical ethic does *not* associate the evaluation of arguments with evaluation of a rhetor's "self." While I agree with Quintilian that the ideal rhetor is a "good [person] speaking well," I am not willing to assert that good arguments are always or only made by good people or the converse (XII.1.1). The necessity of placing brackets in this line in order to eliminate Quintilian's exclusionist use of the word "man" ("vir bonus dicendi peritus") underscores the difficulty posed by such a connection. Rhetorical arguments generate their own lines of force, and it is not possible to determine, at the point of utterance, what will be effected by one's having articulated something. Invention is committed to the discovery of any and all possibilities alternative to those that are currently envisioned by parties to discourse. Granted, this process is never disinterested. On the other hand, the goal of complete investigation is never achieved, and a rhetor's control of the process is never guaranteed. As Victor Vitanza is fond of saying, words want to be written. Sometimes they write us.

To associate personalities with arguments is a hangover from liberal rhetorical theory, where invention indeed depends on the particular qualities of individual minds. The association between individual minds and beliefs is supported by psychology, where (admittedly impressive) empirical studies establish, for instance, that so-called authoritarian personalities tend to subscribe to right-wing political beliefs (Altemeyer).[12] Psychologists' analyses of the relation of belief to personality are useful to a postmodern rhetorical theory to the extent that they posit reflexive relations between psyches and environments. I argue in the next chapter that beliefs are "ours" only to the extent that we wield them in argument on occasion; beliefs and arguments actually circulate in the reflexive relations between culture and "selves" that Pierre Bourdieu calls "the *habitus.*" Thus if one is concerned to imbue an argument with "goodness" or "badness," as I am, she is forced to examine its relation to the circulation of evaluative discourse within the relevant context. The liberal focus on individual minds, then, is far too limited to enable us to grasp the ethical quality of rhetorical inventions.

3

BELIEF AND PASSIONATE COMMITMENT

According to Cicero, rhetoric has three goals: "the proof of our allegations, the winning of our hearers' favor, and the rousing of their feelings to whatever impulse our case may require" (*De Oratore* II.115). This list of objectives, which were called the "offices" or "duties" of rhetoric by medieval and Renaissance rhetoricians, was interpreted by them to mean that the aims of rhetoric are to teach, to delight, and to move (Vickers 50). This formulation allowed rhetoric teachers to establish a hierarchy of preferred genres, with eloquence (*movere*) ranking as the highest rhetorical endeavor because it is the most demanding. But Cicero's Latin in this passage may be read otherwise, to say that a rhetor must of course provide evidence to support her claims, but she must also insure that her audience respects her character and her argument. In addition, she must arouse whatever emotions are necessary to move an audience toward acceptance. Cicero suggests, then, that rhetorical effect is achieved by means of affect: the beliefs and behavior of audiences are altered not only by the provision of proofs but by establishment of ethical, evaluative, and emotional climates in which such changes can occur. This reading of the passage renders Cicero's advice distinctly out of step with liberal rhetorical theory, wherein emotion is configured as irrational and where values are irrelevant. On the other hand, it aligns Cicero's advice with contemporary scholarship on the relation of affect to belief.

Belief—which sophistic rhetoricians called *doxa*—can be paradoxical. People can hold contradictory beliefs; for example, in America super-patriots brook no dissent from obeisance to national policy despite the fact that free speech is an important American value. People can also subscribe to beliefs that have bad consequences for them: those who will never become capitalists nonetheless remain staunch supporters of capitalism; women cling to patriarchal values in the face of feminist analyses of the dangers posed to women by patriarchy. A liberal might say that more and better education would resolve these paradoxes: if people knew more about the ideologies to which they subscribe (that is, if they were better educated), they would remember that dissent is protected by the First Amendment, or they would realize that capitalism and patriarchy work against the interests of many. On the other hand, if one claims, alongside Slavoj Zizek, that people in fact know what they are doing but keep on doing it anyway, it follows that something other than knowledge or understanding motivates people when they accept claims that are contradictory to one another or are detrimental to their well-being (*Sublime* 31–33).

While persuasion can of course be effected by means of reasoned argument, I posit that ideology, fantasy, and emotion are primary motivators of belief and action. Take, for example, George W. Bush's characterization of Osama bin Laden as evil, a claim that was reportedly widely accepted by the American people during the months following September 11, 2001.[1] On its face such a conclusion can reasonably be drawn from empirical evidence and testimony connecting bin Laden to the horrible events of that day—granted that "evil" is defined as a human capacity. However, the persuasive force of Bush's claim is enhanced by its appeal to a racist ideology that Edward Said names "orientalism," which calls up images of the "evil Arab" that stalked characters in old Disney cartoons. There is another persuasive layer at work here as well—the Christian imaginary in which evil is associated with the figure of Satan. Within this context, and for some believers, the word *evil* can excite a network of emotions habitually associated since childhood with the devil. In this context the claim that Osama bin Laden is evil can legitimate Bush's desire to track him down and eradicate him. It has the further persuasive advantage of aligning Bush with the forces of good.

The workings of all of these sources of motivation have their own logics—that is to say, the relations between and among the moments of belief, fantasy, and myth can be traced, and these relations can be shown to make a kind of sense that is not covered by the term *reason*. I borrow the term *moments* from Ernst Laclau and Chantal Mouffe, who define them as "differential positions, insofar as they appear articulated within a discourse" (105). A "moment," then, is some belief that is more or less firmly situated by a history of its use within one or more discursive contexts. Following the practice of Laclau and Mouffe I use the term *position* interchangeably with *moment*. Both terms operate here as they do in the statement "she took up a position." Again following Laclau and Mouffe I use the term *articulation* in a double sense, to describe formulations of moments, as well as connections made among them. Stuart Hall nicely captures the double sense of this term: "'articulate' means to utter, to speak forth, to be articulate. It carries that sense of language-ing, of expressing, and so on. But we also speak of an 'articulate' lorry: a lorry where the front and back can, but need not necessarily, be connected to one another. The two parts are connected to each other, but through a specific linkage, which can be broken. An articulation is thus the form of the connection that can make a unity of two different elements, under certain conditions. It is a linkage which is not necessary, determined, absolute, and essential for all time" (141). I coin the term *ideologic* to name articulations in the second sense, connections made between and among moments (positions) that occur or are taken up within ideology. For example: a worker who defends capitalism has taken up a position, has articulated (in the sense of "formulated") a discursive moment that could be otherwise, although the potential for alternative readings is limited by the present hegemony of capitalism. In forwarding this belief the worker selects a moment from a plenitude of others occurring in any number of belief systems. He or she can then deploy a familiar ideologic, articulating (in the sense of "connecting") this moment with others. A common move in the defense of free-market capitalism, for instance, is to connect belief in it to the belief that poor people are so because they are lazy, thus excusing capitalism from its structurally inevitable unfair distribution of income.

Articulations may be new or as old as the hills. New articulations are relatively rare because habitual and timeworn articulations actually construct communities, at least in part. (New articulations can of course come into a given community when it comes in contact with another.) Hall takes note of the very old articulation of religion with politics: "Anyone interested in the politics of contemporary culture has to recognize the continuing force in modern life of cultural forms which have a prehistory long predating that of our rational systems, and which sometimes constitute the only cultural resources which human beings have to make sense of the world. . . . There are powerful, immensely strong . . . 'lines of tenden-tial force' articulating that religious formation to political, economic, and ideological structures" (142). Rearticulation and disarticulation of com-mon elements occur all the time within a given community, and these processes constitute rhetorical lines of force. Hall reminds us that "since those articulations are not inevitable, not necessary, they can potentially be transformed, so that religion can be articulated in more than one way" (142). Apocalypticism, for example, as it is currently constituted depends on a nineteenth-century rearticulation of elements contained in the apoca-lyptic narrative appearing in the Book of Revelation. The details of this rearticulation, called "millennial dispensationalism," have been continu-ously refined (that is, rearticulated) since that time, both to keep the apoc-alyptic narrative current with historical events and to fulfill conservative Christians' desire to engage in politics (see chapter 4).

The moves I designate as "articulations" are not equivalent to what liberals mean by "reason." Liberal reasoning is grounded on observations or perceptions.[2] Moments of ideology, on the other hand, occur as beliefs, while moments of desire are staged as fantasies (Zizek, *Plague*). Groups can share collective desires that give rise to collective fantasies, and myth is a special case of collective fantasy. One difference between ideologic and rea-son, then, has to do with the sources from which its positions (moments) are drawn—belief, passion, values, desires—rather than empirical evi-dence. But ideologic also entails more means of making connections than are acknowledged in liberal accounts of reason. For one thing, an appeal to a belief can stimulate an emotional response that in turn can activate other, closely related beliefs. For another, ideological means of connection include webs of analogous and/or metonymic historical associations (that is, articulations) built up over time. A burning cross evokes a set of such associations for racists, as well as for those who are targeted by racism. The associations evoked for members of these two groups are very different, but they stem from the same history of uses of a fiery cross.

Because its evocative power draws on emotional, historical, and other contexts, ideologic cannot easily be reduced to a logic. That is, the move-ment of ideologic cannot be generalized across belief systems but must be studied, rather, in the context of given belief systems. Outside of the con-text of racism, for example, a burning cross can be given an anti-Christian reading, although this alternative articulation is not as powerful as that made within white racism because its use therein is densely connected to other beliefs in that system, as well as an appalling history of intimidation, abduction, and murder. The connections (articulations) that are typically made between moments in a given belief system are also specific to that system, and so their "logics" are also dependent on the contexts in which they are used. Once made, however, ideological connections can be endlessly repeated, and their endurance is remarkable. A fiery cross was first used as an instrument of intimidation during the 1870s, and as recently as 2003 cross-burning was the subject of litigation brought before the Supreme Court.

Discourse, Hegemony, and the *Habitus*

The assumption that human beings operate in relation to some medium is characteristic of postmodern thought, whether this medium is called "discourse" (Foucault), "writing" (Derrida), "the symbolic" (Lacan), "hegemony" (Gramsci), or "the *habitus*" (Bourdieu). Of course these constructs differ from one another, and selection of one of them as a theoretical frame creates inevitable consequences, possibilities, and limitations for whatever follows. Because Pierre Bourdieu focuses explicitly on the body and on practice, I adopt his notion of the *habitus* as a context for locating more precisely what I mean by belief. In Latin *habitus* signifies a stable condition or situation, but the word is also related to terms meaning "aptitude" and "dwelling," both of which uses survive in English as "habit," "inhabit," and "habitation." For Bourdieu the *habitus* is "the system of structured, structuring dispositions . . . which is constituted in practice" (*Logic* 52). The *habitus* includes cultural representations such as history, memory, ideology, fantasy, myth, and lore, and it also includes culturally habituated practices, what Bourdieu refers to as "bodily *hexis*"—"a durable way of standing, speaking, walking, and thereby of feeling and thinking" (*Logic* 70). According to Bourdieu, the *habitus* is "a product of history" (*Logic* 56). Because of this the *habitus* has a material dimension: subjects are formed by embodied habits drawn from culture, such as shaking hands and not blowing one's nose at the table. The *habitus* also provides templates for the production of buildings such as schools and churches; artifacts such as uniforms and Bibles; judicial, political, and ethical practices such as trials, elections, and giving to charity. Some habits endure over vast periods, while others emerge and disappear in a relatively brief period of time. Wearing garments is a very old cultural practice, adopted in part, no doubt, to protect the body from weather and other dangerous features of the environment. But the practice of wearing jewelry, which has additional uses (ornament, signification of kinship or economic status), is also very old (Hublin et al.). Its earliest use signals the emergence of fashion, which changes far more rapidly than the function of protection requires.

The *habitus* may be more inclusive than Foucault's notion of discourse, which Lee Quinby handily defines as "a 'system of dispersion' of statements that define, designate, circumscribe, and sometimes eliminate certain objects of its authority" (Quinby, *Anti-Apocalypse* xv; Foucault, *Archeology*). "Discourse" refers to language-in-use, but in light of his later work Foucault's "discursive formations" may be read more inclusively to designate institutions (church, school, prison, media, state) and practices such as "ethical technologies of the subject" and "relations of governmentality" (*Technologies;* "Governmentality"). Outside of a Foucauldian context, however, the term *discourse* can signal a more restricted conceptual reach that, read strictly, may be thought to exclude nonlinguistic manifestations of human being. Since I do not want to get into the complex and ultimately futile business of distinguishing between discursive and nondiscursive arenas of human being, I stick with Bourdieu's term for the most part. On those occasions when the word *discourse* is the least cumbersome available alternative, readers should understand that I mean by it language-in-use as well as actions and artifacts.

One more theoretical concept is necessary to my analysis of belief. Following the work of Laclau and Mouffe, I assume that some discourses and practices achieve hegemony. A hegemony is any set of signifiers and practices that achieves a powerful, near-exclusive hold on a community's beliefs and actions. Earlier I characterized liberalism and Christianity as hegemonic discursive practices. To say this is to imply that these formations influence realms other than the strictly political or religious. According to Laclau and Mouffe, within hegemony meanings become fixed around "nodal points" that stabilize moments or positions in such a way that they seem natural rather than constructed (112). They borrow their concept of nodal points from Jacques Lacan's *points de capiton,* literally "quilting points" (Lacan, *Ecrits;* Torfing 98). Nodal points seem to arrest and even stabilize the movement of difference, and hence they limit the possibility that openings or spaces for dissent may appear within hegemony. Laclau and Mouffe write that hegemonic nodal points are "highly overdetermined: they may constitute points of condensation of a number of social relations and, thus, become a focal point of a multiplicity of totalizing effects" (139). "God" and "the Bible" are nodal points in contemporary Christian apocalypticism, for example, while "rights" and "freedom" function as master signifiers in liberal discourse. It is important to remember that hegemony does not name an entity; a hegemony is a *relation* among competing ways of constructing the world. Because of the antagonistic relations among actual hegemonies and discourses that are competing for that status, the achievement of hegemony is temporal and local, although a hegemony as powerful as Christianity, say, can be relatively extensive over both space and time. Christianity has been practiced for over two thousand years, and nearly one-third of the world's population are professing Christians. Many of these people live in areas where Christianity is not hegemonic, and because of this their religious beliefs and practices are experienced very differently from those of American Christians. While one is in a hegemonic relation, its strictures can seem totalizing, whether or not one subscribes to the hegemonic discourse in question. Thus the beliefs and practices of Americans who are not Christians are nonetheless affected by the hegemonic status of Christianity in this country. (I insist on this relation despite the claim made by some Christian political activists—that liberals are trying to erase Christian belief and practice.) To give another example, it is difficult to "not-think" capitalism in America at this time, even though most Americans seem unable to bring to consciousness their awareness of its effects on all of us. Even writers of science fiction find it difficult to conceptualize what a fairer redistribution of resources might look like. Nevertheless, like all emanations of the *habitus,* Christian and capitalist discourses and practices are products of history, and they have antagonistic "constitutive outsides"—for example, Islam and the democratic socialism practiced in parts of Europe.

Belief and Ideology

Beliefs do not exist in isolation. Belief in the superiority of a vegetarian diet, for example, is connected to systems of belief about human health, animal welfare, and/or protection of the environment. Vegetarianism, environmentalism, and animal rights are ideologies, and, as the example of vegetarianism suggests, ideologies can govern practice.[3] It is possible to abstain from eating animal products (or anything else) on the ground of taste, of course, but generally people who have a choice of diets and who refrain from eating this or that food do so because they are ideologically motivated. For my purposes here I characterize beliefs as moments of ideology and ideology as the medium within which beliefs are articulated with one another. Someone may conceptualize (that is, articulate) the belief that consumption of animal products is to be avoided either before, while, or after she connects (articulates) that belief to any others she may hold concerning her health, the environment, or the rights of animals. Beliefs and their articulations in ideology are rhetorical forces in the sense described earlier. They may be deployed within a rhetorical encounter to alter the alignments and directions taken by other rhetorical forces at work in a given situation, such as factual evidence.

I use the term *ideology* to refer to any system within which beliefs, symbols, and images are articulated in such a way that they assemble a more or less coherent depiction of reality and/or establish a hierarchy of values. Ideologies are always interested, in the same way that beliefs serve certain investments. In American patriotism a set of beliefs about the country's exceptionalism, which dates back to its earliest settlement by Europeans, is currently articulated with the flag, yellow ribbons, images of people in military or civic uniforms (police officers and firefighters, for example), as well as other moments in the ideology (Cecilia O'Leary). Any of these may be articulated with any other that normally circulates within the belief system. Symbols represent belief, but they also produce it. Moreover, their representative relation to belief is indeterminate; that is to say, what is "intended" by a representation is not necessarily what is conveyed because culture, history, and situation play constitutive roles in the determination of meaning. Some people have difficulty disarticulating support for American troops from a prowar stance, for instance, and so they might take a display of yellow ribbons as support for war as well as for the soldiers who are fighting it. However, the meanings of symbols can become sufficiently common and widespread in a given community that they become relatively stable. When this happens they can exert persuasive force. When I see yellow ribbons tied around a tree or affixed to a lapel, I am invited (or even subtly coerced) to acquiesce in supporting our troops. Like symbols, images are also both representative and persuasive (De Luca). A series of videotapes of a calm-featured and apparently unscathed Osama bin Laden was released in the months following the U.S. invasions of Afghanistan and Iraq, and his image on these tapes, apart from what he says, is certainly intended to persuade his followers (and his enemies) that he is still alive and able to lead.

Belief circulates within the *habitus* and must conform to the inclusions and exclusions built into it. That is to say, the *habitus* allows some beliefs and belief systems to emerge while others are unavailable, repressed, or forgotten. Because science currently enjoys hegemony in Western culture, its dispersions are extremely influential, and so competing fields of inquiry such as alchemy and astrology subject or inhabit far fewer people than they used to. Today people generally accept that the earth rotates around the sun and no longer believe that the earth is the center of the universe. Even though this change in belief may not on its face seem to have affected everyday life very much, its consequences for the subsequent achievement of hegemony of science were enormous. Acceptance of a solarcentric universe inaugurated the antagonistic relation of science to religion, as the clergy who opposed publication of Galileo's work clearly realized (Margolis). Despite the current hegemonic status of science, however, scientific theories can be controversial: evolutionary theory, cloning, and gene therapy, for example, are all hotly contested. Evolutionary theory is controversial because it counters a story of origin forwarded by (some versions of) Christianity. On the other hand, few people doubt that scientists can manipulate genes, but this capability evokes substantial controversy about values. Interestingly scientists themselves can become outsiders to scientific discourse in arguments about evolution or gene therapy if they are subjected to another hegemony that informs them more thoroughly (on occasion or always) than does science. Feminist theorists have shown, for example, that genetic research has been influenced by the patriarchal assumption of dimorphism (Butler, *Gender* 106–11; Fausto-Sterling). This line of analysis suggests that a pecking order may occasionally coalesce among discursive formations (in this case patriarchy trumped the scientific method), although this order is never stable because the relative power of a given discursive practice to subject its adherents varies from context to context.

I distinguish ideology from hegemony rhetorically by asserting that ideological belief is relatively more open to controversy than is hegemonic belief. Another way to put this is to say that hegemonic discourses and practices "go without saying." They are so thoroughly naturalized, so imbricated in daily life, that they are seldom brought to consciousness. Ideological belief, on the other hand, is available for contest. It requires more frequent defense because ideological discourses and practices subject fewer people, for shorter periods of time, than do hegemonies. One is much more likely to encounter a liberal or a Christian during one's daily rounds than a vegetarian or an alien abductee. I realize that this distinction-by-extension is a slippery business. It is not always easy to maintain, particularly when discussing a belief system such as patriarchy or white racism whose hegemonic status is currently undergoing challenge. Neither of these formations any longer "goes without saying," at least in large public venues. Fusses are now made when politicians and other public figures utter racist or sexist comments, and sometimes offenders are even disciplined for their transgressions. This is not to say that either of these belief systems has lost its grip on Americans—far from it. Nonetheless, their current status does differ from that which obtained during the 1950s, when it was possible to claim with some assurance that a home in a white suburb was a manifestation of patriarchy, or when all public institutions maintained separate lavatory facilities for African Americans and whites. In contrast, one may still claim with confidence that a church is a manifestation of Christian religiosity. This analysis suggests, by the way, that any ideology may be a dethroned hegemony, or, more ominously with regard to patriarchy and racism, a hegemony-in-waiting.

The Conjectural Nature of Belief

Beliefs can perform many tasks. They may be representative in the sense that they depict some state of affairs ("America is the world's only remaining superpower"); they may assess value ("America: Land of the Free and Home of the Brave"); they may draw boundaries and place limits ("Protesters are traitors"); or they may advocate policy ("Love it or leave it"). There are many other possibilities as well. Students of ancient rhetorics will recognize my allusion in these examples to the questions or places of stasis: conjecture, definition, quality, and policy. Ancient rhetoricians treated assertions about the way things are—what exists, what human nature is, how the world operates, what society demands—as conjectures rather than facts.[4] The Older Sophists were far more suspicious of the representative accuracy of facts and testimony than are moderns. Gorgias claimed that nothing exists, and if it does, it can be neither known nor communicated (Sextus Empiricus vii.45). What can be communicated is language (*logos*), whose representative relation to reality is always to be taken as fortuitous. Aristotle was contemptuous of empirical proofs on the ground that they did not have to be invented but only used; he was far more interested in the rhetorical uses of conjecture (*Rhetoric* I.ii.1356a; II.xix.1392b).

I argue that the ancient notion of conjecture is compatible with the postmodern insistence on indeterminacy. Derrida argues that the movement of difference installs an instability in reference that renders it productive rather than representative: "In order for this history to have taken place, in its turbulence and in its stases, in order for relations of force, of tensions, or of wars to have taken place, in order for hegemonies to have imposed themselves during a determinate period, there must have been a certain play in all these structures, hence a certain instability or non-self-identity, nontransparency. Rhetorical equivocation and mobility, for instance, must have been able to work within 'meaning.' *Differance* must have been able to affect reference" (*Limited* 145). In other words, the meanings and uses of terms are influenced by language, history, and culture; their extension can be limited by these forces, but meanings are never stable either, because of the movement of *differance*. (The French term reminds us that differing occurs in time as well as across spaces.)

Although ancient rhetoricians used a different theoretical vocabulary in which to articulate the tenuousness of representation, they also assumed that meanings are assigned within situations and are influenced by them. A standard example of conjecture in classical sources involves characters borrowed from Homer. Ulysses happens upon the body of his enemy Ajax, who has committed suicide. Teucer finds Ulysses near the body with bloody sword in hand and charges him with murder (*Rhetorica ad Herrennium* I.ix.18, II.xix.28–30). Quintilian demonstrates how any discourse that emerges from this incident must be conjectural: "Teucer accuses Ulysses of murdering Ajax, and states that he was found in a lonely place near the lifeless body of his enemy with a blood-stained sword in his hands. To this Ulysses does not merely reply that he did not do the deed, but adds that he had no quarrel with Ajax. . . . He then goes on to say how he came to be in the lonely place, how he found Ajax lying lifeless and drew the sword from the wound" (IV.ii.13). Teucer and Ulysses are conjecturing, inventing different ways of reading the scene. Quintilian notes as well that this fictional example can be generalized in order to be of wider use as a common topic: "every [forensic] question is based on assertion by one party and denial by another" (Quintilian III.vi.7; see Aristotle, *Rhetoric* II.19.1392b–93a). In ancient rhetorics, then, descriptions of events are assessments. They are interested insofar as they serve desires and needs; they are representative only to the extent that they depict "takes" or "views" or "stances" on truth and reality. These terms suggest performances rather than references, inventions rather than interpretations.

I propose that beliefs are conjectures: that is, beliefs are views or attitudes or assessments about nature (including human nature) that serve the interests of the believer and/or some other person, group, or institution. Barbara Herrnstein Smith observes that beliefs are maintained if they "turn out to be conceptually congenial, practically reliable, and otherwise serviceable over a broad range of conditions" (*Belief* 44). That is, beliefs must be useful. They need only be true (in the sense of "seemingly consonant with reality") within contexts where such consonance is useful to the believer. The relation of belief to empirical reality is actually indeterminate. This holds even for those beliefs that evolutionary psychologists assume to be hardwired into the human genetic code ("avoid large predators"; "this plant is edible") insofar as such beliefs coalesced precisely because they served proto- and early humans' interest in survival (Mithen). That such beliefs were once related to survival does not entail that they remain serviceable in all times and places, much less that they are universally true. Nevertheless, they may be retained within the *habitus*. Herrnstein Smith notes that "the acquired beliefs of a cat whose beliefs kill her are unlikely to survive the cat, but those of a human creature very well may" (*Belief* 48). Unlike cats, humans can hang on to empirically mistaken or useless beliefs long past their recommended expiration date.

Following Bourdieu, I assume that beliefs are not only "mental" (*Pascalian* 11–12). Beliefs can be learned by means of discourse, but they can also be learned through adopting bodily positions, making gestures, and performing movements. Beliefs acquired in any of these ways become habitual through repetition. For example, religious believers kneel or prostrate themselves when they worship. These bodily positions, and their repetition, both construct and express belief. Herrnstein Smith argues further that the embodiedness of belief in part constructs the self: "our 'environments' also include our own bodies, which are not themselves separable from our own beliefs in the sense of perceptual/behavioral tendencies. These continuities imply . . . that our *beliefs* are continuously formed and transformed by our . . . lifelong interactions with our . . . *selves,* including our own other and prior beliefs" (*Belief* 47).[5] That is to say, the constructive relations among environments, bodies, selves, and the formation/deformation of beliefs are continuously reflexive. Slavoj Zizek in fact refers to embodied belief as a "*belief before belief.* . . . By following a custom, the subject believes without knowing it, so that the final conversion is merely a formal act by means of which we recognize what we have already believed" (*Sublime* 40). If a friend gives me a red, white, and blue ribbon, I may wear it on my lapel in order to make her happy. I might say to myself that I wear the ribbon ironically, believing myself to be maintaining distance from its persuasive force. Nonetheless, anyone who sees the ribbon on my lapel misses the irony, unless I explain at length, and in any case such an explanation protests too much. By wearing the ribbon I enact belief in its message whether I agree with that message or not. Zizek might say that my arrival at this awareness is merely a formality.

Commonplaces

The *Oxford English Dictionary* tells me that *belief* refers to "the mental action, condition, or habit, of trusting to or confiding in a person or thing; trust, dependence, reliance, confidence, faith." I like the emphasis given here to trust, dependence, and reliance, all of which point up the necessity of relatedness and otherness to belief. That is to say, beliefs and belief systems are social, taken as true or relevant on the basis of trust and confidence in an other, be that other an individual, a group, an institution, or a tradition.

Given the social character of belief, it seems accurate to say that many beliefs are commonplaces. In ancient rhetorics the defining characteristic of a commonplace was not its truth value but the frequency of its use; that is, the chief mark of a commonplace is its wide dispersal among members of a community. Phrases such as "family values" and slogans such as "support our troops" are commonplaces in contemporary American discourse. Each of these commonplaces presupposes and encapsulates fairly extensive arguments that are not often uttered but that can be deduced and reconstructed. A commonplace can remain unspoken by a given individual who nonetheless accepts it, and people can be surprised to learn of their subscription to this or that common belief. To my chagrin I am often moved by commonplaces that circulate within belief systems I find repugnant, for example, beautifully orchestrated flyovers of baseball games by air force pilots that are, among other things, celebrations of my country's capacity for surveillance and killing. The surprise sometimes happens during argument, when a hitherto unsuspected commonplace articulates itself without warning, but it can also occur during reflection. I confess, for example, that I still register a negative reaction to a woman wearing white shoes after Labor Day. This happens despite my commitment to feminism, which teaches me that this reaction—learned literally at my mother's knee—is sexist. The ideologic within which the commonplace is entailed is itself sexist: one of its premises is that women who wear white shoes during winter have no taste. But more deeply occulted beliefs are at work as well: that women who would do such a thing have the wrong class affiliation and, further, that their moral (read "sexual") standards are not those of respectable bourgeois women. I am not quite sure how I know all of this, because I was not able to articulate the full argument until long after I first absorbed the commonplace. This bit of ideologic seems silly now, given the relaxation of standards in both sexual morality and fashion since the 1950s. Its arbitrariness has become wholly apparent to me since I moved to the desert, where winter is less an empirical fact than a state of mind. Nevertheless, the commonplace still operates on me whether I like it or not (I don't). What's more, I am not alone in being "in its grip"—in 2004 a group of women students, whose average age was then twenty-four, told me that they too were familiar with this bit of lore.

Some commonplaces may be so hoary with use that they have become proverbial ("a stitch in time saves nine"), while others are both durable and current. In 1990 Howard Zinn listed these examples from American moral and sociopolitical discourse: "There are unjust wars, but also just wars"; "Freedom of speech is desirable, but not when it threatens national security"; "If you work hard enough, you'll make a good living. If you are poor, you have only yourself to blame" (3). All of these are still in circulation, although the particular circumstances to which each can be applied change over time and location. Zinn may have been thinking about arguments over Vietnam when he compiled this list, but the commonplace about the relation of free speech to national security was powerfully revived in the aftermath of 9/11. Commonplaces are known to all who participate in the communal discourse in which they circulate, and because they are widely accepted, rhetors may use them as discursive sites from which to launch arguments that are not so likely to be met with general approval.

The terms *liberty* and *equality,* when situated in liberal discourse, signal chains of argument that were revolutionary when they emerged during the eighteenth century. Used as commonplaces they encapsulate two important moments in the history of human belief: that human beings are custodians of their own persons and that all individuals are equal before the law. Moreover, the history of their use has articulated a firm connection between these terms. In 1791 Mary Wollstonecraft argued that women need access to education in order to achieve equality and freedom. In 1854 Elizabeth Cady Stanton used these same values to argue against American laws restricting women's freedom of movement and rights of inheritance (Karlyn Kohrs Campbell 145). Cady Stanton's arguments met with some success almost immediately, while Wollstonecraft's did not; this difference may be accounted for in part by the fact that the tenets of liberalism were radical in 1791, while they had become widely accepted, if not hegemonic, among the nineteenth-century New Englanders to whom Cady Stanton appealed. The commonplaces of liberty and equality were also put to successful use by nineteenth-century abolitionists and by proponents of civil rights during the mid–twentieth century. As I write, they are being deployed once again to argue for the extension of a variety of civil rights to homosexuals. Clearly these liberal values are still in wide circulation—that is to say, they retain the status of commonplaces—even though liberal politics and policies have lost ground since the 1980s.

One function of hegemony and ideology is to create identity, to disguise or hide the flow of difference.[6] Manuel Castells defines identity as "the process of construction of meaning on the basis of a cultural attribute, or related set of cultural attributes, that is/are given priority over other sources of meaning" (6). Castells argues that identities are constructed using "building materials from history, from geography, from biology, from productive and reproductive institutions, from collective memory and from personal fantasies, from power apparatuses and religious revelations" (7). All of which is to say that identities are constructed by the *habitus*. Because of this, identities are shared to some extent. Shared identities can be said to mark the boundaries of a community. Bruce Lincoln points out that the "distinctive aspects and characteristic marks" of a group may "include seemingly superficial, but emotionally evocative signs such as wearing certain clothes, holding or moving one's body in a certain manner, and eating certain food, either as part of one's regular practice or on ceremonial and public . . . occasions" (51). Communities almost never prescribe everything unless they are highly ritualized, like monastics, and even here an abbess or prior is in place to evaluate infractions as they occur. But communities generally allow a "range of possibility within which difference and discussion are permitted, even encouraged" (Bruce Lincoln 51). If a range of possibilities were not available to a community, it could not adapt to changing circumstances.

As I noted earlier, Chantal Mouffe argues that the formation of an identity such as "an American" depends upon a rigorous exclusion of differing or competing nationalist identities such as "a Brit" or "an Iraqi" (*Return* 141). Such exclusions create an outside or a limit beyond which the epithet "American" cannot be thought to apply. This outside, then, establishes a category of an other or others who are not-us. The fact remains, however, that the establishment of identity is always imperiled by the movement of difference (Laclau, *Emancipations* 52–53; Laclau, *New Reflections* 32; Laclau and Mouffe 122–27). This means that both categories—"us" and "not-us"—are always in flux, always open to challenge. According to

Laclau and Mouffe, the antagonisms that exist at the limits of hegemony are managed discursively by imposition of a logic of equivalence, whereby difference is reduced to sameness (127–31). In heterosexist discourse, for example, all nonstraight people are classed as deviant whether they are gay or lesbian or bisexual or transgendered, ad infinitum. Within a logic of equivalence, that is to say, "they all look alike." This is of course a strategic sort of commonplace move, a discursive tactic that reduces the multiplicity of difference to a manageable binary. The resultant binaries (straight/gay, normal/abnormal) occult to some extent the threat posed by difference to maintenance of the dominant category itself.

Commonplaces are part of the discursive machinery that hides the flow of difference, that firms up identity and sameness within a community. It is a commonplace among conservatives, for instance, that liberals tax and spend. The commonplace serves in-group identity (*we* practice fiscal responsibility; *they* do not) at the same time as it reduces a range of available economic possibilities to a binary. Commonplaces generally become available for discussion only when (a) believers wish to solidify identity and community or (b) they encounter unbelief—that is, they become aware of counterclaims. To put this in the vocabulary of ancient rhetorics, commonplaces require utterance when believers need for some reason to engage in *epideictic* rhetoric. The Greek term means "display" or "demonstration." Epideictic rhetoric puts community values on display, either by reinforcing them or by challenging the beliefs/practices of miscreants and outsiders (Aristotle, *Rhetoric* 1358b). In the face of unbelief or countering behavior believers must articulate their beliefs in both senses: they must remind one another of their commonalities, and they must defend the common belief system from disarticulation. My study of feminism brought to consciousness the inherent sexism of my belief about women who wear white shoes after Labor Day, along with other more damaging beliefs about women that I had absorbed during childhood (women should compete with one another for men's attentions, women can't be trusted, and so on). These commonplaces "came out," so to speak, because my encounter with a dissenting discourse challenged the arguments encapsulated in them. That is to say, commonplaces can be made available for scrutiny by encounters with difference. And if this is the case, then (following Laclau and Mouffe) commonplaces that circulate within a hegemonic belief system must bear a relation of antagonism toward commonplaces at work in other hegemonies. Hegemony in fact functions to monitor the frequency and intensity of encounters with difference, seeing to it that the impact of such encounters does not threaten its hold on believers. It follows that believers who are isolated from countering discourses have a better chance of preserving their beliefs intact than do those whose belief systems are exposed to difference.

To the extent that beliefs held in common are defining of community identity, awareness of disbelief can be troubling, first of all, because it calls believers' attention to the nonfixity of belief, to the limits of its extension, and hence to the arbitrariness not only of commonly held beliefs but of the community's antagonistic boundaries as well. Second, the appearance of disbelief renders belief available for contest. If commonplace beliefs are important to the maintenance of group solidarity, an encounter with disbelief requires their defense in order to ward off the possibility of the group's dissolution. Depending on the extent to which commonplace beliefs are defining of community identity, encounters with disbelief can result in social and political antagonism toward unbelievers, which is ordinarily handled by argument, although other means, such as withdrawal, coercion, or violence, are certainly available.

Not all beliefs are commonplaces. Some beliefs describe natural or empirical relations: I believe that the sun will set tonight and that it will rise tomorrow. Such beliefs are (arguably) universally held, and while this fact certainly renders them common, it also renders them unavailable for contest. On the other hand, no beliefs are singular. Just as there can be no private language, there can be no private beliefs because beliefs participate in the *habitus; doxa* is always already in circulation. If I alone believe that Harry is a sexist pig, that belief nevertheless borrows a phrase from communal discourse. Without access to that discourse, I could never have articulated such a belief. If I share my belief with Harry's spouse, it may become controversial, but it is not a commonplace until it is widely accepted in some relevant community.

Beliefs and ideologies can circulate among relatively small communities, however. At the present time, for example, a minority of believers holds that extraterrestrial aliens abduct human beings and perform invasive medical procedures upon them (Dean, *Aliens;* Denzler). On occasion minority beliefs and ideologies come to be accepted by great numbers of people or by people who have privileged access to mainstream channels of communication. In these cases minority ideologies can become mainstream or even hegemonic. Vegetarianism and animal rights are minority ideologies at the moment, but both show signs of enlarging their sphere of persuasive influence, just as environmentalism did during the 1970s. It is

possible that the circulation of minority ideologies is enhanced by the existence of countering hegemonic beliefs; vegetarianism and animal rights are
challenges to the cultural practice summed up in the marketing commonplace that asserts "Beef! It's what's for dinner." In other words, resistance
cannot be discounted as an impetus to the circulation of minority beliefs.
Alien abduction narratives are not taken very seriously outside of ufological circles, perhaps, because they challenge no community belief/practice
that is comparable in scope and importance to meat-eating. Christianity
also fosters belief in sentient extraterrestrial beings (angels and demons),
and scientists tend to be open to the possibility, if not the fact, of sentient
alien life forms. Liberals tend to be skeptical toward claims of alien abduction because reported phenomena are not supported by factual evidence.
Until it faces contest from some powerful opponent, then, belief in alien
abduction may be unlikely to inform a much larger group of believers than
it now does.

Ideologic

Beliefs that circulate within one ideology can be borrowed for use in another. As I state earlier, I use the term *ideologic* to name the connections
that can be forged among beliefs within a given ideology and/or across belief systems. Ideologies are constructed by connecting and disconnecting
beliefs that circulate within a given ideology or among several ideologies.
This borrowing and construction happens whether or not people are aware
of its workings. That is, an ideology can cohere below the level of consciousness. When beliefs and ideologies are actually brought to consciousness,
they become arguments. An argument is a statement or connected series of
statements (what ancient rhetoricians called "premises") forwarded in order to serve some interest. An argument can be had with oneself, obviously,
and in such a case it is not necessarily uttered (it is, however, articulated in
both senses of that term). If an argument is shared with an other, however,
it must be couched in speech or writing or gesture or some other medium
of human inscription (dance, painting, music, and so on). Arguments may
or may not accurately represent belief or ideology, because language is im-
perfectly representative and because the acts of speaking and writing can
actually alter belief. Arguments usually include some commonplaces, but
just as not every belief is a commonplace, not every statement that appears
in an argument is a commonplace. Arguments must contain statements
that allow participants to move from one premise to the next. In an argu-

ment about the justice of the United States' invasion of Iraq, for example, a participant has to connect that event to whatever definition of "just war" is operating within the argument (for example, "The invasion of Iraq by the United States in 2003 was a just war because it ended Saddam Hussein's oppression of the Iraqi people"). Because of their instrumental character, such statements may not be commonplaces, although in this example the instrumental premise is (or once was) a commonplace.

The morpheme -*logic* is intended to convey that, within ideology, beliefs connect, disconnect, and reconnect with regularities that can be traced. Theorists have named a number of possible ideological movements: Lacanian psychoanalysis discerns metaphoric and metonymic relations among desires, while an older faculty psychology settled on associations between ideas such as resemblance and contiguity (that is, metaphor and metonymy), plus succession, enumeration, cause, and effect (Bracher 49–52; Warren). Laclau and Mouffe's "logic of equivalence" is also an ideologic. But there are many other possibilities for the articulation, disarticulation, and realignment of beliefs that constitute ideologies. Given their plenitude and the multitude of contexts in which ideologic relations appear, I am not confident that a complete list of possible relations can be constructed. The same commonplace can function in several ideologies—for example, the commonplace definition of "family" used by Christian Right activists (nuclear, heterosexual, patriarchal) influences a number of belief systems, including antifeminism, antiabortionism, heterosexism, heteronormativity, and homophobia, among others, although it connects with other beliefs in each of these systems in different ways. Some commonplaces are so thoroughly connected to one another in a given belief system that arguments about the one are almost always used to support arguments about the other. As I note earlier, this is true of liberal commonplaces about freedom and equality. It is hard to argue within a liberal context that equality for women does not include reproductive freedom, or that freedom of speech does not apply equally to all citizens. Outside of liberal ideology, of course, it is perfectly possible to disarticulate these values. Neoconservatives have adopted the liberal value of individual freedom in order to legitimate their interest in free-market capitalism. However, conservatives generally resist the liberal connection between freedom and equality, arguing instead that individual freedom rewards those who are most fit to prosper.

Claims that connections can be made between beliefs and belief systems (that is, claims about ideologic) appear regularly in contemporary argument. In an essay on the aftermath of September 11, for example, Dave

Whyte claims that "neo-liberals explicitly associate free markets with ideas of economic democracy, human freedom, and development" (151). In other words, Whyte argues that neoliberals conflate a political practice (democracy) with an economic one (free-market capitalism), while at the same time connecting this new equation to a set of values (freedom and progress) drawn from classical liberalism. The emergence of neoliberalism illustrates how beliefs in hegemonic values and practices may be rearticulated in a moment of realignment, a moment that in this case legitimates free-market capitalism and globalization by associating them with democracy and traditional liberal values. Martti Gronfers argues that the war in Afghanistan was not a war about religious difference, as some supposed, but rather "a man-made war, men on both sides committed as men to wage terrible acts of violence on other men" (201). He notes that since "men do not suffer public humiliation lightly," they are likely to exact retribution for perceived insults (204). That is to say, Gronfers connects a certain model of masculinity to a proclivity for violence, thus articulating a moment wherein, perhaps, a connection may become apparent between a conjecture about gender and the practice of making war. Gronfers's articulation also suggests that this conjecture may operate across national lines, forging a connection of similarity between warring states. In respect to masculinism, "they" are perhaps not so different from "us."

The concept of ideologic may serve rhetorical criticism insofar as its analysis can demonstrate how beliefs connect to one another. Such an analysis might also help rhetors to invent means of disarticulating beliefs that circulate within a given ideology, and exposure of untenable connections might assist with the project of disarticulating systems of belief. I do not wish to be overly optimistic about any inventional potential that may be yielded by an examination of ideologic, however. Exposure of weakness or deception in a belief system does not guarantee defection from it. Analysis of ideologic can nonetheless assist invention insofar as it may reveal whether a rhetorical appeal concerning a specific issue can be persuasive to someone whose belief system affects potential receptivity to arguments concerning it. If subscription to a given belief system forecasts and limits the ways in which new events and information can be read, it follows minimally that a small range of persuasive possibilities may remain open in any given case. In the worst case, rhetorically speaking, some believers cannot be persuaded to entertain dissenting arguments at all. This can occur on a larger scale when the available rhetorical space is simply swallowed up by a dominant and dominating discourse, as it was in the weeks and months following September 11, 2001. Dana Cloud notes of that period that it was "impossible to watch television, go to a movie, drive down the street, or listen to politicians talk without being sucked into the imagined unity of American nationalism. Recently, I purchased postage stamps at my credit union. The teller gave me a sheet of American flag stamps, each of which bore the motto "UNITED WE STAND" (76).

Was it possible after the events of September 11, 2001, for someone who accepted the ideologic of American super-patriotism to hear arguments against carpet bombing in Afghanistan? And could such a person, if able to hear such arguments, remain open to persuasion by them? As with most rhetorical questions (meant here in the sense of "questions concerning the available means of persuasion"), the appropriate answer is "that depends." The answer depends in part upon the relative density with which beliefs are articulated within a given belief system. I hypothesize that the more densely beliefs are articulated with one another in a given belief system or across belief systems, the more impervious they are to rhetorical intervention. The pathways typically taken in some ideologics are so tightly connected with one another, so routinely and regularly traveled, that they become a sort of automatic "first response" to encounters with new or countering beliefs and belief systems. Despite the challenge mounted to white racism by the civil rights movement, for instance, people who live in a *habitus* saturated with racist discourse find it difficult to resist its typical pathways whether or not they consciously or willingly subscribe to it. That the movement had an impact on racism is beyond doubt; this impact is testified to by the ubiquity of the commonplace assertion "I am not a racist, but . . ." At the same time use of this phrase exhibits the inability of the movement, successful as it was, to thoroughly disarticulate racism. Racist commonplaces cannot now be uttered in public venues without some qualifier, but they continue to be believed nonetheless. Indeed, the pathways of racism and sexism are so often trod (I am tempted to write "so well greased") that connections between and among their lines of force are predictable. In May 2004 a million people marched in Washington, D.C., to protest the adoption of measures they perceived to be harmful to women's interests. The next day, surfing the Web, I found that a common response to this event was "Women who protest are ugly." Clearly this response had been anticipated by actress Ashley Judd, who wore a T-shirt to the march that said: "This is what a feminist looks like."

Beliefs incorporated into a densely articulated ideologic resonate with one another. I borrow the term *resonance* from Linda Kintz, who borrows it in turn from acoustics, where it is defined as "the intensification and pro-longation of sound produced by sympathetic vibration" (*Between* 6). Kintz redefines resonance for rhetorical purposes as "the intensification of politi-cal passion in which people with very different interests are linked together by feelings aroused and organized to saturate the most public, even global, issues" (*Between* 6). Resonance is an intensification of passion stemming from "sympathetic vibration"; belaboring the metaphor, I suggest that beliefs encompassed within densely articulated ideologics resonate more sympathetically, and with more intensity, than do beliefs operative within ideologics that are less tightly woven. If this is the case, it follows that be-liefs that are new to a densely articulated ideologic arouse less intense pas-sion than does a challenge to some belief already in the system. On the other hand, less densely articulated belief systems, as well as less densely articulated styles of believing, such as skepticism, are relatively open to reception of both new and countering beliefs because activation of a given belief triggers neither closely connected beliefs nor intense emotional re-sponse. A skeptic need not necessarily abandon her skeptical worldview (or her friends and family) when she changes her mind about a religious or political issue. Unlike skepticism, a densely articulated ideology "explains everything," and so its disarticulation is very costly to a believer. Many other beliefs must be given up, and others rearranged, in order to abandon one. In some cases disarticulation might require abandonment of an entire ideology or even a hegemony; such a sweeping change entails emotional upheaval and changes in identities, not to mention possible abandonment of communities that still cling to the discarded belief system. For these rea-sons beliefs that threaten the integrity of a belief system must be highly res-onant as well. They must "ring your chimes," as the commonplace would have it, before they can be noticed.

Powerful Emotions and Passionate Commitments

Ancient rhetoricians assumed that beliefs could be altered by appeals to the emotions, no doubt because they witnessed occasions on which power-ful speakers such as Demosthenes or Cicero moved an audience to decision by arousing anger, pity, or fear. In the second book of *On Rhetoric* Aristotle analyzes the persuasive appeal of emotions such as anger, mildness, love, hatred, fear, confidence, benevolence, shame, shamelessness, pity, indigna-tion, envy, and emulation (II.2–12). Cicero provides a somewhat different list in *De Oratore:* wrath, love, hate, fear, compassion, jealousy, joy, and hope (II.i.203). Quintilian touts the benefits of a figure called *enargeia*. He argues that *enargeia* is effective because human beings are naturally empathetic with the plight of others. He illustrates as follows: "I am complaining that a man has been murdered. Shall I not bring before my eyes all the circumstances which it is reasonable to imagine must have occurred in such a connection? Shall I not see the assassin burst suddenly from his hiding-place, the victim tremble, cry for help, beg for mercy or turn to run? Shall I not see the fatal blow delivered and the stricken body fall? Will not the blood, the deathly pallor, the groan of agony, the death-rattle, be indelibly impressed upon my mind?" (VI.ii.31). This *enargeia* is expected to provoke sympathy with the victim, which in turn should awaken pity and fear.

Rhetorical pedagogy remained indebted to ancient thought well into the Renaissance. Because the grammar school curriculum was primarily devoted to the study of rhetoric, its strategies were available even to those who possessed little Latin and less Greek. Shakespeare was a master of *enargeia;* consider, for example, the moving scene in *Julius Caesar* where Antony displays Caesar's bloody cloak:

> Look, in this place ran Cassius' dagger through.
> See what a rent the envious Casca made.
> Through this the well-beloved Brutus stabbed,
> And as he plucked his cursed steel away,
> Mark how the blood of Caesar followed it,
> As rushing out of doors, to be resolved
> If Brutus so unkindly knocked, or no. (III.ii.178–84)

Waving a bloody shirt in court was a stock trick even in Cicero's time, but in the right circumstances this act is persuasive because it rouses emotions—sympathy, fear, anger—that inform and underscore belief.

Discussions of the persuasive potential of emotional appeals were fairly standard in premodern treatises on rhetoric and psychology. Thomas Hobbes, for example, devoted a section of his *Leviathan* to emotions—"the interiour Beginnings of Voluntary Motions, commonly called the Passions; And the Speeches by which they are expressed" (I.6). Hobbes took the ancient association of emotions and persuasion (*movere*) quite literally, treating the passions as "motions" expressed in bodily movements. Desire "moves" human beings toward whatever causes it, and aversion occurs "when the Endeavor is fromward something" (I.vi). These bodily motions are mirrored or reflected in the emotional responses called "love" and "hate." These emotions in turn convert bodily responses into values:

"the object of any mans Appetite or Desire; that is it, which he for his part calleth Good; And the object of his Hate, and Aversion, Evill" (I.vi). Here Hobbes repeats elements of a faculty psychology that associated arousal of passions with movement of the will, hence tying emotional response to value judgments (Warren).

A second, philosophical, tradition of speculation about emotions portrays them not as sources of invention but as unfortunate features of human nature that are disorienting and untrustworthy. According to this line of thought, emotions can engulf reason, can force people to do things they might regret when they are no longer afraid, or ashamed, or enraged. This point of view is represented by a powerful image in Plato's *Phaedrus,* where the soul is depicted as a charioteer struggling to control two horses: a dutiful and obedient white horse represents rationality while an unruly and headstrong black horse signifies bodily appetites (246). Judith Butler remarks that in a certain strand of modern philosophy, as well, desire is configured "as immediate, arbitrary, purposeless, and animal"; it is "that which requires to be gotten beyond; it threatens to undermine the postures of indifference and dispassion which have in various different modalities conditioned philosophical thinking" (*Subjects* 1). Obviously this second tradition sets up a binary between reason and emotion; within it reason and logic are "mental" attributes that confer the power of abstraction, while emotions mire humans in the concrete physicality of the body (this binary is gendered of course).

By the early nineteenth century the triumph of this second, negative attitude toward emotional appeals had actually contributed to the declining cultural capital of rhetoric. Bishop Richard Whately remarked in his textbook on rhetoric that "there is . . . no point in which the idea of dishonest artifice is in most people's minds so intimately associated with that of Rhetoric, as the address to the Feelings" (180). By the end of that century Anglo-American rhetorical theorists had banished emotional appeals from the arena of legitimate argument altogether (Crowley, *Methodical* 107–18). The philosophical attitude toward emotion is still very much alive; writing at the end of the twentieth century, political theorist George Marcus and his associates assert that "much of the Western tradition in the arts and especially in the sciences emphasizes the tensions and disjunctures between the emotional and the rational. Further, Western tradition tends to derogate the role of affect in the public sphere. Being emotional about politics is generally associated with psychological distraction, distortion, extremity, and unreasonableness" (1–2). That is to say, those who become emotional about politics are somehow missing the point, mistaking extremes for more sedate middles, behaving irrationally.

Contemporary research in neuroscience and cognitive psychology calls this account into question, however.[7] Antonio Damasio, a neurobiologist, works with patients who suffer from brain injuries. While treating them he discovered that reason cannot operate without emotion; the frontal lobes, the site of consciousness, are virtually helpless when they cannot receive input from emotional body states. Working from this insight Damasio developed a reflexive model of cognition that posits repeated reciprocal relations among emotional response, experience, memory, and cognition (*Descartes'* 165–201, 214). Nico Frijda and his colleagues in cognitive psychology also argue that emotions and belief are reciprocally influential: "Beliefs . . . are regarded as one of the major determinants of emotion and . . . one might easily regard emotions as being among the determinants of an individual's belief. They can be seen as influencing the content and the strength of an individual's beliefs, and their resistance to modification. . . . Beliefs fueled by emotions stimulate people to action, or allow them to approve of the actions of others in political contexts" (1). Frijda and his coeditors invoke Aristotle's *On Rhetoric* as a warrant for these generalizations, thus bringing into a full historical circle the argument about the influence of emotions on belief and behavior.

Damasio tracks a large variety of bodily responses and activities that might be called emotions, dispositions, or feelings. Simplifying enormously, here I define *emotions* as body states that come about in response to environmental cues or messages from the brain and nervous system (Damasio, *Descartes'* 139). I use *emotion* and *passion* as synonyms.[8] I rely on Brian Massumi's definition of *affect* as a "prepersonal intensity corresponding to the passage from one experiential state of the body to another and implying an augmentation or diminution in that body's capacity to act" (xvi). Affect, then, describes the relative strength or weakness of bodily responses to one another and to environmental cues. Most bodily states come into being and pass away without our conscious awareness; the body calls attention to its situation only when necessary, and it does so by means of affect. I use the term *conscious* here not in the Freudian sense but as shorthand for "the portion of the body-mind system that engages in cognition." Damasio's work makes very clear that "body" and "mind" are unhelpful ways of characterizing human being; indeed, "mind" is more accurately read as "nervous system." This system has many parts and functions in addition to the brain, and only a small bit of it is devoted to reasoning. The system works with body states that are as much chemical as organic, and relations within it are always in flux.

Cognitive psychologists Gerald Clore and Karen Gasper posit that emotions have two functions: they provide information about an environment, and they focus attention on discrete aspects of that environment. The second of these functions is most important to a theory of belief. Affect focuses attention; it is connected to objects or events "as an inherent part of the perception of events," which implies that attributions of affect to objects or events are not deliberate but automatic (16). I take this to mean that attributions happen too fast to be thought about (Damasio, *Descartes'* 133–39). It is only after I have startled with alarm that I realize the phone is ringing. But Clore and Gasper's "immediacy principle" posits that affective states are attributed to whatever is being thought about when emotions are aroused (16). So even as the phone rings I might attribute my alarm to whatever fear-inducing thing is "in mind" at the moment. The end has come! No, it's only the phone. None of this rationalization occurs unless the affective response is sufficiently intense to awaken conscious recognition.

Intense emotional response apparently makes the events, objects, or ideas that arouse it seem more important; strong emotional response "may influence beliefs because it provides experiential information or feedback about one's appraisal of objects to which the feelings appear to be a reaction" (Clore and Gasper 12). The feelings "appear" to be a reaction because attribution, that is, the assignment of the response to this or that object, is accomplished outside of conscious awareness. On the one hand, then, we pay attention to events or objects that arouse more intense emotional reactions, thus singling them out from the array of other potential stimulants in the environment. On the other hand, belief can affect the attribution of emotional responses to objects or events. Clore and Gasper posit that the assignment of meaning to an affective state depends in part on the prior meaningfulness of the object or event to which the arousal of emotion is attributed: "such attributions then allow affect to serve as a basis for new beliefs or as validation of prior beliefs about the object" (18). One function of ideology, then, is to channel attention.

The relative intensity of an emotional response can either alter or reinforce belief. Thus emotion and belief can constitute a feedback loop. This reflexive relation between emotion and belief might be exemplified as follows. On rainy days, say, I habitually become gloomy because dark clouds are lowering overhead. I will have constructed this habitual state by means of a history of such associations, which may stem from cultural as well as physiological experiences.[9] If on one rainy day I have an altercation with my department chair, I may begin to associate my gloomy state with him. My emotional response may, in turn, alter my prior beliefs about him and about the future of our relationship as well, particularly if my new belief can easily be articulated with some other belief in my ideology (let's say that as a rule I don't trust men to behave well). In this example an emotional state alters beliefs. But the relation works the other way around as well. If I am generally suspicious of masculine motives and behavior prior to my encounter with my male department chair, I am likely to expect bad behavior from him. Hence I am more likely to notice any behavior I can interpret negatively. That is, if I see anything at all in his behavior that I can interpret in accordance with my beliefs, particularly if this occurs on a gloomy day, I may manufacture an emotional response ("Yuck!") that thus confirms their validity. This possibility is complicated by Damasio's speculation that the brain can arouse an emotion without the body's actually experiencing anything that would create such a state; as he puts it, "the brain learns to concoct the fainter image of an 'emotional' body state, without having to reenact it in the body proper" (*Descartes'* 155). If my department chair exhibits behavior that I can interpret as coinciding with my beliefs about male behavior in general, then my assessment of our encounter on one occasion may color my interaction with him on all others; moreover, my memory of a gloomy occasion may serve "as a kind of experiential evidence" that I was right about men all along (Clore and Gasper 20). In other words, I interpret my emotional response—imagined or actual—as experience, thus conflating my beliefs with "reality." Of course all of these connections are made very rapidly, and most (all?) are made below the level of consciousness. Because of this it is relatively more difficult for me to focus attention on countering behavior that my department chair may display, such as generosity or sensitivity. He must display generous or sensitive behavior often and in rather sensational fashion in order to evoke sufficiently intense responses from me such that I notice it at all.

This is all very distressing to a rationalist. But Clore and Gasper are not finished yet. Borrowing terminology from stylistics, they formulate an "elaboration principle" that posits that "the extent of affective influence depends on whether the experience is elaborated or punctuated, and the potential for elaboration depends on the structure of beliefs regarding the object of attribution" (18–19). An elaborated experience is one that is connected to other experiences and memories of such encounters; a punctuated experience is not so connected. The "potential for elaboration," that is, the potential for a believer to connect an emotional response aroused on a given occasion to a structure of beliefs and past experiences, depends on the density with which the relevant belief is articulated with others. This potential is most potent within densely articulated belief systems. Clore and Gasper note that extremists are "bad affective grammarians" who parse everything as connected to everything else (20). I prefer to put this the other way around, arguing that densely articulated ideologies construct bad affective grammarians who pay intense notice to objects and events that can be threaded into the intricate tapestries of their belief system(s). They notice because almost everything that is made legible by their belief system(s) is weighty with affect for them. If this account is correct, extremists have difficulty taking notice of events or objects that neither support nor attack their beliefs. That is to say, whatever is new and neutral in relation to their system of beliefs is likely to pass unremarked. However, if a new or neutral piece of information or event is noticed by, say, a member of Christian Identity, he or she can immediately take up a position concerning it because that belief system is so densely articulated that it can explain everything (Barkun, *Religion*). Confronted by an alien being interviewed on CNN, such a person could make immediate sense of this new development, could decide instantly upon a course of action regarding it. A skeptic, on the other hand, and apart from his or her immediate affective response, would require time to decide on the appropriate belief system or systems with which to articulate this new information; she might engage in additional deliberation before she could decide on an appropriate course of belief and action in regard to it.

Let's say that Dick learns he has not achieved a hoped-for promotion. He will no doubt respond to this news with sadness and anxiety, emotions provoked by his belief that harm may befall him and his family because of his failure to be promoted. Then he learns that a woman has been promoted in his stead. If Dick does not harbor sexist beliefs, this bit of news will not affect his response unless he is acquainted with the woman, in which case he may feel joy (if she is a friend) or frustration (if he does not respect her ability). If he does hold sexist beliefs, however, he is likely to greet this bit of knowledge with a more intense response that is less likely to be tempered by friendship, if such a relation exists. Perhaps he will become angry that someone who is defined within sexism as an inferior has been promoted in his stead. Aristotle defines anger as "desire, accompanied by distress, for conspicuous retaliation because of a conspicuous slight that was directed, without justification, against oneself or those near to one" (*Rhetoric* II.2.1378a).[10] In our culture sadness and anxiety may be provoked by disappointment in oneself or by failure to achieve goals, but anger is still provoked by perceived insults to one's status or dignity. Recall that affect influences attention, and so if intense anger is aroused by this bit of knowledge the rejected worker will focus on the slight, perhaps obsess over it, see similar slights occurring everywhere. It is not easy to accept rejection or defeat. However, if one is equipped with a densely articulated ideology that is implicated in nearly all one's emotional responses to environments, responsibility for the rejection can be shifted; Dick can more easily believe that he has been victimized by affirmative action than he can accept his own failure. And here is where the elaboration principle can come into play: he can take his anger on this occasion to confirm the righteousness of sexist analyses in general; he can, in fact, mistake it for experience of a reality in which the cards are always already stacked against him.

And so Kintz is onto something when she writes that in the present ideological climate "depth of feeling is increasingly important as evidence of truth" ("Culture" 8). Affect can substitute for reality itself. In Lawrence Grossberg's words, "the affective investment . . . enables ideological relations to be internalized and, consequently, naturalized" (83). Super-patriots witness an antiwar protest; they experience anger because they read the protest as an insult to their belief that citizens should adhere to national policy without demur. The anger may arouse a desire to retaliate because super-patriots may mis-take their emotional response for reality as they construct it, confirming their belief that dissent from national policy is outrageous "in the world," or at least impossible for rational people who look like they belong to "us." In this example anger arises when people witness enactment of a countering ideologic, but the cycle works as well with experiences that reinforce belief. When Dittoheads listen to Rush Limbaugh articulate positions that confirm beliefs they already hold, they must experience satisfaction and pleasure, which in turn must reinforce their belief in the accuracy of assessments made within Limbaugh's (and their own) ideologics (Land). They may in fact derive additional pleasure from the knowledge that an extended community of listeners shares in that satisfaction as well. I suspect that Limbaugh's audience also enjoys knowing that his rants irk people who don't share their positions on issues. The joy of resistance is enhanced by a feeling of solidarity.

Rhetoric and Visceral Belief

Obviously the research reviewed above validates the views of ancient rhetorical theorists regarding the role played by emotional response in persuasion: emotions affect belief, and beliefs arouse emotion. Belief is stimulated, supported, or changed by emotional responses to an environment. Emotions can be stimulated, in turn, by appeals to beliefs already in place. Ancient rhetoricians knew that language can move people to shout or weep just as circumstances do, and anyone who has cried or laughed at a movie or book—or cowered during a sermon—knows this too. Lynn Worsham defines *emotion* as a "tight braid of affect and judgment, socially and historically constructed and bodily lived, through which the symbolic takes hold of and binds the individual, in complex and contradictory ways, to the social order and its structure of meanings" (216). People respond emotionally to what they find in the *habitus;* these responses can in turn affect an individual's perception and understanding of the *habitus.* An individual's receptions, perceptions, and understandings can then reenter the *habitus,* altering it once again. In these views, then, human being has what Bourdieu calls a reflexive relation to the *habitus* (*Pascalian* 10).

The reflexive relation between emotion and belief explains the persuasive appeal of images such as the display of a battered American flag over the ruins of the World Trade Center or the arrival of a flight-suited president on the deck of an aircraft carrier. The first image sets off a chain of ideologic that concludes with something like the claim "America can survive anything, even the loss of thousands of innocent lives and the destruction of our tallest monuments to capitalism"; this conclusion in turn activates civic pride, which in its turn might activate other beliefs that are closely articulated within the ideology of super-patriotism, such as "America can survive anything because God is watching over us." The second image suggests the military competence of the president, which implies in turn that he can make able foreign policy decisions. This conclusion in its turn inspires trust, which reinforces the rightness of the ideologic. The weakness of such arguments is readily apparent when their ideologic is fully articulated—the fact that New York City survived one attack has little predictive value; a military costume has no necessary connection to competence in foreign policy. But to presume the weakness of ideologic is to overlook its visceral pull.

Aristotle's term for standard sets of ideological connections was *enthymeme* (*Rhetoric* I.8.1356b). The Greek root of this term is *thumos*—viscera. Words, performances, images, and other representations appeal to the gut. They trigger emotional responses that can set off a chain of ideo-logic that can in turn arouse additional emotional response. The resulting affect may seem to underwrite the empirical truth of whatever conclusion is drawn. William Connolly notices that visceral affect may be intensified by the fact that some beliefs are widely shared: "representational discourse itself, including the public expression and defense of fundamental beliefs, affects and is affected by the visceral register of intersubjectivity" (*Why I Am Not* 26). If Connolly is correct, the very fact that some beliefs are common enhances their affect, allows them to "write scripts upon prerep-resentational sites of appraisal" more efficaciously. Widely shared beliefs appeal to the visceral register. This explains why the ideologic underly-ing hegemonic commonplaces can literally "go without saying," why the repetition of timeworn slogans is effective although their immediate, spe-cific relevance is virtually nil. A masterful rendition of the "Star-Spangled Banner" prior to a football game can move spectators to tears, despite the fact that the flag memorialized in the song was hoisted during a relatively inconsequential battle in a war that is now nearly forgotten.

Ancient rhetoricians taught that the placement of premises in en-thymematic argument does not require the rigorous formality that is nec-essary in logic. Nor are rhetors obligated to offer a set number of premises, as logicians are. Rather, an enthymeme may articulate as many premises as are needed to secure the audience's belief in the conclusion. But rhetors do not ordinarily state all of the premises and conclusions of an enthyme-matic argument. Indeed, skilled rhetors often omit all but a single premise ("The president is wearing a flight suit"), trusting that the ubiquity of com-monplaces about American patriotism will allow audiences to work out other premises and make the desired connections. Their participation in the construction of the argument may even create a kind of visceral satis-faction for the audience, thus closing the circle of acceptance.

What Counts—Affect and Mattering Maps

Value (quality) is an important topic in ancient systems of invention. An-cient rhetoricians were able to list values held in common by their com-munities—honor, justice, expediency—with enviable ease. Unless they are motivated to argument primarily by religious beliefs, Americans don't ordinarily frame disagreements as arguments about values. Our lack of ex-plicit talk about values permits fraudulent value arguments to be accepted regularly. In the summer of 2004, for instance, conservative pundits accused the Democratic presidential ticket of having "Hollywood values," which in the context of conservative ideology apparently means "liberal" in the sense of "libertine." As far as I was able to discern, there was no discussion of the content of this charge in the media; the commonplace association of "Hollywood" with "libertinism" was simply taken for granted. Values can exert great rhetorical force when subscription to them is necessary to establish or maintain hegemony. The liberal value of individual freedom, for example, can be successfully appealed to even by conservatives, and the bourgeois value of taste is a nodal point in the current class system (Bourdieu, *Distinction*). Every ideology forwards a system of values. We have seen that liberalism values equality, freedom, and tolerance. And we shall see later on that Christian Right ideology values God, nation, and family. People function very differently depending on whether they value financial success or social justice.

On an elementary level of analysis it seems that values must be associated with emotions and the formation of belief. From childhood, emotions tell us which circumstances or objects produce pleasure and which stimulate pain. As a result of emotional experience we make value judgments: eating a pear gives pleasure, which we probably generalize at a later time into a judgment along the lines of "fruit tastes good"; putting your hand on a hot stove hurts, which can be generalized as "hot surfaces are bad." Alison Jagger notes that "values presuppose emotions to the extent that emotions provide the experiential basis for values. If we had no emotional responses to the world, it is inconceivable that we should ever come to value one state of affairs more highly than another" (137). Like my naive analysis, this account holds well enough within a modern dispensation. Ancient thought, however, located value judgments within the wisdom of the community rather than in personal experience. Apparently descriptions of community values were commonplace in ancient Athens. Aristotle simply assumed, for instance, that Athenian citizens would be moved by appeals to goodness, justice, and honor (*Rhetoric* I.3.1358b). In Book II of *On Rhetoric* he asserts that certain categories of citizens hold values appropriate to their station in life; for example, old men "expect the worst, through experience—[in their view] the greater part of things that happen are bad," while young men "choose to do fine things for they live more by character than calculation, and calculation concerns the advantageous, virtue the honorable" (13.1390a, 12.1389a). Medieval thinkers, in contrast, looked to the "book of nature" rather than to the community as an emblem of the Great Chain of Being, God's hierarchical and harmonious creation (Foucault, *Order* 17–25). In this worldview values were made apparent through study of the natural and spiritual orders.

Both of these premodern schemes externalized and communalized values. However, liberal thought internalized values and, in doing so, relativized them. As a result values became at once unimportant and unavailable for argument. Locke's *Essay Concerning Human Understanding* (1694) can again serve as a sort of signpost, this time marking the inauguration of a distinctly modern attitude toward values. While he retained the ancient association of emotions with values, Locke departed from tradition by tying assessments of good and evil to bodily experiences of pleasure and pain rather than to communally derived assessments of worth: "that we call good, which is apt to cause or increase pleasure, or diminish pain in us; or else to procure or preserve us the possession of any other good or absence of any evil. And, on the contrary, we name that evil which is apt to produce or increase any pain, or diminish any pleasure in us: or else to procure us any evil, or deprive us of any good" (II.xx.2). In this view each individual builds a unique system of values based on experience. Locke's departure thus throws into question values derived from community or tradition. As Anthony Arblaster notes, here "values are not woven into the fabric of the universe . . . nor can they be laid down by any form of traditional or institutional authority, whether secular or religious" (17). Furthermore, this move effectively isolates moral judgment from empirical knowledge. Arblaster points out that in this model an individual "should assess the factual situation as objectively as possible. But the facts cannot, and will not, tell him what he ought to do. If he believes that they do, that is because he has confused fact and value, and that is logically inadmissable. Between the facts and the moral evaluation of facts there lies a gulf which no logic can bridge. A starving child crying for food, a wounded man screaming in agony— these are facts. But to say that they are bad facts, as most people would, is not to describe them, but to evaluate them" (17). The distinction between fact and value poses a difficult problem for liberal argumentation, which of course relies on (liberal) values while pretending that it does not and while insisting that nonliberal values are inadmissable in public disagreements.

As Wayne Booth demonstrates in *Modern Dogma and the Rhetoric of Assent,* this argumentative climate posed massive challenges to students and university administrators who clashed—sometimes violently—over issues of governance during the 1960s.[11] Students drew their premises from feelings, intuitions, and values, as is demonstrated by Booth's citation from a Chicago magazine called *Seed:* "resist spiritually, stay high . . . praise god . . . love life . . . blow the mechanical mind with Holy Acid" (*Modern* 3). The Faculty Council countered by trying to "reason" with students, as in this memo cited by Booth: "Before resorting to the civil authorities, the University will seek once again to deal with present disorders through disciplinary means lying in its own jurisdiction. It must be recognized, however, that circumstances—including the refusal of persons concerned to submit to University disciplinary action—may at any time make civil action necessary. . . . In light of the foregoing facts . . ." (206). This is clearly a threat to call the cops if the students do not respond properly to "circumstances," which, the passage implies, are of their own making. "The University" admits no culpability—shares no blame for "present disorders"—at the same time as it smuggles its values (order, discipline, justice) into seemingly rational arguments based on "circumstances" and "the facts." As I suggest earlier, liberal argumentation is equally at a loss in the present argumentative climate, where large numbers of citizens appeal to values derived from the Christian Bible. Liberals have no means of countering appeals to "family values" that carries anything like the level of authority that legitimates the nuclear family within fundamentalist Christian thought. Given this situation, it seems wise for would-be rhetors to consider how appeals to values can responsibly be made.

Barbara Herrnstein Smith offers a useful suggestion in this regard, one that reclaims some features of both modern and premodern thought about values. For her values are contingent on their location in a variety of bodily and cultural systems: "All value is . . . an effect of multiple, continuously changing, and continuously interacting variables or, to put this another way, the product of the dynamics of a system, specifically an *economic* system" (*Contingencies* 30). Literally any thing can become valued (a pet rock, for instance) if it can be inserted into some economy that ranks it vis-à-vis the values accorded to other items in the system. As Herrnstein Smith puts it, things, ideas, or events come to be valued (or devalued) because of their relative positioning within "psychophysiological structures, mechanisms, and tendencies," as well as "innumerable social, cultural, institutional, and contextual variables operating at every level of analysis, from broad through culturally specific ways of classifying objects to the most subtle and minute contextually specific circumstances of individual encounters with them" (*Contingencies* 38). In short, values are continually produced and reproduced by means of reflexive relations in the *habitus,* relations that obtain between and among individuals, cultures, histories. This is not to deny that within some communities, at some times and locations, agreements about valuation coalesce such that values "operate for them as noncontingency" and are "interpreted by them accordingly" (Herrnstein Smith, *Contingencies* 40). "Family values" are held within Christian Right discourse to be noncontingent, having been authorized by God, the Bible, and powerful preachers.

Like Herrnstein Smith, Lawrence Grossberg adopts the language of economics to discuss the "affective investments" that people make (82). He argues that the affective plane has a structure organized "according to maps which direct people's investments in and into the world." He calls these "mattering maps." Such maps "tell people where, how and with what intensities they can become absorbed—into the world and their lives. This 'absorption' constructs the places and events which are, or can become, significant" (82). In Grossberg's model of affect values are the nodal points around which beliefs and emotional intensities cluster. Rhetors who would alter the landscape described by such maps must attend to the ways in which beliefs and affective responses are imbricated with the economy of values they represent.

Desire and Fantasy

For a long time now I have wondered how rhetoricians can do without a theory of desire. People engage in rhetoric, after all, because they *want* something. Even rhetors who advocate maintenance of the status quo want things to stay the same. Despite this, psychoanalysis is almost alone among modern arts and sciences in focusing attention on desire. And so I turn to the work of Freud and Lacan as ways to begin thinking about rhetorical desire.

Jacques Lacan claims that three competing registers shape and maintain subjectivity. These registers are the symbolic (language and culture), the imaginary (produced by egos), and the Real. Lacan argues that human beings acquire subjectivity when they realize that their immersion in the symbolic cuts them off from the Real. That is, at the very moment one becomes conscious of oneself as a subject, as an entity constituted by the flow of language, one also realizes one's separation from the pre- or nonlinguistic. Because we are cut off from the Real (it is not available within the symbolic register), we cannot name or describe it; nonetheless, we mourn its loss.[12] Once an individual moves past the original awareness of lack, theorized as "the mirror stage," desire follows the movement of difference; that is, desire works by means of metonymic substitutions of other objects for the lost Real (Lacan, *Ecrits* i, xi). According to Lacan, desire requires lack; there is no such thing as fulfilled or satisfied desire. In his model desire is produced and reproduced in much the same way that meaning is produced in a Saussurean model of linguistics—that is to say, through difference. The nearer one approaches the object of one's desire, the more it recedes. A subject's very difference or distance from the object of his or her desire allows its significance to emerge. And so subjects represent or stage desire either metaphorically and/or metonymically, by creating fantasies that represent (chains of) analogous or contiguous desires. For example, if I want a promotion, I may fantasize achieving an analogous kind of success, such as becoming president of my organization; or I might fantasize a metonymic scenario in which rather than getting a promotion I get a raise.

My invocation of psychoanalytic discourse does not mean that I have forgotten my emphasis on the importance of bodies to belief. Freud rejected a body-mind distinction when he commented on the relation of body to ego: "A person's own body, and above all its surface, is a place from which both external and internal perceptions spring. It is seen like any other object, but to the touch it yields two kinds of sensations, one of which may be equivalent to an internal perception. . . . Pain, too, seems to play a part in the process, and the way in which we gain new knowledge of our organs during painful illnesses is perhaps a model of the way by which in general we arrived at the idea of our body. The ego is first and foremost a bodily ego; it is not merely a surface entity, but is itself the projection of a surface" (19–20). Egos are bodily entities. Because of the way human perception works, the ego not only depends upon the body for its formation but projects itself as an imagined body, as the surface it imagines itself "to inhabit." The body, then, is both the site and the mechanism that allows human being to represent itself in language and behavior. Desire is expressed through the body. Speech and gesture, writing and dance and painting and so on, are bodily expressions of desire.

Desire may also be staged or performed by fantasies. Slavoj Zizek remarks that fantasy "constitutes our desire, provides its co-ordinates, that is, it literally 'teaches us how to desire.' . . . Fantasy mediates between the formal symbolic structure and the positivity of the objects we encounter in reality—that is to say, it provides a 'schema' according to which certain positive objects in reality can function as objects of desire, filling in the empty places opened up by the formal symbolic structure" (*Plague* 7). Zizek exemplifies this notion with a fantasy about eating a strawberry cake;

his point is not that the fantasy substitutes for reality but that the fantasy tells him he desires to eat strawberry cake rather than, say, bread.[13] Fantasy structures and shapes desire, governs its expression, tells desire how to manifest itself. Hunger is a need, not a desire. When Zizek fantasizes eating strawberry cake, he may indeed be hungry, but his need to eat could be satisfied by anything edible. It is fantasy, through its implication in the symbolic, that alters that need into a desire for strawberry cake. (One of capitalism's greatest accomplishments, in my view, is to have persuaded people that certain desires are in fact needs. Nobody *needs* an SUV.)

Fantasy, like belief, is a conjecture. However, fantasy depicts not "what is" but "what is desired," what is missing. As I point out above, subjectivity is initiated, for Lacan, by the realization of loss and subsequent desire for an other. This other is at first the unattainable Real, but desire for that Big Other is easily transferred to small others by means of fantasy. According to Mark Bracher's reading of Lacan, desire may manifest in several ways: as desire for identification with an other, for instance, or as a desire to possess an other (44). In the first sort of desire—Freud called this "narcissistic"—one can actively desire to become the other through either love or identification, or one can passively desire to become the object of an other's love or recognition. That is to say, an other can be either the subject or the object of one's narcissistic desire. One stages narcissistic desire, then, either by means of a fantasy that depicts oneself as, say, Brad Pitt, or by means of a fantasy that depicts oneself as the recipient of Pitt's affections. In the second sort of desire, anaclitic desire, one can actively desire to possess an other, or one can passively desire to be possessed by an other. What is important for rhetoric about all of these manifestations of desire is their social character. They are enacted by fantasies that depict the desire of an other; that is, the desiring subject imagines an other's desire, constructs fantastic conjectures about what an other wants. Passive narcissistic desire, for example, mimics or repeats a childlike desire to get back to undifferentiated wholeness, literally to identify with an other, to meld/melt oneself with/in an other.

In order to entertain a fantasy, then, it is necessary to imagine or depict what an other feels and wants. Such representations or depictions utilize signifiers made available by the *habitus,* although these may be modified within a given subject's imaginary. It has been persuasively argued, for example, that antiabortionists entertain fantasies of identification with the fetus, which explains at least in part why they are so fond of lurid depictions of fetal dismemberment (Bracher 114; Kintz, *Between* 264–65). Carol

Mason recounts the awful story of Daniel Rudolph, brother of Eric, who cut off his own hand at the wrist with a circular saw and subsequently mailed a videotape of the act to reporters. Mason links Rudolph's self-mutilation to the "gory images of mutilation that characterize pro-life protests and testimony" (29). That is to say, sensational photographs of aborted fetuses may be prominently displayed at antiabortion demonstrations not only because they intimidate those who seek or provide abortion but also because they resonate with antiabortionists' narcissistic fantasies of dissolution. To put the matter in ideological rather than psychoanalytic terms, such images remind protestors that reproductive freedom for women weakens the hold of patriarchy, hence threatening the ideologic of male supremacy and perhaps their personal desire for power over women as well.

A given discourse, practice, or event is particularly influential if it touches on ego attachments that partly construct a subject's sense of identity. Psychoanalysts call such attachments "libidinal investments"; this term roughly means that people put a lot of energy into maintaining them or, more precisely, defending them from assault. The ego attachments constructed by individuals are analogous to what Lacan calls "master signifiers" on the communal level of belief (Alcorn 67–71; Bracher 59–63; Zizek, *Sublime* 87–89). Just as ego attachments require a good deal of nurturing and policing, some signifiers are awarded special attention within a given culture. People who fantasize identity with whatever is depicted by one or more master signifiers—God or nation, for example—do so because they desire love or recognition from a culturally sanctioned Big Other. When they believe that significant groups of people do not desire identification with the same master signifier that motivates their fantasies of identification, they can become alienated and even enraged by this implied challenge to a fantasized communal identity. Such a challenge can be signaled merely by someone's appearance. The owner of a gas station near my home was dark skinned and bearded and wore a turban; these features sufficed to identify him as an enemy to the person who murdered him on September 15, 2001 (Walsh). In this case the knowledge that Sikhs do not profess Islam, that Indians are politically and militarily opposed to Muslims in some regions of the world, would probably have had little impact on the murderer's desire to act out his fantastic identification with America and the flag. This example reinforces Zizek's claim that "the desire 'realized' (staged) in fantasy is not the subject's own, but the *other*'s desire. The original question of desire is . . . 'What do others want from me?'" (*Plague* 8–9).

This event exemplifies the sort of fantasy that primarily interests me here, that is, those fantasies that are motivated by identification with master signifiers in such a way that they stimulate political action as a means of identifying with some valued other or group of others. Kintz provides a serviceable definition of this sort of fantasy: "The historically specific social imaginary of a culture that is for the most part unconscious and unremarked, which is more often simply 'felt'" (*Between* 5). Collective fantasies differ from the private fantasies that psychoanalysts and psychiatrists treat.[14] Jacqueline Rose observes that a popular sense of fantasy mistakenly conjectures it as "what you get up to when the surveying mind and surveying society are both looking the other way. Fantasy is supremely asocial. Doubly licentious, it creates a world of pleasure without obligation" (*States* 2). This popular view of fantasy, as a private boudoir or abattoir, is simply wrong. Even supposedly "private" fantasies about sex and violence participate in the *habitus* and are served by many cultural institutions and practices—pornography prominent among them.

The most powerful signifiers in American discourse, in my opinion, cluster around sex, race, power, and money. Individual and collective fantasies are repeatedly enacted or performed by the desire to identify with the master signifiers thrown up by heterosexism, racism, and capitalism, and such fantasies influence civic life even though they may never be explicitly invoked in political or judicial discourse. In *Excitable Speech,* for example, Judith Butler performs a brilliant reading of a racist decision handed down by the Supreme Court (43–69). Butler demonstrates that the justices' fantasy about urban rioting motivated their decision in a case about a crossburning on an African American family's lawn, so that effectively their judgment condemned the offended family for being black. In other words, even though the suit brought before the court was about free speech, the judgment rendered was motivated by white racist fantasies.

Rose argues that shared fantasy binds even relatively large groups of people to one another. Nationalist fantasies are the "psychic glue" that holds together the "unconscious dreams of nations" (*States* 3). For Rose, Israel is a fantasy that manifests a collective desire for identification with selected others, a desire for community. Such fantasies appear "when a historical desire, drawing its energy from the legacy of ages, emboldens and actualizes itself" (*States* 4). A nationalist identity need not be tied to an actual piece of land. A fantasized homeland will do nicely, as the history of Jewish peoples prior to 1948 demonstrates. Collective fantasies perform persuasive work, such as defining who is an outsider. When history throws

up situations and events as complicated as those surrounding the establishment and maintenance of a Jewish state, fantasy simplifies the daunt-
ing task of sorting "us" from "them."

Myth

Myth is a special case of collective fantasy. Cultural historian Richard
Slotkin notes that myth "performs its cultural function by generalizing
particular and contingent experiences into the bases of universal rules
of understanding and conduct; and it does this by transforming secular
history into a body of sacred and sanctifying legends" (*Fatal* 19). In his
massive study of the "myth of the frontier" Slotkin shows how the story of
Custer's defeat at Little Big Horn, among other historical narratives, was
abstracted and assimilated into a myth that legitimizes belief in American
exceptionalism: "according to this myth-historiography, the conquest of
the wilderness and the subjugation or displacement of the Native Americans who originally inhabited it have been the means to our achievement
of a national identity, a democratic polity, an ever-expanding economy,
and a phenomenally dynamic and 'progressive' civilization" (*Gunfighter*
10). To put it crudely, the myth of the frontier teaches that Americans must
repeatedly fight those defined as "other" in order to renew their sense of
identity as a unified people who share a unique destiny. Americans must
defeat these strange or supposedly hostile "others" in order "to preserve
the American way of life," as the commonplace has it. All of which is to say
that myths perform persuasive work.

Slotkin makes a generic distinction between ideology and myth. He
posits that while "the vehicles of ideology proper are discursive and argumentative in form, and are typified by the rhetorical structure of the credo,
manifesto, polemic, and sermon . . . the language of myth is indirect, meta-
phorical, and narrative in structure; it renders ideology in the form of sym-
bol, example, and fable, and poetically evokes fantasy, memory and senti-
ment" (*Fatal* 21). That is, myths are narrative and poetic, while ideologies
are argumentative and prosaic. Slotkin's language establishes a hierarchy
between narrative and argument, a hierarchy I resist in part because I hear
in it echoes of a similar distinction that is often made between literature
and rhetoric. While it is true that myths are ordinarily narrativized from
historical events, Slotkin himself remarks that the effectiveness of myth
depends upon "instant and intuitive understanding and acceptance of a

given meaning," thus associating myths with commonplaces (*Fatal* 21). Commonplaces are, of course, arguments.

Roland Barthes defines myth as "depoliticized speech": "myth does not deny things, on the contrary, its function is to talk about them; simply, it purifies them, it makes them innocent, it gives them a natural and eternal justification, it gives them a clarity which is not that of an explanation but that of a statement of fact. If I state the fact of French imperiality without explaining it, I am very near to finding that it is natural and *goes without saying*" (143). For Barthes the important thing about myth is that it naturalizes history. Its point is to amplify and sustain accounts of how things are, to render them so forcefully that challenge is literally unthinkable. Myth generalizes history in such a way that the moral derived from the event becomes more important than the incidents recounted. Hence narrative is a less important distinguishing feature of myth than is its psychosocial meaning, to borrow a phrase from Rene Girard, who defines "psychosocial meaning" as whatever contemporary significance resonates in myth for groups of people who may or may not have forgotten the historical event around which it coalesced (74). The narrativity of the originating event can remain compelling, but it is more or less irrelevant to the cultural uses to which the story is put. While students of popular history retain a certain level of interest in the adventures of General Custer, from the point of view of the dominant (white racist) ideology his cultural importance lies in his mythic status: he is one of "our" guys who was defeated by "others" and whose example, therefore, goads "us" never to forget the dangers that lurk beyond the boundaries that define "us." In other words, once an event becomes mythologized, ideologic trumps narrative. It is the moral—the commonplace—that matters.

Ernesto Laclau argues that myths appear during periods of social disruption (what Laclau and Mouffe call "dislocation") and that hence "the 'work' of myth is to suture that dislocated space through the constitution of a new space of representation" (Laclau, *New Reflections* 61; Laclau and Mouffe 142). Myth rearticulates elements of actual disruptive events or circumstances into what Laclau calls "an unachieved fullness" that covers over dislocation and the failure of the actual order to live up to mythological expectations" (63). Girard agrees. Scapegoating rituals, he argues, are based on disturbing historical events; there is always a historical victim or victims toward whom community violence was once directed (74–75). However, once a story is generalized into myth, the community can put the myth and the practices it authorizes to use as means of rearticulating intractable problems whenever one appears. Crops fail? Scapegoat someone—call her a witch, or a communist, and run her out of town or kill her. Then generalize her example into a warning against deviance by other people who want to remain "inside."

In this way myths can become premises in an ideologic. In a Girardian reading of Custer's Last Stand, for example, Custer was mythologized as a scapegoat for white America's failure to drive Native Americans from western lands and hence remove this reminder of difference from its midst. To use Laclau's terminology, the "unachieved fullness" of the American dream remained as long as peoples mythically represented to be enemies of America nevertheless flourished within her very borders. Custer was killed by Sioux warriors because he was dangerous to them, and revenge cannot be discounted as a motive for their action. But Custer was an outsider to Native American communities, and outsiders are not chosen as scapegoats. Rather, insiders are chosen and ritually killed or banished precisely to demonstrate the dangers posed by outside-ness. Within the white community, then, Custer could function as a scapegoat, and the story about the handy dispatch of the general and his men by warriors of the Sioux nation was rapidly integrated into the myth of the frontier as both a moral lesson and a political justification for the near genocide of Native peoples that was already well under way when Custer fell. In the analogy of the Battle of Little Big Horn it is not hard to see how the myth of the frontier could provoke actions of the kind that followed upon the events of September 11, 2001. The ideologic encapsulated in that myth—that America retains its identity by violently subjugating those who differ from that identity—legitimated the subsequent wars in Afghanistan and Iraq. To be sure, I am not claiming that this ideologic occurred at the level of consciousness; no one explicitly compared the fall of the World Trade Center to Custer's Last Stand. However, the enraged man who murdered a Sikh businessman a few days later actually did kill an Indian, although the terrible irony of this act was no doubt lost on him.

H. Bruce Franklin asserts that myth is "a belief that runs counter to reason, common sense, and all evidence but . . . is widely and deeply held by a society" and "appears as essential truth to its believers" (*Vietnam* 177). I agree, with one important exception: myths do not counter common sense, although they certainly do depart from empirical reality. Rather, they encapsulate and intensify the persuasive force of commonly held beliefs by providing a scenario or images that can perform or stage collective fantasies. Franklin studies the POW/MIA myth, writing the history of the (false) belief that American soldiers were imprisoned, and perhaps tortured, in Southeast Asia long after the close of the Vietnam War (*MIA; Vietnam*). Images of American prisoners of war, such as those incessantly purveyed in movies such as *The Deer Hunter* and *Rambo Part II,* provided compelling and memorable emblems of American defeat. Such images aroused powerful emotions and passionate commitments, and their circulation initiated compensatory beliefs and practices such as survivalism and paramilitarism (Gibson). These images resonated because they graphically contradicted mainstream belief in the myth of American exceptionalism (not to mention the myths of American military superiority and machismo). Collective desire to achieve the fullness of the American dream was severely compromised by the fact of retreat from Vietnam, and fantasies have been generated in order to enact a desire that things turn out differently. The collective fantasy that "we could go back in" and rescue mythic POWs served the same purpose as fictional rescue missions generated in novels and films. Tales about the Vietnam War were told and retold to satisfy a desire that events might turn out differently, to reconcile history with collective fantasy, in order that "we get to win this time," as Rambo plaintively puts it in the second film in the series.

As Laclau notes, myth resonates most intensely when events or circumstances bring about social or political dislocation. When events evoke mythic levels of belief, as they did on September 11, 2001, it is very difficult for people whose patriotism resonates at mythic levels to be persuaded to an antiwar position. In fact I doubt that super-patriots are even able to hear antiwar arguments at such moments because such arguments are not commonplace in American discourse. That is, antiwar arguments may be new (but not neutral) vis-à-vis super-patriotism. Those who encounter a peace vigil or other evidence of dissent from the dominant system of belief, then, are unable even to grasp that "real" Americans could hold such beliefs, which is why they invite dissenters to leave the country and/or to cohabit with the enemy.

My review of argumentative possibilities in this chapter demonstrates, I hope, that there are many more factors at work in belief and persuasion than are dreamed of in liberal philosophy. While people do reason by connecting factual evidence to premises, premises are themselves drawn from ideologies or from systems of belief that are even more resistant to change, such as metaphysics, theology, or hegemonic discourses. Furthermore, the term *reasoning* has to be stretched nearly beyond recognition if it is to be applied to the sort of connections that are often articulated in arguments about civic issues. Images can stimulate visceral responses, which can in turn reinforce belief, for example, while myth and fantasy can inspire belief and motivate action more powerfully than reason does.

4

APOCALYPTISM

In the fall of 2003 I borrowed an audiotape of a novel entitled *Left Behind* from my local library, thinking it was similar to the other light fiction I often listen to while commuting. What I heard stunned me. While waiting for class to begin one day, I mentioned to some graduate students that I was listening to a frightening narrative involving mass disappearances, earthquakes, firestorms, and the general collapse of civilization. The students recognized the tale immediately. One picked up its thread while others joined in, and they recited the entire narrative of the apocalypse: from the Rapture, when Christians who are saved will be taken bodily into heaven, through the Great Tribulation and on to the Glorious Appearing, when Christ will return to establish his thousand-year reign on earth. I was the only person in the room who had never heard of John of Patmos or read the biblical book of Revelation. Fascinated by the story, and a bit ashamed of my ignorance, I began to study Christian apocalyptism.

The percentage of religious believers in America is higher than in any other industrialized country—according to historian Randall Balmer, 94 percent of Americans believe in God (*Blessed* 2). In another survey, undertaken in 2001, only 16 percent of Americans described themselves as "predominantly secular" (ARIS). Susan Jacoby observes that some among this group must believe in God nonetheless, because in this same poll "less than

1 percent described themselves as atheists or agnostics" (7). Not all who believe in God are Christians, of course, and not all Christians believe in an impending apocalypse. While Catholic doctrine acknowledges the notion of a Second Coming, for instance, Catholic bishops have taken a fairly dim view of the elaborate end-times scenario painted by *Left Behind*.[1] Mainline and liberal Protestants are also less likely to entertain apocalyptism than are evangelicals and fundamentalists.[2]

Scholars disagree about the definitions of these last two groups. Balmer uses *evangelist* to refer to conservative Protestants in general (*Mine Eyes* xii). Christian Smith asserts, on the other hand, that the word *evangelical* has a substantive content, indicating a commitment to spread the gospel to others by "taking a stand in the world" for religious belief and practice (*American* 243). And not all evangelicals are fundamentalist by any means. Nancy Ammerman points out that prior to World War II one might use "either name to describe those who preserved and practiced the revivalist heritage of soul winning and maintained a traditional insistence on orthodoxy"; more recently, however, evangelical Christians "saw benefits in learning to get along with outsiders," while fundamentalists insisted that "getting along was no virtue and that active opposition to liberalism, secularism, and communism was to be pursued" ("North American" 4). Apparently George Marsden is not joking when he defines a fundamentalist as "an evangelical who is mad about something" (*Understanding* 1). Fundamentalists, according to Marsden, are ordinarily "militant in opposition to liberal theology in the churches or to changes in cultural values or mores, such as those associated with 'secular humanism'" (*Understanding* 1). This militancy stems from the distinguishing character of Christian fundamentalism, which is the priority awarded to correct belief: according to William Dinges, "for the fundamentalist, 'holding right views' and uniformity of belief is normative for all other elements of religious self-understanding" (82). This priority is instantiated in American Protestant fundamentalism by the doctrine of biblical inerrancy, which insists that the Bible cannot be mistaken. Ammerman takes inerrancy to be a distinguishing feature of fundamentalism, along with premillennialism—that is, the belief that the Christian faithful will be taken bodily to heaven prior to the tribulation and the end of days ("North American" 6). In other words, Ammerman identifies fundamentalism with apocalyptism.

In 1992 Paul Boyer estimated that the circle of core believers in Christian apocalyptism was relatively small. However, he acknowledged that the work of this group influenced more millions of Americans who can be classified as "believers who may be hazy about the details of biblical eschatology, but who nevertheless believe that the Bible provides clues to future events" (2). Since members of this second group do not actually read the Bible, Boyer opines, they may be "susceptible to popularizers who confidently weave Bible passages into highly imaginative end-time scenarios" (3). A third, larger circle includes "superficially secular individuals" who in "times of crisis . . . may listen with more than passing attentiveness to those who offer the Bible as a guide to events, or be particularly receptive to ostensibly secular works that are nevertheless apocalyptist in structure and rhetoric" (3). The membership of Boyer's second and third circles may now be quite large. In 2004 *Newsweek* published a poll in connection with a cover story on Tim LaHaye and Jerry B. Jenkins, the authors of *Left Behind*. According to this survey, 36 percent of Americans "believe that the Book of Revelation contains 'true prophecy'" (Gates, Jefferson, and Underwood 48). That is, over one-third of Americans accept biblical inerrancy, at least regarding John of Patmos's vision of the Second Coming. Over half (55 percent) believe in the Rapture. According to the same poll, three-quarters of Americans (75 percent) believe in Satan; among evangelicals the percentage increases to 93 percent. Certainly LaHaye and Jenkins's fictionalized retelling of biblical prophecies about the end time has become a veritable money machine, with over sixty-two million copies of the dozen novels that constitute the series having been sold (as of this writing).

The numbers reported here suggest that belief in bits of the Christian apocalyptic narrative may have become commonplace independent of Americans' religious affiliations. Daniel Wojcik argues that religious practice has become increasingly privatized in America, thanks in no small part to the proliferation of television, radio, movies, and audio/video resources purveying "poignant testimonials" and "do-it-yourself spiritual techniques" (17). In this setting "interest in apocalyptic ideas is a personalized expression of belief, largely unsanctioned by formal religious institutions and authorities yet existing at an informal level among millions of individuals" (Wojcik 17). Susan Harding argues that Bible prophecy has become a folk practice among believers, a practice in which "everyone prognosticates" (*Book* 239). If this sort of speculation is accurate, bits and pieces of apocalyptist belief have indeed filtered into popular culture.

Earlier I hypothesize that densely woven ideologies articulate identities for individuals as well as for communities of believers. Such ideologies resonate for believers at a visceral level because they connect intimate experiences of life with larger questions and issues. A tightly articulated ideology can smooth over contradictions that might give rise to dissonance or doubt because it has a ready response for every possible occurrence. My task now is to show how Christian apocalyptism is tightly articulated with fundamentalist beliefs, demonstrating how this tie authorizes a worldview to which a politics is inevitably attached. Two theological principles underpin Christian fundamentalism: the doctrines of personal salvation and biblical inerrancy. These beliefs are worked out in a genre of conservative Christian discourse called "prophecy interpretation," wherein authors demonstrate how readers should interpret biblical prophecies concerning apocalypse. While anyone versed in the Bible can take up the work of proselytizing biblical interpretation, this work is most influentially carried out by professionals. I define a professional proselytizer as anyone who profits from his or her articulations of apocalyptist scenarios. This includes writers of prophecy interpretation like Hal Lindsey, as well as televangelists such as Jerry Falwell and Pat Robertson. Moreover, it includes any "spiritual leader" who takes money or gifts in return for preaching apocalyptist belief.

Paul Boyer's analysis of American apocalyptism suggests that lay believers buy into apocalyptist ideologic with varying levels of intensity and completeness. The critique that follows thus may or may not hold for those who fit into Boyer's second and third circles of belief, nor does it obviously hold for people who have picked up bits and pieces of the apocalyptist narrative by reading popular accounts such as Lindsey's *Late Great Planet Earth* (1970) or novels in the *Left Behind* series. Indeed, the violent implications of doctrinaire end-time thinking are so ghastly that lay believers sometimes draw back from them. Charles Strozier reports that "it is simply not the case that [fundamentalists] actively want nuclear war, suffering and widespread death to bring Jesus back sooner"; rather, his informants seemed "to have an anticipation of destruction, but it is a kind of half-wish from which, once expressed, they quickly back off" (72). Professional proselytizers, on the other hand, have a material stake in sustaining the tradition of apocalyptist prophecy interpretation. And since empirical data establishes that members of this group are also far more interested in political engagement than are members of the "evangelical public," it is probably not a coincidence that specifically political positions are explicitly advocated within popular prophecy interpretation (Green 15–16).

The End and the Elect

Lee Quinby argues that apocalyptic desire saturates contemporary American discourse. Apocalypticism embraces two beliefs, according to Quinby: that "a supernatural or exceedingly powerful force, like nuclear disaster, for example, will bring world destruction" and that "an elect number will be granted a new, transformed, earth" (*Millennial* 4). She names these two claims "endism" and "electism," respectively (*Millennial* 2–3). She observes that the range of apocalyptic belief operating in contemporary American discourse "stems from evangelicals predicting Armageddon to political officials calling for the United States to lead the way toward a 'New World Order'" (*Anti-Apocalypse* xii). Endism and electism need not occur together. Endism can be found among neoliberals who assert that we have come to the end of history, ludic postmodernists who argue that nothing matters any longer, environmentalists who worry about the potentially disastrous effects of global warming, and pacifists who fear the catastrophic results of nuclear war. Electism circulates among New Agers and alien abductees. At first glance endism and electism may not seem to pose serious problems to the maintenance of democracy. But Quinby thinks otherwise: she posits that apocalyptic "principles and practices interfere with the goals of democratic societies" because endism represents the future as already written, while electism can support the rightness of established hierarchy and privilege (*Millennial* 5).

Concern about nuclear winter demonstrates that apocalyptic thought need not be inspired by religious faith. However, its oldest forms are associated with some of the world's great religions. According to Norman Cohn, apocalypticism is very old, dating to the sixteenth century BCE, when the Iranian prophet Zoroaster promised a "total transformation of existence, a total perfecting of the world" at the end time (*Cosmos* 96). Jews probably encountered Zoroastrianism during the Babylonian captivity; at any rate apocalypticism appeared in prophetic Old Testament texts composed around 600 BCE (Paul Boyer 22). Thereafter it reemerged on occasion, producing, for example, the haunting vision in the Book of Daniel of a gigantic statue with feet of iron and clay (2:31–45). However, it was not until the coalescence of what Cohn calls "the Jesus sect" that apocalyptic thought found truly fertile ground for development. Cohn argues that Christ was himself an apocalypticist, and John of Patmos was no doubt closely connected with early Christian communities (*Cosmos* 196).

John's vision in the Book of Revelation is perhaps the most powerful account of apocalypse ever written. Here is a bit of Revelation's account of the "blowing of the trumpets": "The seven angels that had the seven trumpets now made ready to sound them. The first blew his trumpet and, with that, hail and fire, mixed with blood, were dropped on the earth; a third of the earth was burnt up, and a third of all trees, and every blade of grass was burnt. The second angel blew his trumpet, and it was as though a great mountain, all on fire, had been dropped into the sea: a third of the sea turned into blood, a third of all the living things in the sea were killed, and a third of the ships were destroyed (8:6–10). The soundings of three additional trumpets poison rivers and lakes, cause the moon and the sun to go dark, and loose a horde of locusts that torment people so severely that they "long for death and not find it anywhere" (8:11–9:12). This and the other horrific visions conjured in this text have frightened and inspired Christians ever since it began to circulate in the first century CE, and people have been predicting the immediate advent of apocalypse ever since (Cohn, *Pursuit;* Kyle; Damian Thompson). Cohn historicizes Revelation, arguing that John wanted to encourage Christians to "see themselves in conflict with the larger society," that is, with the Romans who ruled Judea with an iron hand and who could easily be mythologized as minions of Satan (*Cosmos* 216). Today, however, scholars are the only people who are interested in situating Revelation within its first-century context. Apocalyptist Christians treat its prophecies as transcendental truth in spite of the fact that their application to historical events must be continuously updated. Paul Boyer remarks that the durability of apocalyptist belief is in fact connected to its adaptability: "in vastly different historical circumstances, interpreters found vastly different meanings in the prophecies" (77).

The continuous rereading of Revelation and other biblical texts to coordinate them with world events has become a veritable industry in recent decades. Its best-known popular explicator is Hal Lindsey, whose *Late Great Planet Earth* sold over eighteen million copies and was the best-selling nonfiction book of the 1970s. Lindsey is chiefly responsible for the popular circulation of belief in a coming apocalypse. John Walvoord's *Armageddon, Oil, and the Middle East Crisis* (1974) is still read by conservative Christians; it was reprinted in 1990 because of the book's supposed relevance to the Persian Gulf War. According to prophecy interpreters, God promised Abraham that his chosen people would eventually return to their homeland, and Walvoord sees the fulfillment of this promise in the founding of Israel in 1948. But this event was not sufficient to trigger the end time, which must wait upon the interim jockeying of other nations for positions of power and glory (Walvoord 79). Continuing unrest in the Middle East can thus be linked to Christ's prediction about "wars and rumors of wars," when "nation will fight against nation and kingdom against kingdom" (Matt. 24:6–7).

As this bit of prophecy interpretation indicates, its practitioners are relatively insensitive to historical and cultural differences accruing from the lengthy period of time that intervened between the composition of Genesis and the gospels.[3] That's because they use apocalyptist standard time. American versions of Christian apocalyptism tend to be dispensationalist, after the innovation of a nineteenth-century British expatriate named John Nelson Darby. Darby worked out a set of ahistorical relations among events prophesied in texts from both the Old and New Testaments. He managed this by dividing time into seven dispensations, beginning with the creation and ending with the millennium. Darby construed each of the several dispensations to be governed by a separate covenant or contract between God and believers. Joel Carpenter explains that during each dispensation

humanity would be tested according to the revelation they had of God's will and the covenants or promises that God made with them. . . . Each dispensation was meant to provide a way of salvation for humanity, and each ended in judgement, as humans failed the test. Thus, for example, the Flood of Noah's time ended the dispensation of Conscience, while the dispensation of Promise, under Abraham, Isaac, Jacob, ended with captivity in Egypt. These various ages were pointing toward a final golden age, when a messianic kingdom would come to earth. When Jesus came and announced the messianic kingdom, Israel, God's chosen people, rejected him, and so the kingdom was postponed. (248–49)

And, according to Robert Alan Goldberg:

In the current age, the last before judgment, God beckoned the community of true believers to spread the gospel and secure souls. The cause was urgent, for the divine countdown to Armageddon would resume without warning with the Rapture of the church, when believers would enter heaven without dying. . . . The tribulation scenario moved quickly after that and climaxed in seven years: the emergence of a ten-nation confederation, the rise of the Antichrist and his subsequent perfidy, the machinations of the false prophet, and the conversion of the 144,000 Jews who would preach the gospel and die for their labors, an invasion of Israel, the assault of the armies of the East, the return of Jesus, and the defeat of Satan and his followers. (72)

Darby's elaborate list of dispensations has been simplified for popular consumption. In *Are We Living in the End Times?* (1999), for example, Tim LaHaye and Jerry B. Jenkins depict only five dispensations (100). Ages Past generalizes into a single dispensation the events of the Old Testament and those recounted in the Gospels, with the important exception of Christ's death and resurrection. The Church Age marks the period of historical time in which we now live. This period ends with the Rapture, which in turn marks the beginning of the seven-year Great Tribulation. The Great Tribulation ends with the Glorious Appearing of Christ on earth, which begins the millennium. A final period, Ages to Come, suggests that the earthly perfection established by the defeat of Satan might extend well past the thousand years prophesied in Revelation.

All accounts agree that the present age is the only dispensation governed by historical time; the others run on prophetic or eschatological time (Barr 192; Harding, *Book* 236). Carpenter notes that because of this some dispensationalists call the Church Age "The Great Parenthesis," a period during which God is gathering a new chosen people from among Gentiles (249). This last point is very attractive to Christians, obviously, because it carves out a place for them in apocalyptic events. Timothy Weber argues that Darby's "absolute separation of Israel and the church as the two distinct peoples of God" actually establishes Christians as a second chosen people (17). Jews are God's earthly people, still bound by Old Testament covenants, but because they rejected Christ as the Messiah, they must now "suffer through Gentile domination" (Timothy Weber 18). In other words, Jews have to wait while God's "heavenly people" get the earth in shape for Christ's return.

Clearly this elaborate scheme solved some knotty theological and hermeneutic problems. For one thing, it allowed Darby to reject the arithmetical approach to prophecy, which entailed riffling through the Old Testament looking for mentions of dates that might be added up to predict the exact time of the Second Coming. This approach had been taken by Archbishop Ussher, who in the seventeenth century famously dated creation from 4004 BCE and whose theory of a six-thousand-year history placed the Rapture in 1996 (Damian Thompson 98–99). It was also used by William Miller, who reckoned by arithmetical means that Christ would reappear in 1843. When that date passed, the Millerites recalculated, settling on October 22, 1844. When the Rapture did not occur on that date, the "Great Disappointment" made laughingstocks of the Millerites and brought about a temporary setback to apocalyptist belief. But dispensationalism solved the problem of predictive failure by relocating the Second Coming outside of history. In this reading Scripture gives no clue as to when historical time, in which we now live, will be suspended once again in favor of eschatological time. The establishment of differing dispensations also explains away the pesky problem of contradictions between older and newer biblical texts. Thanks to the ahistoricism built into the system, prophecy interpreters are free to plunder all the books of the Bible at once, cobbling together prophetic arguments from texts composed hundreds of years apart and treating each snippet as though it is equally relevant to the present moment—which just might be the moment that precedes the Rapture, the moment that restarts eschatological time.

Prophecy interpreters disagree about the exact sequence in which apocalyptic events will occur. LaHaye and Jenkins's depiction of the end time is premillennialist, so called because it asserts that the tribulation will occur prior to Christ's return to earth. Premillennialists believe that Christians who are saved will be raptured before the tribulation begins.[4] Thus they will be spared its horrors, which, according to Revelation, will be visited on all who are alive at the time. But Jews will suffer the most severe depredations, and only a tiny "remnant" of Jews will remain alive after Armageddon. The remnant will of course finally convert to Christianity and be taken into heaven when Christ arrives on Earth to dispatch Satan once and for all and to condemn unbelievers to eternal damnation. Postmillennialists, on the other hand, reject the notion of a tribulation, or else they believe that the Church Age is itself a tribulation. According to Timothy Weber, postmillennialists "believe that Christ will return after the church has established the millennium through its faithful and Spirit-empowered preaching of the gospel" (9). Until quite recently premillennialism was far more popular among prophecy interpreters than other possibilities, including the belief held by the few hardy "mid-tribbers" who think that the Rapture will occur halfway through the Great Tribulation (Timothy Weber 10). Thoroughgoing premillennialists are pretty much inclined to believe that life here on Earth is difficult and "sin-challenged," and so they see conversion as their major Christian duty. Bob Jones, founder of Bob Jones University, is a strict premillennialist in this regard: "The church is not told to change the moral climate of the world. The commission of the Church is to save men and women out of the world. Anybody who knows and believes the Scripture recognizes that the moral situation of the world is going to grow worse and worse as we go further and further into the apostasy" (qtd. in Boone 53). Premillennialism can thus manifest an utter disregard for the secular realm. Kathleen Boone remarks that "the philosophical and political consequences of premillennialist thought can hardly be overstated: human efforts to effect changes for the good are not only utterly futile, but by definition contrary to the divine plan" (53). The task for premillennialist Christians is simply to practice their faith as well as they can in a fallen world and wait for the Rapture.

Postmillennialism, on the other hand, more optimistically implies that a Christian kingdom can be established on Earth prior to Christ's return, and it also holds out hope for the eventual perfection of human being. Some postmillennialists believe that the Second Coming will not occur until every person in the world has been witnessed to—that is, until they have heard someone preach the truth of the Bible. Postmillennialism is thus a powerful warrant for missionary work, and at the turn of the twentieth century it authorized a number of projects dedicated to the achievement of social justice as well (Carpenter; Morone). Most important for my argument, however, is the fact that postmillennialism can be used to authorize political activity by Christians. It is perhaps not coincidental that postmillennialism has become more widely accepted in prophecy interpretation during the last twenty years (Cox). Susan Harding notices that dispensationalism acquired a new wrinkle among popular prophecy interpreters during the 1980s:

Major national preachers and writers, including Hal Lindsey, Tim LaHaye, Billy Graham, and Jerry Falwell, created a new kind of time within the end-times, a potentially progressive period in what was otherwise a hopelessly regressive era. The tribulation, as ever, was a time when God would judge the Jews according to immutable, irreversible, Biblical prophecy. But the outlines of another, pretribulational, judgment, a little tribulation that preceded the great tribulation, also precipitated out, one that had not been clearly foretold in the Bible. The period before the rapture, the end-time, was now understood to be a time in which God would judge Christians, as opposed to Jews. And his judgment was not fixed by biblical prophecies. It was, in other words, reversible. If Christians responded to God's call through holy living and moral action, God would spare them and the American nation. Thus, with this little tribulation, Bible prophecy teachers opened a small window of progressive history in the last days, a brief moment in time when Christians could, and must be, agents of political and social change. (*Book* 241)

The "little trib" provides a postmillennial rationale for converting unbelievers and disciplining the fallen away while leaving intact the more rigorous determinism of premillennialism. And if Christ's second advent can be hurried along by the creation of a perfect Christian society, prophecy interpreters are authorized to view historical time as something other than a long period of passive longing and waiting. Rather, they can characterize it as an opportunity to change the world.

Jesus Saves

A characteristic feature of fundamentalist Christianity is the notion that a person must be "born again" in order to achieve heavenly life after death as promised by Christ.[5] This belief distinguishes fundamentalist groups from churches that teach that salvation requires the performance of good works, as well as from those that hold that Christ's death on the cross achieved salvation for all humans. Substitutionary atonement, as this last doctrine is called, can be read to authorize election, that is, the assumption that one can be saved by doing nothing at all, by merely relying on Christ's sacrifice to wash away one's sins. The problem posed by election was solved in American Protestantism by the emergence of belief in the necessity of personal salvation. James Barr explains this concept as follows: "God's gift, which is grace, has to have the response of faith: faith is the acceptance of God's grace. When faith is born, when a person accepts Jesus Christ as personal Lord and Saviour, then God's atoning love in Christ becomes effective. . . . He is born again and becomes a new creature" (29). The experience of being personally saved does not mean that the effect is permanent, by any means. According to Barr, one must "work to make his calling sure: the study of the Bible and personal prayer are his instruments in this work. This task can also be described as a fight or struggle: the believer is assailed by temptation and by the devil, for although justified he still has the root of sinfulness in him" (29). Although backsliding is a concern in fundamentalist communities, the experience of personal salvation also seems to provide believers with a certain degree of moral assurance (Balmer, *Mine Eyes*). One of Amy Frykholm's informants had "no doubt that she will go in the rapture"; moreover, she was "fairly certain she can identify those who will go with her," which suggests that those who are saved can discern the spiritual condition of others (50). Sincere words are not sufficient to mark a state of salvation, though—one needs to look for "outward signs," such as changes in behavior or the "clearing out" of life problems (Ammerman, *Bible* 83). This belief provides a powerful theological rationale for the enforcement of social conformity.[6]

The happy situation of those who are saved, and who will thus be raptured, interests apocalyptist authors far less than does the fate of those who are condemned to suffer the most horrible tortures imaginable during the tribulation. Of course gory depictions of suffering are admonitory, just as they were when they first appeared in Revelation, where John's visitor sends "straighten-up" messages to seven churches. But the lingering and graphic attention lavished on the horrors of the tribulation in the *Left Behind* novels and in prophecy interpretation proper suggests as well that apocalyptist Christians are not entirely happy about missing out on this period of eschatological time. Harding tells the story of a Christian fundamentalist who buried a Bible in a cave in the Valley of Petra, the spot where Jews who survive the Great Tribulation are to be converted and hence saved. She argues that this gesture represents fundamentalists' desire to "hope themselves in, if not will themselves into, God's plan for the last days" (*Book* 231). Furthermore, the emergence of the "little trib" suggests that at the very least apocalyptists want to extend eschatological time backward into the historical present so that Christians can believe they are preparing the earth for Christ's return. Steven O'Leary notes that "the promise held out by [Hal] Lindsey" is "nothing more than the preservation of the American way of life for a few more years until the rapture; and presumably, after believers are evacuated in the divine airlift, Fortress America will crumble and the catastrophic conclusion of history will proceed as predicted" (179). This blend of premillennial determinism and postmillennial hope is not quite theologically (dare I say it?) kosher, but it lends a quite useful advantage to prophecy interpretation. As O'Leary remarks, "this is surely only a minor qualification of Lindsey's original historical pessimism, but it is enough to make a crucial difference in his political philosophy" (179).

John's vision of the tribulation includes the four horsemen representing warfare, famine, pestilence, and death, as well as "an earthquake and other upheavals in the natural order: the sun grows black, the moon turns to blood, stars fall to earth" (Paul Boyer 37; see Rev. 6). Here is LaHaye and Jenkins's evocation of the horde of locusts loosed by the blowing of the sixth trumpet:

The sky was black as pitch and the racket deafening. Buck spun to look at Chaim, whose face matched Buck's own terror. Metal against metal clanged until both men covered their ears. Rattling, thumping against the windows now, the rumble had become a cacophony of piercing, irritating, rattling, jangling that seemed it would invade the very walls. Buck stared out the window, and his heart thun dered against his ribs. From out of the smoke came flying creatures—hideous, ugly, brown and black and yellow flying monsters. Swarming like locusts, they looked like miniature horses five or six inches long with tails like those of scorpions. Most horrifying, the creatures were attacking, trying to get in. And they looked past Buck as if Chaim was their target. (*Left Behind* 304–5; see Rev. 9)

Chaim is a Jew who will not convert to Christianity. As a result he suffers terribly during the tribulation and eventually commits suicide in an attempt to kill Antichrist. The *Left Behind* series includes many such vivid depictions of the horrible punishments God has reserved for those who refuse to accept the right kind of religious belief.

This scarifying talk about worldwide earthquakes and killer metal locusts might be about as important to American culture as the latest disaster film were it not for the fact that Christian apocalyptism mandates a politics. Vincent Crapanzano argues that for fundamentalists the Bible describes with unquestioned authority the course and truth of history. It not only provides a model for understanding the chain of events that we come to call history, but it actually modulates the perception of the events and their concatenations. For the fundamentalist Scripture is to history as Scripture is to experience: its truth, its authority, the formulations it provides, override "empirical reality" as it is perceived by those who have not submitted to God's Word (161).

Events occurring in apocalyptist time are *more true* than those that happen in secular time; moreover, apocalyptist time determines how interpretations of events occurring in secular time will be understood. Harding in fact asserts that apocalyptist belief is a "narrative mode of *knowing history.* Dispensationalist readings of events such as the Persian Gulf War are not merely religiously correct interpretations, as if that war, those events, existed outside those interpretations; dispensationalist readings *are* those current events for many Americans" ("Imagining" 60). That is to say, eschatological truth governs and dictates history; eschatological reality is worked out in empirical reality.

Because of its determinism apocalyptism advocates passive acceptance of all sorts of horrors. Even worse, readings of Middle Eastern wars as fulfillment of biblical prophecy can lead premillennialist believers to support policies that foment such wars. In other words, apocalyptism can serve believers as an instruction manual for decision making about international politics. In *The Book of Jerry Falwell* Harding makes the point that apocalyptists believe that "Christians through their actions today cannot alter God's plan, but they may be enacting it. Their actions may prefigure or typify the events of the Second Coming" (230). And so believers can't make mistakes; whatever they do fits in with God's plan.

If belief in the apocalyptist narrative, however unconscious, motivates politicians who hold powerful positions in government, this does not bode well for America's relations with other countries because apocalyptism requires that wars among nations occur prior to the end time. Nor does it bode well for democracy. Christian apocalyptism devalues unbelievers, characterizing them as pawns of history, deluded secularists, or misguided apostates who are condemned to suffering, pain, and death. From the point of view of a Christian apocalyptist nonbelief in their worldview constitutes evidence of failure to be saved. This explains why Jerry Falwell, speaking to Pat Robertson on the latter's television program, could so readily blame the horrible events of 9/11 on those who oppose his views:

The ACLU has got to take a lot of blame for this. And I know I'll hear from them for this, but throwing God . . . successfully with the help of the federal court system . . . throwing God out of the public square, out of the schools, the abortionists have got to bear some burden for this because God will not be mocked and when we destroy 40 million little innocent babies, we make God mad. . . . I really believe that the pagans and the abortionists and the feminists and the gays and the lesbians who are actively trying to make that an alternative lifestyle, the ACLU, People for the American Way, all of them who try to secularize America . . . I point the thing in their face and say you helped this happen.[7]

Falwell does not accept the terms of secular historiography—this historical event is caused by that set of beliefs and practices. Rather, he reads events in terms of their significance within an already written historical narrative whose protagonists and antagonists are always already defined. For Falwell the events of September 11 were literally an act of God—both retribution and a sign to unbelievers that resistance can only lead to death and suffering. This confirms Strozier's observation that "for fundamentalists, the nonbeliever is death tainted"; he or she "lives a constricted life and suffers the pain of death without hope of redemption. There are, in other words, severe consequences for refusing to accept Jesus in one's life. In the immediate and visible present the effects show themselves in a failure to understand the Bible" (90). The only evidence necessary to determine who is an antagonist, then, is evidence of unbelief as defined in apocalyptist theology. Clearly Falwell's worldview supplies a cosmic warrant for the "friend-enemy" relation that constitutes the political (Mouffe, *Return* 2–3).

Those who contest his beliefs are enemies of an angry God who is capable of wreaking terrible vengeance.

Harding notes that secular intellectuals tend to discount the importance of apocalyptist thought on the ground that belief does not necessarily influence action ("Imagining" 59). But as I argue earlier, this disjunction is theoretically and practically suspect. Jerry Falwell certainly does not separate belief from action, and neither should critics who are concerned about the political and ethical fallout from Christian apocalyptism.

Biblical Inerrancy

No doubt most outsiders associate the Christian Right with Pat Robertson and Jerry Falwell. But Tim LaHaye is probably the most influential intellectual in the movement at the moment, given his long history of political activity, as well as the sheer number of his publications and their astonishing popularity. In 2001 the Institute for the Study of American Evangelicals named LaHaye the most influential Christian leader of the past quarter century. He edged out Billy Graham and James Dobson for this honor. Nonevangelicals who recognize his name have probably seen it on the cover of the *Left Behind* novels. But he has been active in conservative Christian politics for a long time. He was on the first board of directors of the Moral Majority, and he directed a voter registration effort for Reagan's presidential campaign (Diamond, *Spiritual* 66). He founded the American Coalition for Traditional Values, among many other religious and political organizations, and he also originated a number of Christian educational efforts, including the PreTrib Research Center and Christian Heritage College in San Diego.

Writing with his spouse, Beverly LaHaye, he has produced works of nonfiction that instruct believers in marital and family relationships and self-help. He has also written about "spiritual growth" and the decline of public morality with other coauthors. He has published at least two books on homosexuality (one entitled *The Unhappy Gays*), but neither of these is currently listed on his Web site (http://www.timlahaye.com). While none of LaHaye's nonfiction is as wildly successful as *Left Behind,* as of this writing over ten million copies remain in print (http://www.pageturner.com). His great ideological contribution to Christian Right activists is to have popularized the thought of Francis Schaeffer, an influential Presbyterian scholar who taught that Christianity exists in fundamental opposition to materialist Western culture (Capps 59–72; Detwiler 111–12). LaHaye accepts

Schaeffer's reading of history, sometimes echoing it nearly verbatim. Walter Capps writes that LaHaye's *Battle for the Mind* (1980) "is hardly anything more than a simplified and condensed highly charged paraphrase of Schaeffer's most potent observation. In LaHaye's restatement, however, some of Schaeffer's contentions are so thoroughly oversimplified as to be distorted" (73). *Battle for the Mind* has since been updated (with evangelical activist David Noebel) and was published in 2000 as *Mind Siege*. In these works LaHaye refines Schaeffer's reservations about Western materialism into a crusade against "secular humanism," and he is no doubt responsible for the widespread assumption among Christian Right activists that their ideological enemy is a religion of that name.

LaHaye also does prophecy interpretation. Recently he published several readings of Revelation that appear to be reworkings of older publications (and near-clones of one another).[8] He claims he wrote these books in response to requests from readers of *Left Behind* who want assistance in interpreting the biblical apocalyptic prophecies.[9] While the names of other writers often accompany LaHaye's on the title pages of his books, I suspect that these others are ghostwriters rather than coauthors. A remarkable symmetry obtains between the accounts of the apocalypse that appear in the *Left Behind* novels and those in the nonfiction titles that make up his "prophecy library." Moreover, the politics remain the same in all of the genres I examined.

According to *Newsweek*, LaHaye attempted to write a novel about the Rapture on his own but decided after one attempt that he needed help (Gates, Jefferson, and Underwood 48). His agent discovered Jenkins, who wrote the *Left Behind* novels using LaHaye's outlines and scriptural commentary. This explains why large swatches of the novels are given over to sermonizing and biblical commentary.

Biblical inerrancy is the major premise of LaHaye's prophecy interpretation. Everywhere in his prophecy works he reminds readers that the Bible is the literal and authoritative Word of God. In *The Rapture* he depicts the current internecine difficulties within the Southern Baptist Convention as a "battle for the Bible against those who would take it figuratively or as an allegory" and crows that "those who believe in an inspired, inerrant, and authoritative Bible have wrestled control of their denomination from those who do not" (20). Those who read Scripture figuratively, note, are not fellow Christians but opponents from whom "control" must be "wrestled." *The Merciful God of Prophecy* is an attempt to repair a popular image of God as "some celestial ogre who delights in inflicting catastrophe" (6). In this work LaHaye asserts that the Bible "remains the only reliable source of who and what God is" (xiv). He does not entertain the possibility that the popular image of God as a "celestial ogre" stems from the very reading of the Bible promulgated by prophecy interpreters.

From the presumption of inerrancy all other arguments follow. One important minor premise is that inerrancy secures the truth of apocalyptism: Revelation appears in the Bible; therefore its narrative must be true. LaHaye asserts that belief in "an authoritative, Holy Spirit–inspired, inerrant Bible" and "the anticipation that Christ could come for His church at any time" are responsible for the spread of Christianity "to every continent on the globe," as if apocalyptism and inerrancy are the most persuasive appeals available to missionary Christians (*Rapture* 20). Apparently he assumes that a dispensationalist reading of Scripture is somehow more persuasive than Christ's gospel of love or the food, clothing, and medical supplies that missionaries often bring with them. LaHaye does not bother to support his claim, preferring to allow the unwritten warrant to do its work; apocalyptism and inerrancy are persuasive because they are true.

A second minor premise depending from inerrancy is the belief that competitors to LaHaye's brand of Bible-centered Protestantism purvey idolatry and apostasy. In order to demonstrate that his religion enjoys an exclusive hold on truth, he develops a history that is, to put it charitably, out of step with secular accounts. He traces "Hinduism, Buddhism, Taoism and Gaia worship" and "every false religion in the world . . . back to Babylon," the ancient city where Satan "introduced idolatry, the first secret societies, and many of the religious practices that continue to the present day."[10] These pagan and false "cultic systems" all "depend on the worship of images" (LaHaye and Jenkins, *Are We Living* 172). LaHaye lumps these religions into a category he calls "Mystery Babylon," connecting them by this means to the Whore of Babylon who appears in Revelation 17. John of Patmos associates the Whore with filth, fornication, and abomination, and LaHaye's treatment does nothing to dispel these connotations (Pippin). His apocalyptist historiography allows him to confound New Age reverence for Gaia with ancient Egyptian and Greek female mystery cults; he conflates Isis, Aphrodite, and Earth herself with John's image of the wanton harlot who betrays kings and is herself betrayed by them, thus taking shots at paganism, feminism, environmentalism, and New Ageism in one economical image. Later on, according to LaHaye, when the Roman Empire ruled the known world, Satan (like any savvy CEO) moved his headquarters to Rome where he once again installed his favorite idolatrous practices, "all of them received from Babylon" (*Are We Living* 173). Satan was thus able to corrupt the early Christian church, that is, Roman Catholicism, with idol worship. "It is said," LaHaye writes, "that the church retained much of the statuary in the pagan temples; it simply rededicated them to Christianity, then chiseled off the names of the pagan deities and replaced them with the names of the apostles, Jesus, and Mary" (*Are We Living* 173). (Anyone who is curious to know by whom this is "said" is out of luck, since this assertion, like all the others cited here, is made without benefit of documentation.) The Protestant Reformation saved the world from idolatry by making the text of the Bible directly available to Christians: the "courageous efforts of a few Christian scholars . . . called Christianity back to the Bible" (*Are We Living* 174). The Reformation arrived not a moment too soon; in France "skeptics like Voltaire and Rousseau" were so angered by Catholic belief and practice that they "became anti-Christian thinkers and began to propagate an atheistic socialism born out of French skepticism, which ultimately merged with German rationalism. Today their intellectual descendants champion a philosophy called 'secular humanism'" (*Are We Living* 175). This breathtaking redaction of European intellectual history cleverly depicts secularism as reactionary, underscoring the point that religious belief antedates it.

And so LaHaye blames Catholicism for the onset of secular modernity. He is also at pains to exclude Catholicism and other religious traditions from the category of true belief: "The idea that all religions point to the same god is blasphemy. So is the idea that there are many ways to God. Buddha, Mary, Gaia, Muhammad, and Christ are *not* in the same category. They do not all carry equal weight with the triune god of the Bible" (*Are We Living* 176). So even though occupants of the papal throne profess to believe in Jesus, their "reverence for Mary" suggests to LaHaye that a pope "could be setting up his church and the religions of the world for the fulfillment of Revelation 17, where 'Mystery Babylon, the mother of harlots' unifies all the religions of the world" during the tribulation (*Are We Living* 177). LaHaye's offensive yoking of Mary with the Whore of Babylon demonstrates that Roman Catholicism is a centrally important target of his narrative. If Bible-centered Protestantism is to be the only true version of Christian belief, the claim to authenticity of this much older tradition must be dismissed. In one place LaHaye dates the emergence of the true, Bible-centered church to 1750, that is, to America's "Great Awakening," erasing centuries of Christian history in the process (*Revelation* 78).[11] Ostensibly he rejects Catholicism because he believes that the Roman church "worships"

Mary and the saints. But this rejection also preserves the truth of dispensationalism. Critics of dispensationalism point out that it was not invented until the nineteenth century, which of course raises the question of why it "was never seen or mentioned by the early Christian fathers or for almost 19 centuries of church history," as LaHaye himself puts the dilemma (*Rapture* 42). In *The Rapture* LaHaye dates premillennial dispensationalism to 1784, that is, prior to Darby's birth, but he gives no reason for doing so (10). Later on he moves the date back to 1742, claiming that evidence for this appears in a book published by a Baptist minister in 1788 (*Rapture* 42). (He does not quote the text in question, nor does he tell his readers where to find a copy.) Premillennialism is very old, and it would not be surprising to find it even in very early Christian texts. But it is dispensationalism, not premillennialism, that legitimates the enterprise of prophecy interpretation. LaHaye must establish a pre-Darbyan date of inauguration for it because he wants to identify premillennialist dispensationalism with the time and place when and where true Christian belief emerged: in eighteenth-century America. And so his history dispenses with Catholic claims on Christianity at the same time as it suggests that the truth of dispensationalism somehow predates Darby.

LaHaye's adherence to apocalyptist standard time creates such howlers that a secular reader may find herself laughing (or crying) as she works her way through his prophecy library. He asserts that ancient Babylon was a "socialist" city (*Are We Living* 132). He also suspects that Saddam Hussein is a Satanist, that he secretly desires to become Nebuchadnezzar or, failing that, wants to play John the Baptist to Antichrist (*Are We Living* 140, 142). LaHaye remarks that Israel is frequently in the news because of the important role Jews are scheduled to play in the end time, as if international interest in Middle East politics is generated by the importance of that area to apocalyptist prophecy (*Are We Living* 45–46). He asserts that "by European standards the Russians were always a backward people" (*Are We Living* 90). Indeed, the Russians were so backward that they allowed themselves to be defeated by the Japanese at the turn of the twentieth century. LaHaye's ignorance of world history is clearly fueled by xenophobia.

In his prophecy interpretations LaHaye is at pains to teach his readers how to interpret the difficult texts they will encounter while reading the Old and New Testaments. In *Revelation Unveiled*, for example, he advises readers to follow "the golden rule of interpretation: When the plain sense of Scripture makes common sense, seek no other sense; therefore, take every word at its primary, ordinary, usual, literal meaning unless the facts of the immediate text, studied in the light of related passages and axiomatic and fundamental truths, clearly indicate otherwise" (17). A resisting reader might well be dismayed by LaHaye's confidence that the "primary, ordinary, usual, literal" meanings of words can so easily be discerned. This approach collapses a complicated history of theories of meaning, stretching from Warburton to Wittgenstein, into a breezy list of adjectives. Nonetheless, it must be admitted that LaHaye's method is a masterstroke insofar as it permits the prophecy interpreter to claim that he sticks to the plain, literal meaning of the biblical texts while at the same time he interprets imagery, constructs points of doctrine, and asserts "axiomatic and fundamental truths" that cannot actually be found in the Bible. He is having his interpretive cake and eating it, too.

In her meditation on inerrancy Kathleen Boone demonstrates that popular prophecy interpreters make very different readings of the same piece of biblical imagery in order to shore up their particular versions of the apocalyptist narrative. For example, the "two hundred thousand thousand horses" in Revelation 9 have been variously described as supernatural creatures, as "missile launching tanks," and as nuclear warheads (Boone 44). Boone concludes from this evidence that for prophecy interpreters the term *literal* denotes "the empirical or ostensively referential. One need not believe that actual fire and brimstone will spew from the mouths of actual horses, whether natural or supernatural, in order to believe that an empirically sensible invasion of death-dealing forces will actually take place at some point in the future" (45). So here *literal* does not mean rejection of allegorical or other sorts of figurative readings. Rather it means "applicable to or referential of the world." Once presumptions about divine time and the inerrancy of Scripture are in place, it is easy enough to assume that God knew all along that he would be using tanks and nuclear warheads; he simply employed language in Revelation that John of Patmos could grasp. A "literal" reading that produces tanks and warheads in place of scriptural horses reinforces the argument about the predictive capacity of Scripture, and the Bible's authority is enhanced in turn to the extent that unfolding world events can be matched to prophecies made within its pages. Thus prophecy interpretation enacts the hermeneutic circle with a certain vengeance. For all his condemnation of moderate Baptists who read Scripture "figuratively," LaHaye does not hesitate to interpret its imagery in mythopoetic terms. He reads the two hundred million horses and their riders as "unnatural, demonlike evil spirits" (*Revelation* 174). If one accepts the existence of a supernatural realm, as LaHaye professes to do, one can forward this reading as a "literal" evocation of actual, empirical beings who will participate in the Great Tribulation.

Many scholars have pointed out the influence of Scottish common-sense realism on nineteenth-century American Protestant theologians.[12] The Scottish philosophers taught that minds had a master sense that controlled each of the physical senses and that mulled over evidence provided to it by them. Thus this sense was common because it participated in all the sensory domains, but it was also common because reasonable people who rightly interpreted the evidence of their senses shared the same knowledge. Thus commonsense philosophy offered a means of escape from radical individualism. Because of this influence, I believe, fundamentalist interpretive literalism also appeals to the "ordinary" or "most commonly used" meanings of Bible passages, just as LaHaye claims it does. Protestantism's originating claim, after all, was that Scripture is legible to any reader. As soon as the Bible was translated into vernacular languages, however, lay people began to read it however they liked, and schisms proliferated. So Protestant theologians cast about for a source of authority that would put a halt to this interpretive free-for-all. Fundamentalists addressed the problem by asserting that the sacred texts represent the actual word of God himself, who miraculously inspired the human authors of both testaments to speak with his voice (Crapanzano 66–69). This innovation secures the divine authority of Scripture, but it exacerbates the difficulty of multiple and proliferating readings: how can the Word of God mean so many different things? Fundamentalists solved this problem with the rationalist notion that the biblical text has a "common sense." LaHaye recommends that readers count on their sense of the "ordinary" or "usual" meanings of words to reveal the meaning of the biblical text—unless they can't, at which juncture they must call upon "axiomatic and fundamental truths." Of course these "truths" are in the custody of prophecy interpreters. The reader of *Left Behind* who writes to LaHaye asking him to help her interpret Revelation does so because his name appears on the cover of many books that supposedly contain the "common sense" of the Bible. That is to say, he is an authority who possesses knowledge that she cannot find either in her own spirituality or in the sacred text. While on its face the claim of common sense seems democratic enough, then, in practice it mitigates against new or deviant readings, legitimating instead the prior claim of an interpretive tradition that inserts a layer of professional authority between the lay reader and the sacred text.[13] Harold Bloom, analyzing a resolution passed at the Southern Baptist Convention in 1988, rails that "fundamentalist pastors have been declared to have the authority of priests, while lay persons have been denounced for what amounts to soul incompetency in spiritual matters" (226). The "soul incompetent" can and do turn to the popular *Scofield Reference Bible* for help, but they will find the common sense of the priesthood ensconced in its pages as well. Cyrus Scofield "canonized" Darby's dispensationalist reading of Scripture "by printing it in the margins of the King James Version of the biblical text" when he first published his reference Bible in 1909 (Goldberg 73). Apparently lay users of this Bible can confuse the biblical text itself with Darby's marginalia and Scofield's annotations (Frykholm 18). Goldberg summarizes the resulting state of affairs nicely: "Human agency had ensured the Bible's infallibility. The literal word had been interpreted, and the interpretation was now raised to the level of the literal word" (73). The Scofield Bible remains a strong seller to this day (Balmer, *Blessed* 52).

The inescapable conclusion is that if lay readers follow the interpretive path laid out for them by LaHaye and his ilk, they are reading dispensationalism rather than the Bible. Prophecy interpreters themselves do not read the sacred text in the ordinary sense of "reading," from cover to cover, say, or from chapter to chapter (Bloom 220). Rather, they deploy verses scattered throughout the text to shore up points in the interpretive tradition that are weakened by the passage of time. Bloom claims that "fundamentalist clergymen . . . are not writing about the [biblical] text, in any sense whatsoever of text, or of that text. They write about their own dogmatic social, political, cultural, moral, and even economic convictions, and biblical texts simply are quoted, with frenetic abandon, whether or not they in any way illustrate or even approach the areas where the convictions center" (222). In other words, prophecy interpreters are shoring up an ideology by supporting its disputed points with supposedly authoritative citations gleaned from Scripture. They are also shoring up their own authority. As Bruce Lincoln puts it, "by minimizing their agency and masking their interests, while simultaneously insisting on the sacred status of the verses they cite, they attempt to claim the same sacred (i.e., authoritative and indisputable) status for the speech through which they advance their own favored views and projects" (47).

In sum: prophecy interpreters excerpt prophetic passages from their biblical contexts, reinterpret them to accommodate new doctrinal crises or historical developments, and drop them back into the ever-evolving dispensationalist narrative of the end time. The recent evolution of the "little trib" demonstrates that prophecy interpreters have evolved a discourse (in the Foucauldian sense) that governs what may be said, and by whom, about prophecies appearing in the Old and New Testaments. The little tribulation is authorized by neither Revelation nor the Old Testament, which of course has nothing literally to say about Christians. Nor, for that matter, is it authorized by Darbyan dispensationalism. Undaunted by these realities, in his recent spate of publications about the end time LaHaye has assembled a web of verses to support it.[14] The identification of the "northern kingdom" called "Magog" also exemplifies the evolutionary quality of prophecy interpretation. Ezekiel 38 prophesies that the prince of this city or kingdom, named "Gog," will someday make war on Israel. Prophecy interpreters began to identify Magog with Russia during the nineteenth century, and during the Cold War this identification clearly served the fear-mongering purposes of American dispensationalists.[15] Since the collapse of the Soviet Union, however, the connection has become more difficult to maintain, and so some prophecy interpreters now identify Magog with various Middle Eastern nations. LaHaye compromises by asserting that "Russia and her Muslim allies are doing everything they can to foment war in Israel" (*Are We Living* 92). Now while it is true that the Soviet Union supported Iran and Syria during the Cold War, more recently Russia has mounted brutal wars against the inhabitants of Afghanistan and Chechnya. So LaHaye's assertion that "Muslims" are allied with Russia requires qualification at the very least. But historical facts may be overlooked if apocalyptist standard time requires their erasure. After supplying his readers with a long list of Russia's current travails, LaHaye observes: "if she is going to be the major power that Ezekiel forecasts her to be, she had better make her move soon, or she won't be able to do so!" (*Are We Living* 92). Uncharitably I read this sentence to mean "Russia had better make her move soon, or I will have to contradict myself!"

Apocalyptism and the Struggle of Nations

The authors of the Old Testament did not think of the vast territory that stretches between southern Russia and northern Africa as "the Middle East," although the Babylonian and Egyptian captivities surely made archaic Jews aware that large land masses surrounded Judea on all sides except the seaward one. For the same reason they were all too aware of what is now called the cultural diversity of the area. But such historical details do not deter LaHaye from generalizing wildly about the role played by "Arabs" in the end time, as though the peoples who inhabit Egypt, Iraq,

Turkey, and Syria are all members of a single "race" (and moreover have always been so). Entire nations are condemned by the dispensationalist script to act as willing agents of Satan during the Great Tribulation. For instance, LaHaye asserts that at the end of this period China and possibly Japan ("the kings of the east") will make "the long trek to the Megiddo Valley" to do battle with Christ (*Are We Living* 217). LaHaye never fails to remind his readers that China is "controlled" by "dedicated communists," a "ruthless group of elite gangsters" who want to "conquer the world" (*Are We Living* 211). Unfortunately China escaped Christian proselytizing (read "civilizing") until recently because it is located on the wrong side of the Euphrates, a "natural dividing line" between East and West. Consequently the Chinese people were "exposed to demons and spirits of devils" for a long time before Christian missionaries arrived to correct the problem (*Are We Living* 212).

These comments manifest a deep and abiding chauvinism. Entire peoples populate LaHaye's imagination only because their existence is required to fulfill biblical prophecy. One way to account for his fervid nationalism is to echo Paul Boyer's point that the notion of strife between "nations" is widespread in the Old Testament, and hence dispensationalists assume that "competition among nations is a natural expression of the divine order of things" (148). A second, less generous way to explain the xenophobia in LaHaye's prophecy interpretation is to filter it through the distinction made in apocalyptism between the saved and the unsaved. In this reading born-again Christians and a handful of converted Jews are pitted against all the other peoples of the world, who side with Antichrist during the tribulation. Apocalyptist invention begins with denial of the other, an other defined as absolutely corrupt. This beginning point allows anti-Semitism and other exclusionist binaries to run rampant through prophecy interpretation. When combined with belief in American exceptionalism, apocalyptism has troubling ramifications for international politics, because disasters and tragedies can be read as evidence that God's plan has at last begun to unfold. To an apocalyptist way of thinking, as Daniel Wojcik notes, "the ubiquitous signs of doomsday are a cause for rejoicing. . . . As portents of the last days, famine, wars, plagues, environmental disasters, and nuclear war are regarded as markers on God's predetermined timetable . . . not as events that one may avert" (58). Prophecy interpreters oppose the United Nations, as well as international efforts to restrain the use of nuclear weaponry, improve trade relations and disease prevention, and protect the environment. For premillennialists the achievement of any of these goals mitigates the determinism of biblical prophecy, while post-millennialists believe that world peace will be achieved by the conversion of everyone to Christianity rather than by means of diplomacy and international cooperation. LaHaye maunders on about the threat of "one-world government," a "world tax," a "world court," and a "world police force" (*Are We Living* 170). He does not see the United Nations only as a threat to America's status as a superpower. For him one-worldism is, rather, a prelude to the rise of Antichrist. He predicts that "liberals and socialists" will take over the world "right after the rapture," thus setting the stage for the takeover of all world governments by Antichrist, who will institute a single government that rules the entire world (*Rapture* 169). In this view internationalists are agents of Satan, working through Antichrist.

Why Apocalyptism Resonates

Students of apocalyptism have offered a number of explanations for the usefulness of the apocalyptist narrative to believers. Randall Balmer reads it as compensation for fundamentalists' loss of religious and cultural hegemony (*Blessed* 104). That is to say, the narrative assures them that even though their beliefs are not dominant, they are nonetheless correct. On the other hand, fundamentalists interviewed by Vincent Crapanzano "seemed to be primarily concerned with their individual salvation, their own spiritual and bodily salvation at the end of history" (174). Because of this Crapanzano risks the argument that for some fundamentalists the collective narrative has become autobiographical, transposing a private fear of death into belief in a triumphant immortality. Steven O'Leary argues more charitably that apocalyptism assures believers of the eventual triumph of good.[16] And Paul Boyer sums up nicely: apocalyptist beliefs "offer the disinherited a means of systematizing their grievances, the powerful an avenue of advancing their goals, and believers far from the public arena a language for expressing their deepest spiritual longing" (55). Boyer is onto something important with his last point: the function of religion, after all, is to delineate rituals and ceremonies that encourage and enhance spirituality. The apocalyptic narrative allows the expression of religiosity outside of church, within popular culture. Bits and pieces of the narrative are featured in films such as *The Rapture* (1991) and *The Seventh Sign* (1988). The first movie in the *Omen* series of four films, which covers the birth and rise to power of Antichrist, premiered in 1976. The Terminator himself, Arnold Schwarzenegger, starred in *End of Days* in 1999. All of these films are shown regularly on cable television. And in 2005 a series called *Revelation* aired on network television; its episodes were available for immediate re-viewing on cable channels as well.

The popularity of these works suggests to me that the apocalyptist narrative also has mythic appeal. James Barr in fact refers to dispensationalism itself as "a remarkable achievement of the mythopoeic fantasy" (195). The scholars whose work on myth I review earlier agree that its function is to cover over contradictions or dislocations that appear in the *habitus*, usually by resolving them into a mastering narrative or by propounding some moral that can serve as a general guide to belief and action. While apocalyptism can fulfill these functions, it has an additional mythic use: it allows believers to read everyday events as embodying cosmic portent. In his book on Antichrist Robert Fuller argues that "with the help of biblical metaphors, many Americans are able to mythologize life by 'seeing' that there are deeper powers at work behind the surface appearance of worldly events. Everyday life is viewed against a cosmic background in which the forces of good are continually embattled by the forces of evil" (5). The perceived tie between everyday experience and an overarching master narrative is a veritable recipe for resonance. In this view the most intimate moments shared with family or friends can be read as manifestations of the divine plan. Amy Frykholm's interviews with readers of *Left Behind* amply demonstrate that the maintenance and quality of relationships with spouses, parents, siblings, and friends are tightly implicated with responses to the apocalyptist narrative: couples quarrel, daughters stop speaking to their mothers, churchgoers become intimates; a death in the family becomes an occasion for thinking more deeply about heaven and the Rapture; the imminence of the end time explains the perceived prevalence of "Satanism, drugs, kids selling drugs" (86).

Apocalyptism also dictates the ways in which believers must interpret national and international developments. Apocalyptism conjectures the world as an eternal struggle between good and evil. Humans are pawns in schemes developed by the forces of evil, while their moral fiber is tested by the force of good. The end-time narrative supplies ready-made warrants for discerning the positions that should be taken on difficult issues, the geographical sites of which are often far removed and the disposition of which is not controlled by ordinary people: who is an enemy, what role should be assigned to which groups as events unfold, which international policies will hasten the advent of apocalypse. Such decisions become easier to make thanks to the industry of prophecy interpreters, who authorize political positions with a scriptural seal of approval. This effect is surely enhanced by the American mythology of exceptionalism, which posits that America is a very special political experiment. Lane Crothers notes that millennialism confluences with exceptionalism in such a way that "the conflict over government policies becomes a struggle for control of the destiny of all humanity in the continual story of good and evil" (48). This combination of apocalyptism and exceptionalism warrants an aggressively nationalist foreign policy. Of course the United States should go to war with Iraq, because Saddam Hussein is clearly a bad guy (perhaps Antichrist himself). Even better, American intervention might trigger the war among the ten kingdoms that brings historical time to a screeching halt, thus hastening the advent of the Rapture. In addition to its usefulness as a rationalization of otherwise inexplicable events, the apocalyptist narrative also prescribes "right action" (Stephen O'Leary 25). That is, it has an *ethical* dimension, which term here includes the ancient sense of *ethos* as character. In the worldview of dispensationalism a person is as she believes; that is to say, her character is signaled by the nature of her beliefs. If she is saved, if she subscribes, she is perforce capable of right action. If she does not believe she is, perforce, an agent of Evil. Thus if leaders speak or act in ways that can be interpreted to accord with apocalyptist prophecy, they act rightly. This is electism with a vengeance.

If apocalyptism enjoys mythic status in America, it also resonates as fantasy. The apocalyptist narrative qualifies as fantasy in the literary sense, a tale of heroes and villains whose struggles have cosmic implications. Revelation invents a veritable zoo of outlandish creatures fit to rival those that threaten the fellowship in *The Lord of the Rings*. But apocalyptism is also a fantasy in the psychoanalytic sense. Surely prophecy interpreters' reading of Revelation stages a passive narcissistic desire to achieve God's recognition and approval. After all, biblical inerrancy on its face requires complete intellectual submission to God's word. Wojcik observes as well that in a nuclear age "rapture belief may serve as a defense mechanism or compensatory fantasy, reducing individual fears and responsibility concerning nuclear apocalypse and transforming anxiety about such predicted catastrophes into passive acceptance of these as foreordained events" (57). Equally likely, apocalyptism fulfills a desire for identification with a community. The reader of prophecy interpretation need not belong to a church, but she can nevertheless participate in a fantasized community of believers that extends across the globe and includes the dead as well. Scholars who interviewed believers report repeated testimonials to the warmth and strength of the social bonds secured by subscription to apocalyptism. Strozier writes that it "brings the believer firmly into a tightly cohesive community, which I suspect is as much a motivation for as a consequence of conversion. Friends, entertainment, ethical guidance, and personal integrity all meet in the community" (160). Frykholm notes that "belonging often takes tangible form in tightly knit, supportive communities of shared religious faith—the people and routine practices of daily life" (45). Apocalyptist community is achieved at a cost, though, because it requires ideological, if not physical, separation from nonbelievers. As Frykholm puts it, "in order for apocalypticism to thrive, boundaries must be constructed, be they the symbolic boundaries of evangelicalism or the physical walls of the Branch Davidian complex in Waco, Texas" (14).

Apocalyptist fantasy can also stage a desire for revenge. Wojcik nicely captures this aspect of apocalyptist beliefs, which "provide individuals with a sense of empowerment as well by assuring them that the suffering they now endure at the hands of the unjust and the corrupt will be rectified by an avenging God. . . . The element of divine retribution and expectations of revenge, even at one remove, may be a means of empowerment to those who feel victimized, disempowered, or alienated. This sense of vindication insists on a larger moral order underlying the universe, making meaningful the perceived crises and injustice of contemporary existence by promising that a new world of complete justice and perfect order will replace a world gone seriously awry" (144).

LaHaye attempts to arouse feelings of alienation by repeatedly telling his readers that Christ and Christians are hated by unbelievers. He writes, for example, that the church has been "persecuted by religions, kings, and dictators" and that Christians are "the most consistently hated group on earth" (unbelievably, this comment follows a passage in which he discusses the history of the Jews) (*Are We Living* 11). In several places he recounts his personal disappointment at being denied a building permit by a city council. From this event he draws the conclusion that "men and women largely hostile to the church controlled our city" (*Battle* 191). Boone notes that this story betrays "an almost laughable persecution complex" (59). Its effects aren't funny though. Apocalyptism assures its adherents that the slights, hurts, and injustices administered by the powerful in this world will be paid back in triplicate in the next, when Christ—presumably locked and loaded—will sally forth to wreak revenge in believers' name.

In *The Geneology of Morals* Friedrich Nietzsche argues that Christian morality is all about resentment and vengeance (x). Nietzsche's disparagement of Christianity served his own philosophical goals, and the sweep of his indictment is unfair to Christians whose beliefs are otherwise motivated. But it is hard to escape the force of his argument with regard to apocalyptism. Robert Solomon and Kathleen Higgins note that "if [Nietzschean] resentment has a desire, it is the desire for revenge . . . entertaining the abstract desire for the total annihilation of its target" (118). With this in mind I excerpt one of LaHaye's accounts of the battle of Armageddon:

When Christ consumes all before Him through the earthquakes, lightnings, and the sword that proceeds out of His mouth, not only will the Holy Land be destroyed but the entire country will be literally bathed in the blood of the unregenerate, God-hating, Christ-opposing people. . . . Who can conceive of a time when the blood of slain men will flow as high as the horses' bridles by the space of a thousand and six hundred furlongs? . . . Millions of pieces of ice will fall to the earth weighing a hundred plus pounds each, melting in the torrid heat of Palestine, and mingling with the blood of those slain until the land of Palestine will be literally bathed in a bloody liquid that is almost too horrible to describe. What a price human beings will pay for rejecting Christ! (*Revelation* 315)

Reading this, it is hard to shake the impression that LaHaye is actually gloating over the horrible punishments that will be meted out to the unsaved.

The Ethics of Apocalyptism

Apocalyptism presents a real problem to rhetoric. Crapanzano notes that fundamentalist Christians "do not argue with theologians from non-evangelical churches. They tend to dismiss these other theologies in a name-calling way, with easy stereotypes. Their understanding of other religions, indeed, other value systems, is limited and judgmental. They have the truth, they have Jesus, they have been chosen—why bother to engage? Engagement, as many of them see it, is always corrupting" (xxiii). If we accept Crapanzano's comments, this belief system allows little space for invention and none at all for argument. Readers may recall that earlier I develop a rhetorical ethic, claiming that rhetors who posit unities that transcend temporal and local contexts are making bad arguments because the assertion of a noncontingent foundation shuts down the search for available alternatives. Christian apocalyptism, as articulated by its professional proselytizers, virtually defines noncontingency.[17]

Prophecy interpretation also raises very serious ethical issues, in my opinion. Interpreters tell their readers that they are being given the truth, secured by divine authority, when in fact they are reading a discourse generated and maintained by a priestlike caste of interpreters who stand to gain financially from its circulation and who are motivated by a political agenda that serves their own interests. A reactionary and divisive mythology is being passed off as the Word of God. Prophecy interpretation has serious ramifications for Christian belief, as well. Kathleen Boone contends that dispensationalist readings raise a doctrinal issue because they date the beginning of the present, historical age from Christ's death and resurrection. This forces prophecy interpreters to give primacy to the Pauline texts rather than to the Gospels, producing what Bruce Bawer calls a "Church of Law" rather than a "Church of Love" (6). That is, reliance on Paul rather than Christ shifts the tone, if not the substance, of Christian belief away from love and onto proscription. The result of this shift, according to Boone, is that "the main significance of Christ is to be found in the act of his death" rather than in the truth of his teachings (51). James Barr in fact calls dispensationalism a heresy because "Christ appears no longer in the role of a saviour calling all men to him but rather as a kind of automaton or switch, whose actions introduce each new stage of the apocalyptic sequence" (205). Dispensationalism renders Christ's teachings as a sideline to its determination of the main act: his triumphant and violent return to Earth. If Barr is correct, apocalyptism represents a serious departure from mainstream Christian belief. Apocalyptists' habit of thinking of themselves as the only true Christians only exacerbates this problem.

In my opinion apocalyptism also poses a danger to democracy. This belief system makes an invidious distinction between good and evil that it then relentlessly repeats across wide swaths of history and applies to large groups of people. LaHaye made this clear when he spoke on Jerry Falwell's talk show. He said: "We're in a religious war and we need to aggressively oppose secular humanism; these people are as religiously motivated as we are and they are filled with the devil" (qtd. in Frykholm 175). Even though apocalyptist believers profess that they are motivated by love, their beliefs can have hateful consequences for gays, Jews, and anyone else who is depicted by the belief system as an "enemy." The exclusions built into apocalyptism follow well-worn lines of force in American culture, and an apocalyptist ethic informs exclusionary political and social agendas. But the absolute binaries posited in apocalyptism, between believers and unbelievers, the saved and the unsaved, do not simply mark an unbreachable divide. Rather, these are hierarchical dichotomies that award moral privilege to the saved. But that is not all. Those of us who accept neither the necessity of being saved nor dispensationalist readings of events are depicted by this narrative not as resisting or indifferent, but as evildoers, as willing dupes of Antichrist, as agents of Evil. More than that, the unsaved become active enemies of all who are saved. Association with the unsaved poses a danger to the saved. If the saved listen to opinions forwarded by the unsaved, their ticket to the Rapture may not be punched when the end time arrives. This is not a recipe for the preservation of democracy.

5

IDEAS DO HAVE
CONSEQUENCES

Apocalyptism and
the Christian Right

In the election of 2004 ballots in eleven states featured initiatives to deny marriage and other civil rights to gays. As I watched the election returns, I saw relatively early in the evening that these initiatives had passed in all of the states considering them. I knew then that the Republican party would win the presidency even though all the votes cast for national offices would not be counted for some time. For a brief moment I wondered whether I needed to continue working on this chapter, the burden of which is to establish a link between apocalyptic theology and conservative politics. I could muster no more convincing proof of the connection between conservative religious belief and political activism, I thought, than that provided by the approval of these initiatives. The election of three born-again Christians to the Senate (Coburn, DeMint, Thune) and of several pro-life, anti-gay-rights conservatives to the House of Representatives confirmed that organizational efforts undertaken by the Christian Right continue to pay off handsomely on the national level. But the victory was ideological as well as electoral. When more than half of the voting citizens of a representative democracy support a given political agenda, one is surely justified in suspecting that the ideology undergirding that agenda is a contender for hegemonic status within that polity.

The success of conservative Christian activists in the election of 2004 does not establish my main line of argument, however: that apocalyptism might be in hegemonic contention with liberalism. For one thing, professional proselytizers are more intensely committed to apocalyptism than are lay believers. Indeed, I suspect that some if not many centrist and right-of-center voters who support born-again Christians and anti-gay-rights legislation would be appalled by apocalyptic belief, were they aware of its implication with conservative Christian politics. Nonetheless, apocalyptism is densely articulated with born-again Christianity if only because fundamentalist Christians accept the principle of biblical inerrancy. But apocalyptism infuses conservative Christian politics in more subtle ways as well, and the task of this chapter remains: to establish a relationship between apocalyptist theology and conservative Christian political activism. With this in mind, in what follows I attempt to articulate the Christian Right's political agenda with conservative Christian beliefs about family and nation and to connect both to the apocalyptic belief system that underpins and motivates them.

What Do They *Really* Want?

In his book on Ronald Reagan Garry Wills notices the necessarily close tie between conservatism and religion: "Attitudes toward the divine tend to be stable, as their object is thought to be. They look back to a past revelation. They observe a prescribed ritual, repeat sacred words, replicate the requirements for priests or initiates. They judge the world against some otherworld of the supernatural and find it wanting—this life is but a falling off from, a dim reflection of, or arduous preparation for, a better one" (453). Belief in an ideal, respect for the past, for standards, and for authority— these aspects of religious belief are all consonant with the traditionalist conservatism associated with modern American thinkers such as Russell Kirk and Richard Weaver.[1] In addition, however, Christian political activists are interested in defending the authority of the Bible and a Protestant fundamentalist tradition of interpretation, chiefly Calvinist in orientation. But religiously motivated conservatives can have a more radical agenda as well. Over twenty years ago Paul Weyrich, a founder of the Christian Right and still one of its most important activists, asserted that "we are no longer working to preserve the status quo. We are radicals, working to overturn the present power structure of the country" (qtd. in Conway and Siegelman 94).

For my purposes here "Christian Right" designates (a) a group of organizations that promote a conservative social and political agenda and

(b) people who subscribe to an ideology—a set of beliefs—that drives this agenda.[2] There are literally thousands of conservative Christian political groups in the country. Those that most often make national news are the American Family Association, the Christian Coalition, Concerned Women for America, the Family Research Council, and Focus on the Family; these organizations were founded by or are chiefly associated with Donald Wildmon, Pat Robertson and Ralph Reed, Beverly LaHaye, Gary Bauer, and James Dobson respectively. In addition, there are think tanks, PACS, and foundations that more or less openly support Christian Right activism. And as we shall see, the Christian Right has its organic intellectuals as well.

The Christian Right styles itself as "pro-family" and "pro-life," which means that it supports prayer in school, abstinence-based sex education, home schooling, and parental rights, while opposing feminism, gay rights, abortion, and pornography. It has also opposed gun control, welfare, affirmative action, and the United Nations. Sara Diamond summarizes its agenda as follows: "Were the Christian Right to achieve its wish list of policy goals, things would certainly be different. For starters, abortion would be illegal. Homosexuals would be, if not invisible, then certainly unprotected from all types of discrimination. Children would pray in the schools, which would be run privately or by local school districts, with no government-mandated curricula. The entertainment media would voluntarily eliminate profanity from the airwaves and movie scripts. The range of ideas and images accessible in bookstores, libraries, magazines, and art exhibits would be sharply curtailed" (*Not by Politics* 7). Scholars who study these groups have claimed that Christian activists mount both a defense and an offense (Diamond, *Facing* 56). In his study of the Christian Coalition Justin Watson characterizes these strategies as "recognition" and "restoration" respectively (2–3). The Christian Right wants recognition of Christian positions and issues in the public sphere. However, members of this group also want to "restore" America to its status as a "Christian nation." What this means for Americans who are not Christian depends upon how, and by whom, the goal of restoration is articulated. Watson's answer to the question "What do they really want?" will not reassure those who want to preserve liberal democracy in America: "they want both. They want 'their place at the table' and they want everyone at the table to agree with them" (175). This can be read to mean that Christian activists simply want to convert non-Christian Americans to their faith. However, a small group of Christian intellectuals has thought through the inchoate desire for restoration that is often voiced by less reflective Christian Right activists. These thinkers are called "dominionists" and "reconstructionists." They are quite open about their desire to replace the liberal democracy authorized by the American Constitution with a Christian state governed by Old Testament law. Both of these ideologies are motivated by postmillennial apocalypticism.

The Political Goals and Achievements of the Christian Right

Christian fundamentalists retreated from civic affairs following upon the rather embarrassing denouement of the Scopes trial in 1925 (Carpenter; Harding, *Book*). During the 1970s, however, new social movements began to effect changes in public policy and discourse that were sufficiently alarming to advocates of this belief system that they became active in politics, thus ending their relative intellectual isolation from the larger American community (Balmer, *Blessed*). Christian political activism began in response to gains made by the civil rights and liberation movements of the 1960s, gains that included affirmative action and the legalization of abortion. Chip Berlet and Matthew Lyons note as well that "a series of Supreme Court decisions—such as the 1962 and 1963 decisions barring prayer in public schools and several rulings that weakened or overturned obscenity laws—provided ammunition to those who argued that godless—perhaps satanic—forces controlled the federal government" (208). Other scholars think that the Christian Right was galvanized by a 1978 decision made by the IRS to question the tax-exempt status of Christian schools that practiced segregation (Hodgson 176).[3] But given the family-centered politics of the Christian Right, the political and legal gains made by second-wave feminism must also be named as a powerful motivation for its generation and maintenance. Randall Balmer argues that "what was especially striking in the American political arena at this point was the extent to which issues relating to gender—the proposed Equal Rights Amendment, the availability of abortion, private sexual morality—shaped [the] political agenda" of evangelical Christians (*Blessed* 82). In 1972 Phyllis Schlafly set up an organization to defeat the Equal Rights Amendment, and this objective was achieved in 1982 when the period mandated for ratification expired. In 1975 she changed the name of the organization to Eagle Forum, and this group is now an educational arm of the Christian Right (Wilcox, *Onward* 67).

The Christian Right was lent a distinct political flavor in the mid-1970s when a set of seasoned conservative politicians—Terry Dolan, Howard

Phillips, Richard Viguerie, and Paul Weyrich among them—sensed that a reactionary ideological wave was just about to crest (Diamond, *Spiritual* 56). In 1979 they drafted Jerry Falwell to head the Moral Majority (Conway and Siegelman 83–99). The Majority's first board of directors included Tim LaHaye, who, along with Falwell, also served on the board of directors of the Coalition for Religious Freedom, financed by the Unification Church of the Reverend Sun Myung Moon (Diamond, *Spiritual* 69). Christian activist groups were supported intellectually by conservative think tanks such as the Heritage Foundation and Weyrich's Free Congress Foundation, which were lavishly funded by wealthy conservatives Joseph Coors and Richard Mellon Scaife respectively (Berlet and Lyons 218; Wilcox, *Onward* 68–69).

Today the best-known conservative Christian political group is probably the Christian Coalition, founded by televangelist Pat Robertson in 1989 and skillfully directed through the 1990s by Ralph Reed. According to a pamphlet published by the Coalition in 1992, its purposes are to "represent Christians before local councils, state legislatures and Congress; speak out in the public arena and in the media; train Christian leaders for effective social and political action; inform Christians about timely issues and pending legislation; protest anti-Christian bias and defend the legal rights of Christians" (qtd. in Watson 52–53). The political goal of the Coalition is to develop activists in every precinct in the United States, thus assuring that its positions are heard on local and regional issues, as well as on the national level. Its grassroots style of organizing, which relies on church mailing lists, telephone trees, and e-mail, is extremely effective at getting out the vote in local and national elections, as well as on state referenda such as anti-gay-marriage proposals. But as their list of purposes indicates, the Coalition is not content simply to get out the vote. Their voter guides, which are usually distributed in churches on the Sunday prior to elections, are intended to inform Christians about the positions taken by candidates on issues important to the Coalition. Here, for example, is the text of a presidential voter guide distributed by the Coalition in 2004:

Dear Fellow American,
You are holding one of the most powerful tools Christians have ever had to impact our society during elections—the Christian Coalition Voter Guide. Right now, this simple tool is helping educate millions of citizens across this nation on where the candidates stand on key faith and family issues. On the front side, you'll find our Presidential Voter Guide. I want to assure you that every Christian, every church and every Christian organization has the right to distribute

this non-partisan guide. And now, it's up to you. I encourage you to read this Voter Guide and pass on this vital information to your friends and family, and finally, please go to the polls on November 2. Make your vote count! This is a crucial election. Too much is at stake for God's people to sit on the sidelines! Finally, please be in prayer for our nation. We need God's hand of mercy. Again, thank you for the stand you are taking as a Christian citizen, and may God bless America!

This letter is signed by Roberta Combs, current president of the Coalition. On the front side of the flyer is a list of issues:

Passage of a Federal Marriage Protection Amendment; Permanent Extension of the $1,000 Per Child Tax Credit; Educational Choice for Parents (Vouchers); Unrestricted Abortion on Demand; Federal Funding for Faith-based Charitable Organizations; Permanent Elimination of the Marriage Penalty Tax; Permanent Elimination of the Death Tax; Banning Partial Birth Abortions; Public Financing of Abortions; Federal Firearms Registration & Licensing of Gun Owners; Adoption of Children by Homosexuals; Prescription Drug Benefits for Medicare Recipients; Placing US Troops Under UN Control; Affirmative Action Programs that Provide Preferential Treatment; Allowing Younger Workers to Invest a Portion of their Social Security Tax in a Private Account.[4]

The words *supports, opposes,* or *no response* are entered on both sides of this list of issues in two columns, one column each underneath photographs of the Republican and Democratic candidates for president. The flyer assures its readers of the accuracy of the Coalition's attribution of candidates' positions on these issues by noting that "each candidate was sent a 2004 Federal Issue Survey by mail and/or facsimile (Fax) machine. When possible, positions of candidates on issues were verified or determined using voting records and/or public statements." Despite the declaration of nonpartisanship, clearly the issues and positions listed here are couched in language that favors the goals of the Christian Right. Such terms include *marriage protection,* which actually means "anti–gay rights," and *death tax,* which is an estate tax. *Partial-birth abortion* is a term invented by a Christian Right activist in order to create "a purely political, neological category of late-term abortion" (Mason 80, 176). The term is not used by the medical profession, and it misrepresents medical procedures that are performed very rarely and only to save a woman's life (Mason 82). *Preferential treatment* limits the effects of affirmative action to those perceived by white males. No presidential candidate from any party in this election supported "unrestricted abortion on demand," a phrase clearly intended to instill fear rather than to impart information. In this case the Democratic candidate is recorded as having made "no response," which may be technically accurate given the Coalition's survey methods but which is not factually correct, given that the candidate spoke of his religious and political positions on abortion during nationally televised presidential debates. Clearly the Coalition's selection and framing of issues elide the possibility that different or more nuanced constructions of issues and positions might be available.

I am not the only person who suspects that the Coalition distorts the facts in their voters' guides. In their study of the Coalition's 1994 guides Larry Sabato and Glen Simpson found "a consistent pattern of lies and distortions concerning the voting records of Democratic candidates" (Diamond, *Not by Politics* 100–101). The 1994 guides used tactics similar to those described above. In 1996 the Federal Elections Commission (FEC) sued the Coalition, alleging that the voters' guides constituted an "in-kind contribution" on behalf of Republican candidates, which, if found to be true, would end the organization's tax-exempt status (Diamond, *Not by Politics* 236; Watson 59). The FEC did not pursue a second allegation, made by the Democratic National Committee, that the Coalition is partisan.

The tactics developed by members of the Christian Right have achieved some stunning political successes. Christian political activists began with local elections, using so-called stealth campaigns (Watson 64). This tactic involves running candidates for low-turnout elections, such as for school boards or city councils. The selected candidates do not advertise their positions to the electorate at large but are put in office by high turnout among Christian activist voters. Depending on one's point of view, the stealth campaign may be read as democracy in action—citizens who vote get what they want—or as a threat to democracy insofar as covert campaigns do not require candidates to state or publicize their positions on relevant issues until they are safely in office. Using these tactics along with more conventional methods of getting out the vote, by 1979 the Christian Right held "some forty seats in the House of Representatives and ten seats in the United States Senate, besides countless seats in state legislatures and places on city councils and school boards and other local offices" (Hodgson 183). During the 1980s Christian activists continued to elect social conservatives to the U.S. Congress, and they began to target liberals for removal as well (Conway and Siegelman 96). Both of these processes continue to this day, as the results of the 2004 election amply demonstrate.

The Christian Right's first success on the presidential level was the election of Ronald Reagan in 1980 (Diamond, *Roads* 233; Berlet and Lyons 184). In that election, according to Berlet and Lyons, two-thirds of Reagan's ten-point electoral margin over incumbent Jimmy Carter "came from White evangelicals," even though Carter is himself an evangelical Christian (224). Reagan was certainly aware of his debt to the Christian Right, whose support he carefully courted. In a speech given in 1983 to the National Association of Evangelicals, for example, he noted that "there's a great spiritual awakening in America, a renewal of the traditional values that have been the bedrock of America's goodness and greatness" (Wills 547). In that same speech he called the Soviet Union an "evil empire." Frances FitzGerald argues that this was a direct appeal to the evangelicals who were in his audience, and her analysis implies that Reagan knew this identification "would trip-wire the whole eschatology of Armageddon" (27). Anecdotal evidence suggests that Reagan himself entertained apocalyptist views (Stephen O'Leary 182–83). In 1983 the *Jerusalem Post* quoted him as telling an Israeli lobbyist: "I turn back to your ancient prophets in the Old Testament and the signs foretelling Armageddon, and I find myself wondering if—if we're the generation that's going to see that come about. I don't know if you've noted any of those prophecies lately, but believe me, they certainly describe the times we're going through."[5] Caspar Weinberger, Reagan's secretary of defense, certainly was an apocalyptist; in 1982 he said, "I have read the Book of Revelation and, yes, I believe the world is going to end—by an act of God, I hope—but every day I think that time is running out" (qtd. in Mojtabai 152). Reagan also named a born-again apocalyptist Christian, James Watt, to be secretary of the interior. According to Sara Diamond, "Watt saw his appointment . . . as a license to enforce his bizarre theological views about human stewardship over the rest of nation. Why bother preserving the environment for future generations, Watt argued, when Jesus was liable to return at any moment" (*Spiritual* 63). Watt once announced to the House Interior Committee that "I do not know how many future generations we can count on before the Lord returns" (Balmer, *Mine Eyes* 52). Both of Reagan's administrations were peppered with social conservatives, and members of his justice department, under the leadership of Attorney General Ed Meese, made heroic if largely unsuccessful efforts to overturn *Roe v. Wade* and other civil rights legislation enacted by the Warren Court (Melich 174–75; Lazarus 230).

Christian Right activists were not particularly enamored of the candidacy of George H. W. Bush, but in 1988 they acquiesced to the Republican

Party's choice for president. In 1992, however, the movement suffered a bit of a setback. Almost half of the delegates to the Republican convention were "self-described born-again Christians," according to Sara Diamond, and they "secured a party platform demanding a ban on all abortion; opposing civil rights for homosexuals; and calling on the government to stop the sale of pornography and condemn 'obscene' art. The platform also endorsed homeschooling and school prayer, and opposed making contraceptives available in public schools" (*Not by Politics* 94). Tanya Melich, who was a Bush delegate to this convention, writes that the gathering "belonged to the right. It belonged to Pat Robertson and Jerry Falwell and their exclusionary vision of Christianity. It belonged to Paul Weyrich and his New Right authoritarians who wanted a Cromwellian America: narrow, puritanical, and intolerant. It belonged to the right-to-lifers and Phyllis Schlafly, and to Marilyn Quayle's petulant antifeminism" (303). This development might have concerned only moderate Republican delegates were it not for the fact that several fiery right-wing orators addressed the convention during prime time. This group included Pat Buchanan, who called for a "culture war." According to Diamond, "conventional wisdom" blamed the defeat of the incumbent president on the popular perception that rightist radicals speaking in prime time had frightened "middle-of-the-road voters away from the Republican Party" (*Not by Politics* 94).

Christian activists recovered swiftly, pulling off a truly spectacular national victory in 1994, when "congressional candidates backed by the Christian Right won 55% of their campaigns. . . . Also, for the first time ever, about a quarter of the elected first-term representatives were themselves members of evangelical churches" (Diamond, *Not by Politics* 100). The House of Representatives tapped Newt Gingrich as its leader, and his domestic agenda—the Contract with America—was written with input from Ralph Reed, then director of the Christian Coalition. In 1995 Reed announced that "as religious conservatives, we have finally gained what we have always sought, a place at the table, a sense of legitimacy, and a voice in the conversation that we call democracy" (qtd. in Melich 336). By the 1996 elections, Melich claims, "more than half of the state Republican organizations were effectively in the hands of the Religious Right" (336). Indeed, the Christian Right's position in the Republican Party was so strong that it "exercised virtual veto power over mainstream Republicans," according to Jean Hardisty (56). Christian activists managed to maintain a pro-life plank in the party's platform over the objections of moderate Republicans and of the party's presidential nominee, Senator Bob Dole.

Conservative Christian groups were active as well in the impeachment of Bill Clinton by House Republicans (Berlet and Lyons 305–22). In
1998 Hardisty attended conferences held by the Eagle Forum, Concerned
Women for America, and the Christian Coalition. At each of these meetings she observed a "broad and passionate hatred" for Clinton (66). At-
tendees were encouraged to "lobby their Congressmen and Senators and to
'hold their feet to the fire' with threats of political retaliation if they didn't
pursue impeachment to the limit" (66). Berlet and Lyons note that "the
roar was visceral" at the Coalition conference that year, "a torrent of sound
fed by a vast unconscious reservoir of anger and resentment" as "speaker
after speaker strode to the podium" to denounce Clinton (305).

The arrival of George W. Bush in the White House in 2000 marked a
milestone in the history of conservative Christian political activism. Bush
is a self-professed born-again Christian, and his religious beliefs apparently comfort Christian Right activists. When asked to comment on the
fact that no religious conservatives were scheduled to speak in prime time
at the 2004 Republican National Convention, for example, Roberta Combs
reportedly said: "That's all right. We have the president."[6] Like Reagan,
Bush has appointed apocalyptists to important positions: his first-term attorney general, John Ashcroft, is an apocalyptist, as is the undersecretary
of defense for intelligence, General William "Jerry" Boykin. Boykin, who
helped establish the interrogation practices used in the prisons at Guan-
tanamo and Abu Ghraib, has claimed on several occasions that America
is a "Christian Nation" fighting "Satan" (Blumenthal). Bush's positions on
a number of issues support those taken by the Christian Right: opposition to stem-cell research, curtailment of abortion counseling for members of the armed forces, proposal of a federal amendment prohibiting gay
marriage, and funding of faith-based initiatives, among others. Prior to
his 2000 campaign, according to Sidney Blumenthal, "Bush confided to a
leader of the religious right: 'I feel like God wants me to run for president.
I can't explain it, but I sense my country is going to need me. Something
is going to happen.'" An apocalyptist might easily read this remark as a
sign that 9/11, and Bush's warring response to it, were part of God's plan
for the end times.[7] Whether or not Bush himself holds apocalyptist beliefs
is an open question. He certainly seems comfortable with a religious vocabulary: in 2001 he used the word *crusade* to describe American retaliation against the attacks of September 11, and in 2002 he revived Reagan's
strategy of demonizing enemies, claiming that three nations constitute an
"axis of evil." And his speechwriters, at least, grasp the Manichean ethical

vision forwarded by fundamentalist Christianity. Charles Kimball notes that Bush's use of "powerful religious imagery" rendered a complex history of international relations as a simple dichotomy: "People and nations had to make a choice. There was no neutral ground. You had to align with the forces of good and help root out the forces of evil or be counted as adversaries in the 'war on terrorism'" (36). And Bruce Lincoln makes the interesting case that the imagery used in Bush's address to the nation on October 11, 2001, was coded in such a way that those versed in the Bible would hear an allusion to Revelation's opening of the sixth seal, among other biblical texts (30). Lincoln concludes that "for those who have ears to hear . . . this conversion of secular political speech into religious discourse invests otherwise merely human events with transcendent significance. By the end, America's adversaries have been redefined as enemies of God, and current events have been constituted as confirmation of Scripture" (31–32). In other words, Bush's speech on that occasion authorized a reading of 9/11 as an event heralding the advent of apocalypse.

Nested Beliefs

Conservative Christian theologians have long preferred deductive argument as a means of reasoning. One variety of this is called "presuppositionalism," which asserts that the discernment of first principles is an act of faith. In this view every thinker, religious or not, has only faith to go on as an assurance that the principles, that is, the presuppositions, from which she begins are true and accurate. When presuppositionalism is combined with a Manichaean worldview, as it was in the work of Calvinist theologian Cornelius Van Til, presuppositionalism becomes exclusive. Van Til argued that "Christians could make no peace with secularization because the world view that grounded secularization was based on fundamentally different faith presuppositions than Christianity" (Detwiler 108). Van Til taught that faith presuppositions are given to Christians by God, while faith in secular first principles is legitimated only by human reason and perception. Presuppositionalists argue, then, that "the truth about God has already been placed in every heart and therefore does not require intellectual defense based on appeals to human reason" (Barron 30).

Van Til, who died in 1987, was among a small group of influential American theologians whose beliefs about faith and reasoning undergird contemporary Christian fundamentalism. In this worldview divine knowledge provides the premises from which all else is deduced. And since

God's knowledge is prior to human consciousness, reality is presumed to accord with God's premises. In Fritz Detwiler's words, divine knowledge reflects "the God-Given order of reality" (109). The presumed consonance between God's knowledge and reality is not open to discussion. Human events do have to be interpreted in order to grasp the ways in which they fit into God's plan, however, and readings of reality deduced from God's major premises can be expanded to cover any number of specific practices. If God's command to "be fruitful, multiply" can be read to oppose nonprocreative sex, for example, it can also be read to oppose all forms of contraception, including those that protect against disease (Gen. 1:28). Abortion is unlawful in any circumstance, no matter the conditions under which conception occurred, including rape or incest. Nor does a threat to a mother's health, no matter how serious, authorize abortion.[8]

In biblically based Christianity God is thought to manifest propositions through the sacred text. Its major premises are derived and interpreted by a priesthood of believers; these premises are not exactly a secret, but one must be well versed in the interpretive tradition used by members of the group in order to decipher the connection of passages from the Christian Bible to current events. However, Christ is thought to speak directly to the heart of the person who is saved during the experience of being born again, and, ideally, whatever knowledge is gained through personal experience is reinforced by Bible reading. I argue earlier that fundamentalist belief relies on a double move to achieve consonance between the realm of experience and biblical injunction: believers must forget that interpretation mediates the text of the Bible and assume instead that God's word is immediately and correctly grasped by those who receive it. People who don't read the Bible in accordance with sanctioned readings, then, either have insufficient faith or are so sinful that they cannot see reality clearly. Catholics and Jews, who base their doctrines and practices on long histories of interpreting the sacred texts, are at best misled because they allow interpretive traditions to stand in the way of direct traffic between God and an individual. At worst they are apostate.

In this deductive model of knowledge God stands in the place occupied by the individual subject in liberal thought, and he enters consciousness through the heart rather than by means of sensory experience, which is the ground of knowledge posited by liberalism. The achievement of direct access to God's word does not entirely eliminate the human capacity for agency, however, because individuals must continually worry about their moral suitedness to act as conduits of God's message.

The set of metaphysical claims just outlined assures conservative Christians of the rightness of their religious and political positions. According to Linda Kintz, this assurance manifests itself in their political discourse as an "ideology of clarity" that "has helped move the center of contemporary U.S. politics far to the right" ("Clarity" 115). Kintz claims that this ideology of clarity is sustained by means of a densely articulated and hence highly resonant set of conjectures that "might be visualized as a closed set of concentric circles stacked one on top of the other and ascending heavenward: God, property, womb, family, church, free market, nation, global mission, God" (*Between* 6). Elsewhere, she elaborates:

The elements of this symbolic structure rise from the womb to the heavens, uniting God as Creator, the family, a divinely inspired Declaration of Independence and U.S. Constitution, a nation defined as God's unique experiment in human history, a belief that the unregulated free market is inherent in human nature, and a claim that the United States has a God-given responsibility to spread free-market democratic capitalism to the rest of the world. At both the beginning and the end of this clear narrative, God's judgement seals a circular logic of God, family, mother, nation, and global duty within a Judeo-Christian Book of the World made coherent from top to bottom, from beginning to end. ("Clarity" 116)

Clearly the elements of this belief system are derived from the beliefs and practices of Christianity, capitalism, patriarchy, and American nationalism. Its recursively spiraling logic produces a sense of seamless coherence that underwrites intimate connections among the positions it dictates on a wide range of issues. Potentially conflicting positions that are available within the structure are overlooked because they are not rationalized. Kintz remarks, for example, that the centrality of the family metaphorically reconciles the competing claims of freewheeling capitalism and cultural traditionalism (*Between* 6).9

Jason Bivins posits that Christian political activism originates in a "sacred register" that is largely "felt" and "experienced" rather than thought (10). He argues that religious activists tend "to politicize what is most intimate to them: their very identity and self-understanding as religious practitioners" (10). The nested structure of belief outlined by Kintz resonates, then, because it taps into the emotionally intimate relationship with God that born-again Christians experience upon being saved. Repetition among and across its elements reinforces the emotional impact of the whole—just as God is the Father of creation, human fathers are the authoritative centers of families. Leaders of the nation deserve the same sort of obedience owed to both earthly and heavenly fathers—that is, when they can be certified as doing God's will. But the structure also resonates because of the central location awarded to family, that most intimate of cultural sites (Kintz, *Between*). The depth of feeling stimulated by appeals to this site can easily be taken as evidence of the truth and rightness of the entire system. This also holds for appeals to nationalism, since the relations thought to be proper on one level of the structure hold for all levels. Furthermore, the entire structure is legitimated by a super-rationality that simply trumps human reason and the evidence of the senses.[10] That is to say, conservative Christian discourse authorizes its political positions with an appeal to divine reason, and it posits as well a divine reality that governs or controls what happens in historical reality. This divine reality runs on God's time, not historical time, and it will culminate in the apocalyptic events described in Revelation. Subscription to these uber-realities requires visceral commitment because they are not obviously validated by empirical data.

Relying on Baudrillard's analysis of media culture, Kintz argues that one important function of the ideology of clarity is its repetition of the same, or rather, its repeated application of the same ideologic to differing circumstances. As she puts it, the aim is to "rediscover in nature what one already knew would be lying there waiting to be found" ("Clarity" 134). This produces what she calls "a jammed representational machinery" wherein "units of meaning" are "structurally the same, even if the contents of these units are different, and the circulation of these structural units constructs what we come to think of as the real" ("Clarity" 134). This is exactly the circuit described by the relation of emotions to beliefs; that is to say, one finds in reality what one expected because one notices what one expected to find. Difference, the unexpected, doesn't resonate because difference is hard to notice; it is hard to notice because in a densely articulated ideology of the same, awareness of difference provides little or no emotional stimulation. Repetition of the same, however, does stimulate emotional response, and because this resonance can be mistaken for experience, emotional response comes to be associated with reality. Another way to say this is that in a densely articulated belief system whose moments are highly resonant (because they are so tightly connected to experience and belief) the believer comes to believe in belief itself. The ideology of clarity becomes reality. As Kintz puts it, inside the representational space occupied by the ideology of clarity, we "find the intense passions and emotions of a super-rationality, a closed atmosphere of emotion that reinforces its unchanging structure because the 'feelings' aroused by absolute values . . . produce a real that feels more real than our ordinary lives" ("Clarity" 134).

Kintz points out that ambiguity is a persistent threat to the ideology of clarity: in fundamentalist Christian discourse "an anticommunist Cold War framework joins absolutist Christianity in such a way as to code ambiguity not only as subversive to a national security state but as a Satanic force that threatens Christian civilization itself" ("Clarity" 118–19). The stability of the structure depends on maintenance of clear and unbreachable divides between God and Satan, saved and unsaved, male and female, gay and straight, capitalism and socialism, America and all other nations. Any claim that questions such divides, or muddies them, must be rejected outright. God's argument is crystal clear to those who are saved. People who wield arguments justified by the theo-political ideology of clarity assume that they possess the truth because their discourse is divinely authorized. They accept no criterion of falsifiability; that is to say, there is no way to prove to a believer that she is wrong. Arguments from complexity or nuance suggest only that those who make them are confused. And for believers the sower of confusion, the agent of complexity, is Satan. In ethical terms a refusal of ambiguity and complexity allows no space for negotiation, no way to generate alternatives or gradations. In rhetorical terms the ideology of clarity opens few spaces for invention; the only modifications permitted are those necessary to adapt the structure to new historical developments.

But Phyllis Schlafly Has a Housekeeper . . .

If inerrancy is the major premise of fundamentalist Christianity, preservation of the nuclear family is the major premise of conservative Christian politics.[11] Belief in the centrality of this family structure to the preservation of Christian morality composes an ideological text the warp and woof of which are patriarchy, antifeminism, and homophobia. This text dictates that all adults ought to participate in heterosexual marriages. Duties within the family are strictly gendered: wives must submit to husbands, and "dads go to work" while "moms stay at home" (Diamond, *Facing* 61). Children must submit to their parents' will, because they belong to their parents in the sense that they are owned by them. The privilege awarded to the nuclear family in this ideology yields positions on a number of issues: reproductive practices, gender performance, and parental rights.

In general, fundamentalist Christians believe that the point of sexual activity is procreation. This belief entails two prohibitions: recreational sex and contraception are forbidden. The prohibition against nonprocreative sex between married partners has softened in recent years.[12] Tim and Beverly LaHaye, for example, coauthored a marriage manual, entitled *The Act of Marriage,* that gives quite explicit advice about sexual enjoyment. However, the prohibition against extramarital sex remains strong, as does that against contraception. Unmarried people are expected to practice total abstinence from sexual activity—including autoeroticism. Their desire that sexual activity be strictly controlled motivates conservative Christians to express concern about the circulation of pornography and the perceived proliferation of nudity, profanity, and sexual explicitness in media and other forms of entertainment (Lienesch 57).

The "family values" agenda of the contemporary Christian Right is clearly a reaction against the achievements of second-wave feminism. Randall Balmer posits that this reaction is secured by invocation of a nineteenth-century notion of "feminine piety as the purest expression of Christianity" (*Blessed* 71). He opines that the fantasy of the pure wife and mother might be thought of as a Protestant counterpart to "popular Catholic pinings for the Virgin Mary"; however, "if the Blessed Virgin ever sorted socks, scrubbed the kitchen floor, or worried about ring-around-the collar, we seldom hear about it" (*Blessed* 72). Balmer's comment underscores the role played by marketing in reinforcing the image of women as wives, mothers, and homemakers. Within conservative Christian circles, however, the ideology of the dutiful wife is supported by an essentializing biology that portrays women as willing partners in a marital contract whose function is to control men's "natural" sexual aggression. Phyllis Schlafly remarks, for example, that "man's role as family provider gives him the incentive to curb his primitive nature" (103). To the extent that such a predatory view of masculinity is accepted, of course, it authorizes abuse of women and children, as well as male-on-male violence. Women's essence, on the other hand, is motherhood; women are thought to have "an innate instinct for maternity," an instinct that cannot be fulfilled outside of heterosexual marriage (Lienesch 65). The antiabortion position taken up by the Christian Right is often represented as a defense of "unborn" life, but the legality of abortion also carves a deep fissure in the depiction of every woman as desirous of motherhood. As Balmer writes, "the very idea that a woman might seek an abortion violated the cherished evangelical ideal of feminine domesticity. If women guarded their purity and contented themselves with their divinely ordained roles as mothers and housewives, abortions would be unnecessary" (*Blessed* 83). The belief that women are in charge of their "purity" suggests that here, as elsewhere, empirical reality often poses real challenges to these gender ideals. In recent years the Southern Baptist Convention has famously struggled with the biblical teaching that wives must submit to their husbands, trying to reconcile it with the social reality of single motherhood and the economic necessity that forces many women to work outside the home. Christian Smith, commenting on a large study of evangelical opinion conducted during the 1990s, demonstrates from remarks made by informants that evangelicals' opinions about the roles of men and women in marriage are far more nuanced in practice than they are typically made to appear, either by leaders of the Christian Right or by scholars and media pundits (see *American; Christian*). For example, evangelical couples assert that headship of the family is often shared between partners. However, Smith's informants offer no evidence to suggest that patriarchal, heterosexual marriage is ever considered to be anything other than a norm. Much less is it critiqued as a norm whose imposition can have harmful effects on those whose practices and desires do not conform to its ideals.

People who live outside of the heterosexual patriarchal family pose a threat to the ideology of clarity because they demonstrate the arbitrariness of the rigid gender boundaries established therein. Michael Lienesch points out that conservative Christian writers revile "aggressive women" (that is, feminists) as "haters of men," which renders them as quite unnatural creatures (58). Quoting one such writer, Lienesch notes that homosexuals also threaten "the clear distinctions between the sexes. God intends men to be masculine . . . not effeminate" (59–60). Indeed, the threat posed to essentialized gender boundaries may account in large part for the conservative Christian proscription of homosexuality. In her extensive study of conservative Christian writing Didi Herman discovered that male gayness is represented there as masculinity "out of control" and "unrestrained," presumably because male homosexuals refuse to commit to marriage with a good Christian woman who would put a stop to that sort of thing (80). Gay people are also depicted as "pathetic and unfulfilled" (71). More telling for my argument, Herman found that the "uniting theme" of Christian writing about homosexuality is "godlessness: a failure to comply with conservative Christian tenets is synonymous with atheism, and atheism is most definitely a satanic strategy. The gay agenda is the secular agenda is the liberal agenda is the devil's agenda" (89). This reading confirms Kintz's insight about the flattening of difference and the reinforcing circularity of the ideology of clarity.

Sara Diamond offers an interesting discussion of the parental rights movement, which asserts "parental *ownership* of children" (*Not by Politics* 114). Diamond claims that this issue "cuts right to the heart of what much of the family values debate has been about. Who will *decide* and who will *control* what happens to children, what children and parents can get away with, what spouses can get away with, what pregnant girls and women can and cannot do, what homosexuals can and cannot do? These are all questions of morality wrapped up with questions of power" (*Not by Politics* 114). Conservative Christians believe that parents ought to be free to raise their children in any way they see fit without interference from government agencies or regulation. In 1995 conservative legislators drew up the Parental Rights and Responsibilities Act, which would "prohibit any federal, state, or local government from 'interfering with or usurping the right of a parent to govern the upbringing of a child,' unless there is a 'compelling interest' such as abuse or neglect" (Diamond, *Not by Politics* 118). Belief in absolute parental rights extends to corporal punishment. According to Philip Greven, fundamentalism authorizes such punishment by teaching that spanking and beating are necessary to "break" a child's will. This has been "the central task given parents by successive generations of preachers, whose biblically based rationales for discipline have reflected the belief that self-will is evil and sinful" (65).[13]

Fundamentalist Christians also believe that their children should not come in contact with values other than their own, and this belief has sparked explosive conflicts with secular institutions. Conservative Christians have protested public school curricula that expose their children to evolution, multiculturalism, and sex education, and they have also opposed critical thinking and collaborative learning pedagogies (Detwiler; Moffett). Many Christian parents have adopted home-schooling as a means of escaping public school curricula and practices that they take to violate their beliefs. The Christian Coalition supports the use of vouchers, which would allow parents to send their children to whatever schools they wish at taxpayers' expense. The Christian Right has also supported the importation of standardized testing into public schools. The primary effect of such testing, of course, is to insure that authority over curricula is taken away from teachers and effectively located in decisions made by parents and school boards. Of course this practice violates the principle of academic freedom, if not a teacher's constitutional right to free speech. Teachers have vigorously protested all of these efforts, which led Rod Paige, George W. Bush's secretary of education, to refer to the National Education Association as a "terrorist group."[14] More radical Christian theorists aim to "hamper" the public schools and ultimately to shut them down (Clarkson 119). This is part of the program of Christian reconstructionism, whose spokesperson, Gary North, declared: "Until the vast majority of Christians pull their children out of the public schools there will be no possibility of creating a theocratic republic" (qtd. in Clarkson 119).

Dominion Theology on Capitol Hill

The "Great Commission" was laid on Christians by Christ's command to "go therefore and make disciples of all nations" (Matt. 28:19). Many Christian churches teach that this command obligates Christians to convert others to their faith when and wherever possible. But Christian Right intellectuals are also drawn to a passage in the Old Testament where God commands Adam and Eve to "have dominion" over all things of the earth (Gen. 1:26–28). Christians of many varieties accept that compliance with this passage requires humans to exercise stewardship over the earth and its creatures. Some conservative Christian thinkers, however, take the passage more literally, reading it as a command to "bring every institution and organ of civil society into conformity with God's will" (Detwiler 104). That is to say, the task laid on Christians goes far beyond conversion of unbelievers; rather, they are required to bring law, government, schools, churches and synagogues, families, and other communal institutions into line with Christian beliefs and moral principles. Such thinkers are known as "dominionists." Dominion theology is tightly articulated with the postmillennial belief that with God's help the Kingdom of God can be constructed here on Earth; this achievement will bring about the end time. Kintz defines dominion theology as "the belief that the future of the nation as well as its God-given mission in the world depends on the reconstruction of U.S. culture so that it is in tune with the natural law of the Ten Commandments and Judeo-Christian values, as natural law and biblical law are conflated. . . . Those values are in fact inherent in nature. Nature, when it is interpreted properly, will reveal the truths of its Creator" ("Culture" 7). Read in this way the passage from Genesis legitimates a widespread belief among conservative Christians that a fallen, secular America must be returned to its original Edenic state, when it was a moral and fully Christian nation. In *Mind Siege: The Battle for Truth* Tim LaHaye and David Noebel claim that America was "founded on the biblical principles taught in the Old and New Testaments" (99). They assert that Europeans who settled in America created a polity where biblical law was the law of the land and where the Ten Commandments and "the civil laws of the Old Testament, formed the basis for our laws and the U.S. Constitution."[15] They buttress this claim with a bit of revisionist history: "Most colonists were Englishmen, and almost all were Europeans, who brought to the New World a Reformation mind-set. Some men, it is true, introduced the errors of Voltaire, Rousseau, and others, but these did not predominate. Therefore, our government was based on a respect and reverence for God and the realization that man was His special creation" (99). This argument revises early American history in interesting ways (not all of the Europeans who settled America were Calvinists or even religious believers, for example). More salient, however, is its erasure of the fact that neither God nor the Christian Bible is mentioned in the Constitution of the United States. The First Amendment famously forwards two clauses concerning the relation of the state to religion: "Congress shall make no law respecting an establishment of religion, or prohibiting the free exercise thereof." The disestablishment clause prohibits the installation of any church as a state religion, and the free-exercise clause protects Americans' right to practice whatever religion they choose, or none at all, for that matter. In addition, Article 6, in the main body of the document, prohibits the establishment of religious tests for anyone who wishes to run for public office.[16]

Isaac Kramnick and Laurence Moore claim that "the U.S. Constitution, drafted in 1787 and ratified in 1788, is a godless document. Its utter neglect of religion was no oversight; it was apparent to all. Self-consciously designed to be an instrument with which to structure the secular politics of individual interest and happiness, the Constitution was bitterly attacked for its failure to mention God or Christianity" (27–28). When the Constitution was circulated for ratification, Article 6 in particular became extremely controversial. Susan Jacoby notes that those who opposed adoption of the document complained about its failure "to acknowledge God as the ultimate governmental authority. The opposition to article 6 frequently took on an anti-Semitic and anti-Catholic tone" (29). One widely circulated essay complained that the Constitution would allow Quakers, Mahometans, Deists, Negroes, Beggars, and Jews to participate in civil affairs (Kramnick and Moore 33).

This bit of history suggests that James Madison was quite correct to be concerned about the divisive effects of religion. The only mention of religion in the Federalist Papers is in Number 10, written by Madison, which considers ways in which a state can neutralize the "violence of faction" (Rossiter 77). By *faction* Madison meant "a number of citizens, whether amounting to a majority or minority of the whole, who are united and actuated by some common impulse of passion, or of interest, adverse to the rights of other citizens, or to the permanent and aggregate interest of the community" (Rossiter 78). One of the factions he mentions is "a zeal for different opinions concerning religion," which has "divided mankind into parties, inflamed them with mutual animosity, and rendered them much more disposed to vex and oppress each other than to co-operate for their common good" (Rossiter 79). Madison's suspicion of passionate commitment to faction sounds very much like that expressed by John Locke and George Campbell. The similarity is not coincidental—according to Kramnick and Moore, "all the important figures of the founding generation, including John Otis, John and Samuel Adams, James Madison, Thomas Jefferson, Patrick Henry, and Benjamin Franklin, were disciples of Locke" (72). Most of these men were Christians as well; apparently they did not see the contradiction between Christianity and Enlightenment that so troubles LaHaye and Noebel.

The First Amendment was also hotly debated when it was proposed for adoption along with the rest of the Bill of Rights in 1791 (Kramnick and Moore 27). Proponents eventually convinced doubters that its disestablishment clause protected religious diversity by prohibiting the emergence of a state-sponsored religion. Thomas Jefferson supported the disestablishment clause because he was confident that a widely shared public morality, grounded in reason, would suffice as a guide to political action. This position earned him the epithet of "the Virginia Voltaire" (Kramnick and Moore 95), a rhetorical strategy of guilt by association with the French that seems never to go out of favor in American politics. In any case, America's founding document locates governmental authority and legitimacy in the principle of natural human rights, drawn from the work of Enlightenment thinkers. For Locke the source of state authority was not God but "the people, who voluntarily contracted to set up governments in order to protect their natural rights to life, liberty, and property" (73). This achievement was a startling departure from historical and legal precedent, where the rule of monarchs was certified by divine authority.

Ever since its ratification the Constitution has been challenged by religious believers who want to substitute divine authority for human rights as the basis of its legitimacy. Such believers apparently do not accept Jefferson's argument that separation of church and state protects religion. Jefferson wrote in his *Notes on the State of Virginia* that "the legitimate powers of government extend to such acts only as are injurious to others. But it does me no injury for my neighbor to say There are twenty gods, or no God. It neither breaks my leg, nor picks my pocket" (qtd. in Kramnick and Moore 87). In other words, the duty of government is to protect citizens' lives and property from injury and to punish those who injure others. According to Jefferson, this power does not apply in the religious arena. If a government enjoying the capacity to punish interferes with the practice of religion, it acts illegally. Much less is such a government authorized to take sides in religious disputes.

Christian Right activists take advantage of this line of argument in an interesting way. Perversely enough they assert that secularism is itself a religion; as such, it cannot enjoy government protection. Nor should legislative or judicial decisions be made on secular grounds. This line of thought implies that secularism is as well organized institutionally as Christianity, sporting sacred texts, supporting a proselytizing ministry, and all the rest. Indeed, LaHaye and Noebel make just this claim, asserting that the Humanist Manifesto of 1933 is the "Bible of the Secular Humanists," whose "dogma has been consistently taught to our youth" (133). To define secularism as a religion is to eliminate the possibility of a nonreligious orientation to the world. At the same time this definition treats all belief systems as existing on the same footing vis-à-vis the state. That is to say, there is no neutral civic space that is free of religious symbolism or significance. This is the ground on which activists oppose judicial rulings prohibiting mandated school prayer and the display of religious artifacts in publicly funded places. In the opening pages of their *A Nation without a Conscience* Tim and Beverly LaHaye write that the First Amendment has been so warped by judicial misuse that it is now producing what it was written to defend against: secular humanism, which is a religion. They claim further that the founders believed that inalienable rights come from God (13). This is a clever argument, but it is based on a category mistake: that civic neutrality toward religion amounts to religious belief. This is borne out by the fact that its supporters must rewrite history in order to make the argument work.

Christian Right intellectuals deploy such arguments because it is crucial to Christian Right theology and politics that America be understood to be a Christian nation, in the profound sense that its government is authorized by divine rather than human law. Michael Lienesch found many more such claims in his study of the work of Christian Right intellectuals, who assert that America is "a chosen nation, singled out by the Creator as part of a providential plan" (141). Consequently they read the Revolution and the founding as "God-guided episodes" (Lienisch 145). However, authors of many of these accounts also claim that God's plan for America was threatened during the twentieth century by "the growing power of government. Standing in stark contrast to the moral and spiritual soundness of America's people, the state is described as a corrupting and secular institution" (Lienisch 152). Of course this is a generalized redescription of specific events, such as the judicial decisions outlawing school prayer and the legalization of abortion, that jolted fundamentalists out of their self-imposed cultural isolation during the mid–twentieth century. These accounts utterly ignore the fact that for some Americans these decisions did not signal "the growing power of the state" but actually defined more accommodating civic spaces.

Christian Right intellectuals are fond of distinguishing between "the state" and "the nation." This distinction allows them to claim that even though the government has lost its spiritual quality, growing ever more secular, the people themselves (that is, the nation) retain their Christian religiosity.[17] As proof, Christian authors offer up the practice of public prayer and the many references to God that appear on monuments, coinage, the Pledge of Allegiance, and the administration of oaths of office. They mean, then, that America remains a Christian nation in the sense that its national ideology and praxis are saturated with Christian symbols, images, and rituals. Thus Christian Right political activism can be configured as an attempt to return the state to its former consonance with the sentiments of the people. Walter Capps in fact defines the Christian Right as a neonationalist movement: "it is nationalistic in intention before it is religious or even Christian" (208).

Preachers and prophecy interpreters are not subtle when they express their desire for dominion. In 1998, at a conference entitled Reclaiming America for Christ, D. James Kennedy, pastor of the Coral Ridge Presbyterian Church and host of television's *Coral Ridge Hour*, proclaimed: "We founded America. It's ours. We want it back!" (qtd. in Detwiler 131). Not content merely to advocate restoration, Kennedy included an apocalyptist warning: "God's will for this nation will be done. Twenty-six other empires have risen, and all have fallen" (Christian Smith, *Christian* 21). Driving home from work on inauguration day, 2004, I heard NPR broadcast the voice of a minister who was participating in the celebration; he solemnly intoned that "Jesus Christ is Lord of the United States."

The achievement of dominion is not exactly a democratic process. Christian Right intellectuals believe that the duty to return America to its fallen state can be undertaken only by those "whose minds and wills are faithful to God. Dominion is reserved for those who remain the spiritual and moral heirs of the Judeo-Christian tradition" (Detwiler 104). For the more radical Christian intellectuals known as reconstructionists the path to restoration requires the rejection of pluralism and of secular democracy. Reconstructionists believe that "contemporary application of the laws of Old Testament Israel is the basis for reconstructing society towards the Kingdom of God on earth" (Clarkson 78). Rousas John Rushdoony, a postmillennialist and the driving intellectual force in this movement, aims to bring about apocalypse by transforming America into God's earthly kingdom as prophesied in Revelation (21:1–4). William Martin provides a fair description of "how a reconstructed America might look" (353). The federal government would be severely curtailed, perhaps limited to providing national defense. Citizens would interact with government at the county level, and each county would boast a "fully armed militia, but citizens would be answerable to church authorities on most matters subject to regulation" (353). There would be no taxes outside of a 10 percent income tax (the traditional tithe), and there would be no welfare-state programs such as food stamps, unemployment, Social Security, or Medicare because families would be expected to take care of their own. This would include home-schooling children because there would be no public education. Families would be organized patriarchally. The only people permitted to vote would be Christians who belonged to "biblically correct" churches. Reconstructionism also requires that the U.S. Constitution and its attendant body of law be rewritten to conform to biblical law, particularly that found in the Old Testament. Frederick Clarkson, who is very concerned about the social and political implications of reconstructionism, writes that under this regime the death penalty would be exacted as punishment for "apostasy (abandonment of the faith), heresy, blasphemy, witchcraft, astrology, adultery, 'sodomy or homosexuality,' incest, striking a parent, incorrigible juvenile delinquency, and in the case of women, 'unchastity before marriage'" (81, citing Rushdoony). And Clyde Wilcox quotes Rushdoony as saying that "a reconstructed America would have no room for Jews, Buddhists, Muslims, Hindus, Bahais, or humanists. There might not even be room for nonreconstructed Christians" (*Onward* 127).

It is a safe bet that very few people have waded through Rushdoony's more than thirty books, let alone those of his quarrelsome disciples. Because of the difficulty involved in reading him, and because his ideas are so radical, scholars are divided in their opinions about the influence of reconstructionism on the larger Christian Right movement. Watson points out that Pat Robertson and Ralph Reed are savvy politicians who understand the need to compromise with unbelievers, and they have been vilified for doing just this in reconstructionist circles (114). Nonetheless, Rushdoony has appeared several times on Robertson's television program, *The 700 Club*. Martin thinks that because reconstructionism is "so radical" it is necessary for Christian Right leaders to distance themselves from it, at least in public venues (354). He cites Jay Grimstead, leader of the Coalition on Revival, as saying that "there are a lot of us floating around in Christian leadership—James Kennedy is one of them—who don't go all the way with the theonomy thing, but who want to rebuild America based on the Bible" (354). Detwiler notes that activists who have not thought through the implications of reconstructionism might be shocked were they to do so; nonetheless, he writes, "the dominion principle . . . is the *sine qua non* of the movement" (130). And Wilcox notes that reconstructionist arguments "are being increasingly incorporated in mainstream writing" by Christian Right activists (*Onward* 128). I side with those who accept the trickle-down theory of ideological transmission. Ideas do have consequences. Clearly the work of relatively obscure theologians like Van Til and Schaeffer has entered the discourse of the Christian Right, thanks to the proselytizing efforts of Tim LaHaye and others. I see no reason why reconstructionist ideas should not filter out of Rushdoony's scholarly tomes and be translated into ordinary discourse in exactly the same fashion, particularly since the major thrust of reconstructionism coincides so nicely with both dominion theology and apocalyptist desire. Furthermore, given that Schaeffer and Rushdoony follow Van Til in making a sharp hierarchical distinction between divine and human reason, in my opinion dominionism presents a distinct threat to liberal democracy to the extent that proponents are willing to act on their beliefs. Bits of evidence are accumulating that suggest that dominionism is far more influential than scholars have realized. Christian hospitals, doctors, and nurses are refusing to prescribe or dispense contraception. Schools are adding creationism to their curricula, either in addition to or in place of evolutionary theory. Even more disturbing evidence suggests that legislators elected by the Christian Right are doing their best to overturn the secularist clauses of the U.S. Constitution.

Theonomic desire obviously motivates a piece of legislation proposed to the House of Representatives by Robert Aderholt, Republican of Alabama, in 2004. Section 1260 of H.R. 3799 reads: "notwithstanding any other provision of this chapter, the Supreme Court shall not have jurisdiction to review, by appeal, writ of certiorari, or otherwise, any matter to the extent that relief is sought against an element of Federal, State, or local government, or against an officer of Federal, State, or local government (whether or not acting in official personal capacity), by reason of that element's or officer's acknowledgement of God as the sovereign source of law, liberty, or government." The point of this bill is to get around the disestablishment clause. If passed, it would permit government officials to enact their religious beliefs while pursuing their duties without opening themselves to the possibility of prosecution. Aderholt's legislation is supported by the Christian Coalition, and it is not the only piece of legislation put before state and national legislatures in the past few years that furthers the dominionist aims of the Christian Right (see http://www.cc.org). Nor will it be the last, given the increasing numbers of federal legislators who are committed, or at least indebted, to Christian Right activism.

Signs of the Time

In her book on pro-life politics Carol Mason points out that since the 1960s pro-life writings have become more and more apocalyptic. In such writings, she argues, abortion itself is represented as "an apocalypse, a revelation of just how immoral America has become" (2). As we have seen, the apocalyptist narrative entails that divine reason has worked out the progress of history before it happens; historical events have always already been forecast. In this sense the legalization of abortion can be read by those so inclined as yet one more symptom of the moral decline forecast by premillennialist dispensationalism. When events are read as fulfillments of apocalyptic prophecies, according to Mason, their recital "fosters a desire—and promotes a way—to 'take a stand'" (137). Apocalyptist time opens a narrative space in which ordinary people can become characters in a cosmic drama, where their actions affect world-shattering events. Those who hand out antiabortion literature, picket women's clinics, harass employees at Planned Parenthood—even kill doctors who perform abortions—can exult that there is cosmic justification for what they do. Robert Jay Lifton echoes this analysis in another register, taking note of the apocalyptist rhetoric emanating from the White House after the events of September 11,

2001. In this case the apocalyptism had postmillennial overtones. Lifton wonders "whether fundamentalists within the Bush administration, who are engaging in violence, do not at some psychological level envision the war on terrorism as a vehicle for our own salvation, for a new American regeneration through violence, for not only destroying evil worldwide but cleansing ourselves of our own sins and revitalizing our spiritual energies through our predominant military power" (123–24). Certainly September 11 was an apocalyptic event in the noncosmic sense. But for the born-again Christians who currently inhabit the White House and who are, presumably, familiar with the apocalyptist narrative, the temptation to represent this event to themselves and others as yet another sign of the approaching end time must be grave indeed.

Clearly acceptance of an apocalyptist structure of belief legitimates an approach to factuality that is very different from that deployed in liberal argument. In this view facts are not proof of the existence of some human or natural reality, as liberals would have it, nor can they be offered as proofs of the ways in which empirical reality or history behaves. They are, rather, signs of God's will. Their relation to divine premises must be interpreted, of course, and this process goes on endlessly in Christian conservative discourse: the election of George W. Bush is a sign of God's approval, the passage of antigay legislation is a sign that God approves of homophobia, and so on.

Aristotle mounts a brief discussion of arguments from sign in *On Rhetoric* (I.ii.16, 1357). He offers no definition of signs, saying only that signs may relate the universal to the particular and vice versa. I take it that signs, then, name relations among things, ideas, or events. Aristotle divides signs into two kinds: the infallible (*tekmerion*) and the fallible, which has no specific name. Infallible signs are both true and logically valid, and hence they seem irrefutable. His examples are these: fever is a sign of sickness; a woman's having milk is a sign she has recently given birth (I.ii.18). These examples are clearly based on observations of the empirical world. Aristotle's example of a fallible sign is this: "since Socrates was wise and just, it is a sign that the wise are just" (I.ii.18). This argument from sign is true in the particular but not so in all cases, which is why it is fallible.

I extrapolate from Aristotle's discussion here that people can be persuaded by fallible signs because they analogize the relations that obtain in human behavior (wisdom accompanies justness) to the true and valid relations that obtain in empirical reality (fever accompanies sickness, mothers' milk accompanies childbirth). His remarks on sign appear in tandem with his discussion of probability (*eikos*), in which conclusions depend from this premise: what happens for the most part has happened in the given case (I.ii.15, 1357a). Here is an argument from probability: "John will be late to work on Monday because he parties hard on the weekends." Obviously probabilities differ from infallible signs because their premises are not always true, nor are their premises always connected to one another in logically valid ways.[18] And yet people reason this way all the time, because human behavior is predictable to some degree (which is one reason why rhetoric works). Fallible signs work because they too depend from a premise about probability: "this is ordinarily connected to this." That is, fallible signs are persuasive because people assume that the relations evoked by them are like the relations between empirical facts such as fever and sickness. We assume, in other words, that relations in human behavior are as regular as those in empirical reality. If I conclude that John's droopy demeanor this morning is a sign that he partied last night, I am basing this conclusion on a history of observing the relation between daytime droopiness and nighttime debauchery either in John's behavior or in that of others.

A rhetorician would treat the claim that Bush's presidency is a sign of God's favor, then, as an argument from fallible sign: true (or not, given the rhetorician's religious beliefs) but not necessarily valid (again, depending on the rhetorician's religious beliefs) because no evidence or argument is supplied (or available?) that unfailingly connects the minor premise (about Bush) to the major one (which is something like "God gives us worldly signs of his pleasure or displeasure").[19] Those who accept the ideology of clarity read the major premise of this argument as infallible (that is, always and everywhere true) and the relation they read between it and the empirical fact of Bush's presidency as valid. Believers assume that the same relation exists between this major premise and whatever other empirical facts they wish to connect to it. Given this assumption, believers can read any fact or event as a sign of the (always true) major premise, assuming that the relation posited between the particular and the universal is valid, in their opinion, in any case to which it is applied. In this model, for instance, creationism offers more satisfactory explanatory power than does evolution, because creationists can interpret the fossil record as a set of signs manifesting God's loving relation to Earth. While the theory of evolution posits the operation of natural selection and other regularities, it offers no commanding major premise that satisfactorily explains the beginning of the process, nor can it predict its end, as apocalypticism does.

Sore Winners

Dissent is a problem for those who accept the ideology of clarity. Departure from its propositions and positions does not merely pose one alternative among others, as pluralist liberals would have it. Rather, dissent indicates misguidedness at the very least and evil at worst. Justin Watson notes that even Pat Robertson, who is ordinarily careful to cloak his apocalyptism with a veneer of pluralist good cheer, has on occasion depicted "his political or intellectual opponents as the enemies of all that is decent and good" (102). Because dissent demonstrates the limits of truth claims made by the ideology of clarity, and because it may be a sign of evil as well, refusal to acquiesce is an obstacle that must be overcome. Resolute believers in this ideology measure all beliefs and practices against their own: nonbelievers don't go to church or they go to the wrong church; they vote for the wrong policies; they are anti-life, antifamily, antiwar, anti-God. Furthermore, those who accept the ideology of clarity assign unbelief to people who can be fitted into the reductive categories constructed by the belief structure: homosexuals, feminists, academics, liberal Hollywood actors, members of the ACLU or People for the American Way—none can be considered truly Christian, even if they profess Christianity, because their political beliefs or other behavior suggest that they oppose some facet of the tightly articulated structure of the ideology of clarity. Such people are an affront as well because they are not obviously potential converts.

This feature of fundamentalist Christian argument moves political disagreement onto ethical ground, a ground where judgments about the efficacy of arguments are based on the character of those who forward them (saved or unsaved?) rather than on the quality of arguments advanced. This is why dissent is often subjected to one of three argumentative strategies that Jean Hardisty claims are typical of right-wing discourse: stereotyping, scapegoating, or demonizing (51). Demonization has proven to be an especially effective argumentative tactic for the Christian Right. Hardisty notes that "when the right mobilizes intolerance against a minority or an out-group (such as lesbians and gay men, welfare recipients, or teenage offenders), it blames and demonizes the hated group, and, at the same time, draws anger away from real sources of social ills. By displacing anger onto such decoys, the right allows for greater dominance by elites, while creating the impression of increased empowerment for those expressing their intolerance" (51). This last phrase is key. I would argue that the Christian Right has developed a fourth argumentative strategy: self-victimization, which, curiously enough, enhances the group's political and rhetorical power by generating sympathy for supposedly embattled Christians. This tactic conjectures public discursive venues as spaces in which Christians are being hunted down and persecuted (like witches?) by angry and venal secularists. While its spokespersons ordinarily stop short of calling their opponents evil, at least in public venues, they are quite ready to cast conservative Christians in the role of persecuted victims. Here, for example, is an exchange that took place between James Dobson of Focus on the Family and ABC news commentator George Stephanopoulos:

Stephanopoulos: Dr. Dobson, you also have a problem with the ranking Democrat on the Senate Judiciary Committee, Senator Patrick Leahy. I want to show something that was reported in the "Daily Oklahoman" during the campaign. In the "Daily Oklahoman," it quoted you saying, "Patrick Leahy is a God's people hater. I don't know if he hates God, but he hates God's people." Now, Dr. Dobson, that doesn't sound like a particularly Christian thing to say. Do you think you owe Senator Leahy an apology?

Dobson: George, you think you ought to lecture me on what a Christian is all about? You know, I think—I think I'll stand by the things I have said. Patrick Leahy has been in opposition to most of the things that I believe. He is the one that took the reference to God out of the oath.

Stephanopoulos: But Dr. Dobson, excuse me for a second. You use the word hate. You said that he's a "God's people hater." How do you back that up?

Dobson: Well, there's been an awful lot of hate expressed in this election. And most of it has been aimed at those who hold to conservative Christian views. He is certainly not the only one to take a position like that. But I think that that is—that's where he's coming from. He has certainly opposed most of the things that conservative Christians stand for.

Stephanopoulos: So no apology?

Dobson: No apology.[20]

As Stephanopoulos noted, Dobson offered no evidence to support his charge that Leahy hates Christians aside from his remark that the senator "took the reference to God out of the oath." This refers to Leahy's having administered an oath to witnesses before the Judiciary Committee without adding the phrase "so help me God." When this omission was called to his attention, Leahy agreed to amend his ways, adding that he had not been chair of the committee for very long.[21] Dobson nonetheless draws the unwarranted conclusion that Leahy's omission of God's name from an oath amounts to hatred of Christians and possibly of God as well.

Dobson's outburst can be read as an example of the conservative Christian habit of conducting argument from premises that are certified, prima facie, to be universally true. In this model of argument anyone who omits God's name, innocently or not, on a ceremonial occasion wherein God has in the past been ritually invoked obviously does not have access to the divine reality wherein all events are dictated by the will of God. But this does not necessarily mean that such a person bears ill will toward Christians. And so Dobson's tirade must be read as an example of Christian self-victimization. Conservative Christian complaints about their victimization at the hands of unidentified others range from LaHaye's plaintive assertion that Christians are the most persecuted group in the history of the world to the carefully crafted and widely circulated meme, current as I write, that secularists are attempting to take Christ out of Christmas.[22] Obviously this tactic aims at securing sympathy for the Christian cause at the same time as it solidifies group identity by painting a picture of beleaguered Christians holding together in the face of onslaught by a powerful enemy, much as Cecil B. DeMille depicted first-century Christians cowering in the arena while slavering lions approached. No doubt there are people who hate apocalyptist Christians because of their beliefs. Discursively, however, the most powerful antagonist of apocalyptism at this cultural moment is liberalism, which is by definition tolerant and pluralistic. Liberals don't burn people at the stake, and generally they don't threaten their opponents with sodomy, violence, or death either. Hatred of a fantasized enemy is required not by liberal secularism but by apocalyptism. Furthermore, secularists are very much in the minority in America. Their relative invisibility is suggested by the fact that organizations and institutions aiming for inclusiveness seldom think to invite participation by atheists, agnostics, or those who simply don't feel the need to believe in supernatural entities of any kind. In the last fifty years America has elected several mainstream Protestants, a Catholic, and two born-again Christians to the presidency, and in recent national elections a Jew ran for major office. The chances of an atheist or unbeliever running for or being elected to either of these positions are virtually nil. For all of these reasons I agree with Detwiler, who suggests that resistance to conservative Christian politics, if any such resistance actually exists, must be coming, at least in part, from mainstream Christians (51).

One way to end dissent is to convert everybody so that no dissenters remain. On February 27, 1860, Abraham Lincoln gave a speech to a group assembled at the Cooper Institute in New York. On that occasion he opined about the difficulty of conducting arguments about slavery with Southerners:

The question recurs, what will satisfy them? Simply this: We must not only let them alone, but we must somehow, convince them that we do let them alone. This, we know by experience, is no easy task. We have been so trying to convince them from the very beginning of our organization, but with no success. In all our platforms and speeches we have constantly protested our purpose to let them alone; but this has had no tendency to convince them. Alike unavailing to convince them, is the fact that they have never detected a man of us in any attempt to disturb them. These natural, and apparently adequate means all failing, what will convince them? This, and this only: cease to call slavery wrong, and join them in calling it right. And this must be done thoroughly—done in acts as well as in words. Silence will not be tolerated—we must place ourselves avowedly with them. Senator Douglas' new sedition law must be enacted and enforced, suppressing all declarations that slavery is wrong, whether made in politics, in presses, in pulpits, or in private. We must arrest and return their fugitive slaves with greedy pleasure. We must pull down our Free State constitutions. The whole atmosphere must be disinfected from all taint of opposition to slavery, before they will cease to believe that all their troubles proceed from us. (28)

I think that a similar discursive set of affairs has coalesced in contemporary politics. The theological distinction between the elect and the nonelect has morphed into an "friend-enemy" dichotomy in conservative Christian political discourse, creating exactly the sort of threat to democracy forecast by Chantal Mouffe (*Democratic* 104). Christian activists do not merely wish to pose their positions as alternatives; rather, they want to erase dissent altogether, to insist that those of us who disagree with their policies "place ourselves avowedly with them." This desire is fully consonant with the Christian mandate to convert unbelievers. The present difficulty has arisen because the political agendas of conservative Christian activists have become so thoroughly implicated with their religious beliefs that they are either unable or unwilling to distinguish between democratic advocacy and apocalyptist desire.

6

THE TRUTH *IS* OUT THERE

Apocalyptism and Conspiracy

Lee Quinby recommends a Foucauldian brand of skepticism as an antidote to apocalyptic thinking. This brand of skepticism "encourages analysis of how truths are culturally established and embodied as experience. Millennial skepticism specifically questions truth claims that are authorized through faith alone" (*Millennial* 8). This approach challenges the situation of apocalyptist belief in a supernatural foundation, pointing up its contingency and confronting the ways in which "the empirical claims of these various sources of authority are framed, looking to their historical constitution to track the relations of power and the cultural conditions that built such edifices of knowledge" (*Millennial* 8). That is, Foucauldian skepticism exposes the worldly and therefore contingent sources of apocalyptist belief. Quinby pursues this project because "many of the obstacles U.S. democracy has faced and currently confronts are rooted in its millennialism" (*Millennial* 6). At the same time, she argues, "the strengths of U.S. democracy stem from the skepticism that is also present in the founding documents" (*Millennial* 6). While I wholly agree with Quinby's analysis, I would distinguish between the liberal skepticism enshrined in the founding documents and the Foucauldian skepticism she forwards and practices. Quinby rightly notes that skepticism is "built into the Constitution's Bill of Rights, especially the separation of church and state, its system of checks and balances, and provisions for amendment" (*Millen-*

nial 6). The founders installed these features in the Constitution because they doubted that human beings can be trusted always to behave according to the dictates of reason and the evidence of their senses (Popkin and Stroll 246–53). Their moral and political skepticism is related historically to the development of scientific skepticism, where dependence on reason and the quality of sensory experience renders necessary a certain mistrust of any claim that cannot be established by those means (Shermer 16–17). Foucauldian skepticism, on the other hand, informs the intellectual work that many academics in the humanities now do, and it produces provocative critiques, such as Quinby's, that are useful to people who want good arguments to substantiate their disbelief in commonsense assumptions. That is to say, Foucauldian skeptical analyses are ordinarily convincing only to other skeptics. Few committed apocalyptists will be persuaded by any skeptical reading—liberal, scientific, or postmodern—that attacks the super-rational foundation of their belief system. In fact apocalyptists are on the lookout for skepticism, and they furiously police the borders of their belief system against invasion by it. Here is one of Tim LaHaye's rants about secular humanism:

It is no overstatement to declare that most of today's evils can be traced to Secular Humanism, which already has taken over our government, the United Nations, education, television, and most of the other power centers of life. Secular Humanism—whether it calls itself Marxist Humanism, Cosmic Humanism, Scientific Humanism, Planetary Humanism, Postmodern Humanism, or sports some other label—is driven by a flaming hatred for Jesus Christ that seeks to eradicate the Christian world view from the media, the government, and especially public education. Secularists scorn creationism, design in nature, man in the image of God, the Fall, traditional or biblical morality, the natural family of father and mother, and the religious and political faith of the majority of America's Founding Fathers. (LaHaye and Noebel 35)

Aside from LaHaye's irritating habit of reading secular disinterest as active opposition, the point to notice in this passage is that skeptics don't believe in anything, or at least not anything important. LaHaye hasn't yet realized that there is a difference between liberal humanism and postmodern skepticism. But he or some other of his ilk will soon figure out that while liberal humanism is scandalous from their point of view because it takes human reason rather than God's word as its foundation, postmodern skepticism is more scandalous yet in its refusal to privilege anything at all, or rather, in its insistence on privileging everything provisionally and contingently.

Such a skepticism posits that systemic reflexive relations among history, culture, and selves are always differing and deferring, always changing. God is not in this picture, although discourse about God is very much on the table as a subject of investigation, as Quinby's studies demonstrate. Which further irritates apocalyptists, who are outraged that anyone can look at a biblical text as a cultural artifact rather than as a direct pipeline from a divine source. From the position taken up by an apocalyptist like LaHaye, academic skepticism is a problem and an obstacle, not least because the very existence of skeptics demonstrates the limits of his claim to fundamentalist truth.

Apocalyptism is now growing in popularity, I believe, at least in part precisely because it is a satisfactory antidote to skepticism. Apocalyptist belief allows adherents to hang onto a clear notion of truth in an age where technology raises awareness of differences across the globe, where unadulterated truths are hard to come by. It also permits the division of a complex and diffuse American polity into two clear camps—us and them—thus legitimating both fundamentalist Christian triumphalism and its adherents' desire to conjecture themselves as victims. The mainstream media have cheerfully adopted this simple-minded dichotomy, dividing America into red and blue states; the presumption is that conservative populists who care about moral values live in the one, while so-called liberal elites who are responsible for moral decline inhabit the other. But things are not quite as simple as this. Feminist and queer theorists, among others, have demonstrated that the notion of a single "public," an "us" that can be labeled "Americans," is a fantasy, even though liberal theorists try hard to hang onto such a notion (Berlant; Warner, *Publics*). And scholars who study minority discourses can easily demonstrate that Americans who have historically inhabited the category of "them" (from a majoritarian point of view) are quite aware that the country's discourse harbors a cacophony of "uses" (Takaki). Nevertheless, theorists and ordinary citizens alike attempt to hang onto a notion of "us," because without such simple identifications it is difficult to imagine civic arenas in which we can all operate peacefully. One of the ideological means through which the notion of "a public" or "the nation" has been maintained is commonsense liberalism—we are all created equal, all of us have rights to privacy and individual freedom, and so on. But these commonplaces, and the liberal strategies of argument by means of which they circulate, have now been brought into crisis by the growing discursive influence of Christian fundamentalism.

There are hundreds of communities whose members think of themselves as part of "us" who nevertheless do not have the same level of access to mainstream media that spokespersons for the Christian Right have achieved. Jodi Dean studies narratives told by members of one such group: people who believe they have been abducted by extraterrestrials. Her analysis of the negative reception accorded to abduction discourse demonstrates that terms such as *reason* and *rational* are words of power, used to legitimate points of view that typically get a hearing while others do not. She notes, for example, that "ufological discourse upholds the very criteria for scientific rationality that mainstream science uses to dismiss it. 'Scientists' are the ones who have trouble with the 'rationality' of those in the UFO community" (*Aliens* 9). In other words, science owns a claim to reason from which ufologists and abductees are excluded even though the latter use precisely the same approach to evidence that is employed by the former. Thus the words *reason* and *rational* can take on an exclusionary overtone. One of the early readers of this book objected to my use of the word *irrational* because of its ambiguity. She knew from the context that I meant "an argument that does not depend on reason," but she worried nonetheless that *irrational* might be taken to mean "crazy," as it often is when applied to those whose discourse departs from common sense. In other words, to be rational is to be sane, to be normal.

Another complication has emerged for liberal argumentation because of the Christian Right's willingness to distort factual evidence to make ideological points.[1] People who hear arguments supposedly authorized by reason and factual evidence do not know whether these proofs are being referred to in the skeptical sense, meaning that the relevant reasoning is warranted by the available evidence, or whether they have been manufactured in order to represent someone's interest (Engel 7). For instance, Dean asks: "How can I know which statement on partial[-birth] abortion reflects 'facts' the pro-life movement wants to disseminate?" (*Aliens* 10). Her example is particularly apt given that *partial-birth abortion* is itself a term invented by pro-life activists in order to recast a rarely used medical procedure in such a way that repeated reference to it advances their political agenda. In other words, that doctors practice partial-birth abortions is a fact only within the confines of Christian Right discourse.

Michael Shermer's response to Dean's work demonstrates that scientific skepticism does not pose satisfactory answers to questions about who can produce accounts that are deemed reasonable. Shermer, who publishes *Skeptics Magazine* and is director of the Skeptics Society, reports that he asked Dean whether she herself believed the UFO and abduction narratives she studies (304). She answered: "I believe that they believe their stories." What interests Dean is the diversity of truth claims; the multiple ways in which people construct and authorize them; and, finally, what this means for notions of community and the public sphere. Because of these interests she treats abduction narratives as though they are artifacts, taking them as seriously as she would take rocks were she a geologist. However, Shermer decided that Dean had ducked his question. What he wanted her to say was "extraterrestrials do not exist," which assertion would support his belief that abduction narratives have no demonstrable relation to empirical reality. He had in fact already decided that "there is no more evidence for the existence of aliens on earth than there is for fairies" (304). Hence he accuses Dean of equivocating "on the veracity question" when in fact she answered forthrightly about her own belief. His assurance that his position is correct is very like the confidence displayed by members of the Christian Right. He is sure that he knows a piece of evidence when he sees one, and narratives told by alien abductees are not evidence of anything he is interested in knowing. He is also quite sure that he recognizes an authority when he meets one, and he cannot understand how scientists and social scientists who accept abduction belief can be considered experts, despite their academic credentials (Dean has a Ph.D. from Columbia, he tells us) (303). This is of course an instance of the liberal habit of blaming an audience who won't come round to agreement. Abduction narratives don't appeal to the sort of truth Shermer accepts—that which is empirically verifiable. He is not interested in investigating such beliefs because he is sure he has nothing to learn from people who believe in extraterrestrials, who, if not insane, are certainly not entirely rational. All of which is to say that Shermer is, of all things, a fundamentalist skeptic.

Because of its refusal to tolerate many kinds of warrants, skepticism may not be a useful mode of resistance to apocalyptism. I hazard that academic and scientific skepticisms may in fact accelerate the spread of fundamentalisms, may be one reason that apocalyptic beliefs of all kinds are embraced by more and more Americans. As I suggest earlier, the emergence of postmodern skepticism, abetted by the rise of global capitalism and the worldwide use of spectacular new communications technologies, calls for profound responses from those who would resist this multiplicitous and uncertain milieu, resistance that we see today among apocalyptists and other fundamentalists who dogmatically assert the truth of their beliefs without offer of proof and who found those beliefs on teachings and sources of authority that are inaccessible to unbelievers.

The Death of Enlightenment Cannot Be
Attributed Solely to Derrida

I argue earlier that apocalyptism mandates a style of argument that does not risk engagement. Its proponents believe that they possess the truth, and they legitimate this assumption by claiming direct access to a super-rationality that trumps human reason. People who oppose apocalyptist readings of divine desire are not simply incorrect; they are, rather, either uninformed fools or liars. There is no rational or empirical way to prove an apocalyptist wrong, because her major premises derive from an ineffable source whose wishes are clear only to believers. Claims that support the worldview are endlessly reiterated: abortion is murder, gay rights are a threat to the sanctity of straight marriage, abstinence is a superior form of birth control. Facts are not always offered in support of such claims, and when empirical evidence is provided it is often incorrect. For example, abstinence-only sex education programs teach that condoms do not protect against sexually transmitted disease and that women are dependent upon men (Waxman 8, 17).[2] Evidence that contradicts these claims is ignored, and those who point out that a vow of abstinence does not protect women and girls against unwanted sex are characterized as misguided at best and evil at worst. Liberal reliance on reason and empirical fact is now being seriously challenged by this style of argument, which derives its truth claims deductively and guarantees them by means of their resonance, by a rightness that is deeply felt rather than rationalized. Apocalyptism is faith in belief itself, belief that the deeply resonant structure of the ideology of clarity is reality itself.

Faith in belief itself as an avenue to truth is not limited to apocalyptism. Anyone who paid attention to popular culture during the 1990s could not have missed the popularity of *The X-Files,* a relatively long-lived television program whose lead characters, Fox Mulder and Dana Scully, were initially portrayed as a believer and a skeptic, respectively. (In case viewers missed this plot point, a poster in Mulder's office announced "I want to believe.") Scully's skepticism was authorized by her credentials as a scientist, while Mulder's acceptance of outré beliefs was legitimated by a backstory involving the mysterious disappearance of a younger sister during his adolescence. But the point of the series was that Mulder *wanted* to believe; his desire to believe in something, anything, proved stronger than his own training in science. As the series matured, Scully was forced by her numerous encounters with unexplained evidence to moderate her scientific skepticism. Mulder's passionate commitment to belief wavered only once during the series' run, a change of heart brought on by his realization that he had been systematically lied to by authorities. His brief flirtation with skepticism was ultimately unconvincing to fans of the show, however, and it was quickly dropped. I recount all of this by way of pointing out that during the 1990s a popular television show was so, in part, because its writers touted belief, rather than skepticism, as a superior means of making sense of the world.

Ominously faith in belief itself has also surfaced in the highest circles of politics. Reporter Ron Suskind recounts an unsettling conversation he had with an unnamed "senior adviser" to George W. Bush. The adviser critiqued Suskind's residence in "the reality-based community," which he defined as people who "believe that solutions emerge from your judicious study of discernible reality." The adviser told Suskind that the world no longer worked that way: "We're an empire now, and when we act, we create our own reality. And while you're studying that reality—judiciously, as you will—we'll act again, creating other new realities, which you can study too, and that's how things will sort out. We're history's actors . . . and you, all of you, will be left to just study what we do."[3] A student of the discourse deployed by the Christian Right cannot help but hear echoes in this passage of that group's messianic self righteousness, its certainty, its disrespect for outsiders, and its utter contempt for factual evidence.

The popular radio talk-show host Rush Limbaugh provides yet another helpful illustration of the status of truth in contemporary conservative discourse. In his discussion of Limbaugh, Jeff Land remarks: "Outside of the Christian broadcast networks, it is difficult to find any parallel in the media landscape where a host so constantly invokes privileged access to the truth to which he testifies" (233). Land's invocation of Christian broadcasting is apt; Limbaugh argues as though the truth he tells is transparently self-validating, even though his ideology is laced "with a vicious and racist core," as Land observes (234). For Limbaugh what matters is how many people agree with him; if his ratings are high, he must be telling the truth. In fact his ratings exempt him from criticism. Linda Kintz notes that according to Limbaugh, "the free market reliably guarantees the goodness—the truth, the democratic moral, fair nature—of whatever it blesses. It would not bless bad things; that is its very logic. Racism, homophobia, and sexism are bad things, therefore, they are not what I do, because the inherently democratic market, sanctioned by God and natural law, does bless me" (*Between* 213). Limbaugh is successful; ergo he is a good and righteous guy who tells the truth legitimated by capitalism. Liberal attacks on his ethics are, ipso facto, lies. Limbaugh's bald equation of truth and justice with the possession of economic and cultural power may be startling, but it cannot be doubted that he grasps the nature of the argumentative climate within which we all now work.

Contemporary intellectual developments, then, taken together, constitute a powerful recipe for a climate of suspicion. Apocalyptism discerns the true and the real by means of deduction from ineffable first premises. Contact with the real is certified by its resonance with beliefs already in place. In addition, many citizens now realize that reason, the liberal measure of truth, is in the service of power. Finally, postmodern thinkers insist that there is no longer any argumentative ground beyond the pull of competing interests from which one can assert a claim to truth. When ordinary standards for measuring truth-telling are under assault, whatever those standards may be in a given time and place, conspiracy thinking can flourish.

They're Out to Get Us

Conspiracy theorists tend to reason from a deductive premise, just as apocalyptists do. In their case the premise is something like "Somebody is up to no good." The nefarious groups invented by conspiracy theorists generally have access to power of some kind that is not widely available. Hence Michael Barkun defines conspiracy theory as "belief that an organization made up of individuals or groups was or is acting covertly to achieve some malevolent end" (*Culture* 3). This definition applies equally well to conspiracies that discover witches in Salem or communists in the U.S. government, but it is difficult to be more specific given the variety of events to which conspiracy theories have become attached. It is possible to conjecture a conspiracy wherein secretive people and powerful agencies have in mind the best interests of all humanity and the entire planet, I suppose, but conspiracy writing seldom follows this hopeful trajectory. Comic book narratives like *X-Men* and Saturday-morning cartoons perhaps come closest to realizing this possibility.

Conspiracy theory differs from apocalyptism insofar as it generally disrespects the word of authorities. It also revels in facts, treating them as a route to truth and depending on data to support even the wildest sorts of conjecture; no conspiracy theory can be persuasive, it seems, without a lengthy rehearsal of evidence that can be assembled to support it. The preferred data is empirical, that is, material, although the testimony of experts is also welcome.[4] Because conspiracy theorists seek to persuade uncommitted believers, they are quite willing to abandon a secondary claim should facts or reasoning render this necessary in order to protect the major claim.[5] Clearly, then, apocalypticism is not a conspiracy discourse, given its reliance on revelation, its relative disregard for factual evidence, and its assurance of an eventual reward for believers. However, apocalyptist prophecy interpretation can take on the character of conspiracy writing when its authors consider the possible identities and activities of Antichrist. For instance, Pat Robertson's *The New World Order* is a veritable compendium of classic conspiracy theory blended with apocalyptist fantasy. In this wild adventure into the dark corners of the human imagination Robertson trots out Antichrist, the Rothschild family, Satanists, and "international financiers," all of whom are in cahoots with the League of Nations, the Trilateral Commission, New Agers, and Presidents Carter and George H. W. Bush in a foul plot to secularize the American family. This stuff still percolates in Christian Right circles. On November 12, 2004, I saw televangelist Jack van Impe warn his viewers against the machinations of the mysterious Illuminati, who had seen to it, among other ungodly things, that secret signals to conspirators are printed on the dollar bill. According to van Impe, the Illuminati are now working through the European Union, a nice touch that allowed him to get in a jab at the French. And of course Tim LaHaye conjectures secular humanism as a conspiracy of God-haters who are out to silence Christians and erase Christian belief and practice from public awareness. All of which is to say that apocalyptists exploit generic features of conspiracy writing when they need to conjecture obstacles to their achievement of dominion.

Scholars who study conspiracy theory can trace it back to America's founding (Barkun, *Culture;* Goldberg). The archetypal conspiracy theory centers on a cabal—the Masons, the Knights Templar, the Priory—whose members are either desirous of world power or own it already, for good or ill. The basic narrative was refurbished into a virulent anti-Semitic screed early in the twentieth century in the infamous *Protocols of the Elders of Zion,* in which, according to Norman Cohn, a "secret Jewish government" is portrayed as working "through a world-wide network of camouflaged agencies and organizations" in pursuit of "an age-old plan and with the single aim of achieving Jewish dominion over the entire world; and it is supposed to be perilously near to achieving this aim" (*Warrant* 22–23). Horribly the *Protocols* has spawned uncounted acts of violence against

Jews. Hitler knew the book well, and Cohn establishes that it was central to his philosophy and policy regarding Jews (*Warrant* 181). In America prior to the Cold War conspiracy narratives circulated primarily among members of cults and subscribers to relatively unpopular ideologies such as nativism and fascism, and anti-Semitic conspiracy theories continued to emanate from conservative organizations such as the John Birch Society well into the 1960s (Bennett; Lee; Stewart). During the 1940s a novel conspiracy narrative entered popular discourse when reports of flying saucers began to circulate in mainstream media (Dean, *Aliens;* Denzler). Conspiracy theories have proliferated since the assassinations of John Fitzgerald Kennedy, his brother Robert, and Martin Luther King in the brief span of five years—from 1963 to 1968—a series of events so unpredictable, so mind-boggling, that they demand larger-than-life explanations (Fenster; Knight). The continuing popularity of the standard conspiracy narrative is certified by its centrality to the plot of Dan Brown's enormously successful novel *The DaVinci Code,* which has spawned a veritable industry of conservative Christian commentary aimed, interestingly enough, at debunking the conspiracist details included in an avowed work of fiction.

Scholars offer several explanations for the postwar popularity of conspiracy discourse. Perhaps the best known of these is Richard Hofstadter's claim that conspiracy theorists are paranoid. However, a confident diagnosis of paranoia requires an agreed-upon notion of truth from which a paranoid can be thought to have departed, and with some exceptions students of conspiracy theory are unwilling any longer to settle for this explanation (Pipes; Robins and Post). Another explanation, one that is perhaps too facile, is that subscription to a liberal concept of the unhampered individual has rendered Americans unable to make systemic analyses of events, analyses that would lay bare the connections among economic, class, and political forces that together motivate historical events. Conspiracy theorists replace such analysis with a deus ex machina, a group of shady, powerful men (they are always men) who manipulate events in order to gain power and to disadvantage others. In his *Empire of Conspiracy* Timothy Melley notes that "the power of social structures frequently comes as a shock" in postwar writing (5). Thus he interprets conspiracy theory as a symptom of "agency panic," which he defines as "intense anxiety about an apparent loss of autonomy or self-control" accompanied by a secondary sense that "controlling organizations are themselves agents—rational, motivated entities with the will and the means to carry out complex plans" (12–13). In this reading victims of conspiracies blame straitened circumstances on people or groups whose movements are hidden but whose motives are nonetheless apparent. This explanation accounts nicely for conspiracy theories developed by right-wing thinkers such as the members of the Christian Identity movement, who see government manipulation at work in cultural and political developments ranging from the founding of the United Nations to the spread of feminism (Barkun, *Religion*; Levitas). But agency panic does not account very well for conspiracy writing in which authors actually seem to feel empowered by the acts of ferreting out pieces of evidence and making connections among them (Dean, "If Anything" 100). I think Melley hits on a more distinctive point about conspiracy theory when he notes that it "arises out of radical doubt about how knowledge is produced and about the authority of those who produce it. . . . It develops from the refusal to accept someone else's definition of a universal social good or an officially sanctioned truth" (13). This is an excellent description of conspiracy writing that attempts to account for the events of 9/11.

A New Day of Infamy

At 8:46 on September 11, 2001, an aircraft crashed into the North Tower of the World Trade Center (WTC).[6] Video footage of this crash was not available until that evening. But CNN broke into its regular programming at 8:48, only two minutes after the first crash had occurred, to begin live broadcasting from downtown Manhattan. Television cameras showed a huge plume of black smoke rising from a gaping hole near the tower's apex. At first television anchors were unwilling to speculate about what could have caused such a horrible thing, and George W. Bush claimed to think that the first crash was an accident, the result of pilot error (Paul Thompson 382). But explanatory narratives quickly began to emerge. In fact the seed of one narrative was planted only minutes after the major events of that day were over. At 11:30 that morning General Wesley Clark said on television that he suspected Osama bin Laden of masterminding the attacks, and CNN soon confirmed that bin Laden was under suspicion (Paul Thompson 462, 465).

In case anyone needs to be reminded, the official account of these events asserts that on September 11, 2001, four aircraft were hijacked by nineteen men associated with Al Qaeda, an organization led by Osama bin Laden. Two of the planes were flown into the Twin Towers of the World Trade Center, another craft was flown into the Pentagon, and yet a fourth was forced to crash in Pennsylvania after its passengers mounted an attack on the hijackers. I use the term *official* because this version of events has been sanctioned by Congress and by mainstream media. The official narrative is retold, more or less, in the 9/11 Congressional Report and the reports issued by the National Commission on Terrorist Attacks upon the United States, known familiarly as the 9/11 Commission (CR). The commission's report rapidly became a fixture on the *New York Times*'s best-seller list, despite its small type and massive documentation.

Conspiracy theories about 9/11 dispute all of these assertions, and they run the gamut from silly to sobering. The silly category includes a photograph that supposedly shows Satan's face in the smoke rising from the towers (http://www.markdphillips.com). However, one alternative explanation for the events of that day demands somewhat more careful consideration, in my opinion. This version, which conspiracy theorists call "revisionist," claims that some degree of government complicity was necessary for the plot to have been pulled off successfully. Michael Moore's *Fahrenheit 9/11* forwards a relatively reticent version of this argument. Moore's film implies that the Bush family's relations with Saudi royalty, and the implication of both in worldwide high finance and oil dealing, are at least suspicious given that members of the bin Laden family also move in these circles and that most of the hijackers were Saudi nationals. This narrative can be dismissed as a leftist take on one-worldism, with capitalist oil barons assuming the role played by Jews in the anti-Semitic right-wing version. Moore's implication is typical of conspiracy theory insofar as all of the information on which he relies can be documented, and other authors have pointed out the connections between the Bush family and Saudi royalty as well (Briody; Unger). In this instance, however, the facts emphatically do not speak for themselves, even though Moore apparently hoped they would.

When fully fleshed out, the central revisionist claim is that the horrible events of September 11, 2001, legitimated the desire of Bush administration officials to invade Afghanistan and Iraq, and perhaps other countries as well, either in order to secure America's status as a superpower, or to gain control of the world's dwindling oil supply, or both (Nafeez Mosaddeq Ahmed 240; Griffin 89–104; Ruppert). A supporting premise must be that administration officials guessed American citizens would support this desire more strongly if the event were spectacular and if the losses of life and property were devastating. The spectacle and devastation can be read to support bin Laden's aims, as well. But this realization can also reinforce conspiratorial suspicion of collaboration between bin Laden and the Bush administration.

In his survey of revisionist arguments, entitled *The New Pearl Harbor*, David Ray Griffin helpfully outlines what "degrees of complicity" might mean with regard to the events of September 11 (xxi–xxii). The lowest level of complicity includes construction of a false account as cover for incompetence or to justify the subsequent attacks on Afghanistan and Iraq. Even though this is the least damning of the possible meanings of "complicity," lying to the American people can have serious consequences for elected officials—as we saw in 1999 when Bill Clinton was impeached for this very offense. Even more serious is the possibility that intelligence agencies and/ or the White House knew the attacks were coming and did nothing to stop them. The most serious possibility, of course, is that high-level officials took part in the planning or the execution of the attacks, either by failing to deter the perpetrators (as in ordering defense systems to stand down) or by actively assisting them (as in helping the hijackers to enter the country—repeatedly—without the proper papers). These last levels of complicity are criminal offenses, and if any of these possibilities is ever validated, the implications would shake American citizens' faith in democracy, to say the least.

Versions of the revisionist argument appear on a number of Web sites devoted to the events of 9/11, as well as in a growing stack of books published by presses with names like Tree of Life and Olive Branch. Reviews of revisionist accounts in the mainstream media generally treat them with scorn. None has made the *Times* best-seller list, although Thierry Meyssan's *9/11: The Big Lie* made a splash in France, where it was originally published in 2002. Some revisionist authors seem more trustworthy than others, and Griffin, whose book reviews and evaluates revisionist arguments, is among these. Griffin is a professor of religion at Claremont, and it is not easy to write him off as a wing-nut alarmist wearing a tinfoil hat. He has taught theology and ethics for more than thirty years, and his list of scholarly publications in these fields is impressive. When he takes on the events of 9/11 he ventures far out of his area of expertise, of course. However, a habit of careful scholarship is everywhere apparent in his book. He is conversant with both the sober and the more wild-eyed literature on 9/11, and he distinguishes among accounts on the basis of their quality. He documents assertions, and he develops his argument in the cumulative way typical of philosophical speculation. He considers possible counterarguments to the revisionist account. He also notes that he cannot evaluate the accuracy of the empirical evidence he assembles, and so he claims only that "these revisionists have presented a strong *prima facie* case for official complicity" (xxiii). That is to say, he thinks the evidence is strong enough to establish a fact or raise a presumption of fact. His credentials and his caution do not prove that he that he has not "drunk the Kool-Aid," of course, and none of this information addresses or erases other sorts of suspicions, such as that Griffin perhaps wanted to write a book, finally, that would make some real money. Of course I am here applying the tests of authority recommended by rhetoric textbooks to Griffin's work. In this case the tests yield no clear conclusions.

Both versions of the events that occurred on September 11 raise questions that have no satisfactory answers. How is it, for example, that the nation's defense apparatus was not scrambled in time to shoot down American flight 77, the plane that hit the Pentagon at 9:37, if not United flight 175, which crashed into the South Tower at 9:03, some seventeen minutes after the North Tower was struck? Contact was lost with American Airlines flight 11 between 8:13 and 8:21, some twenty-five to thirty minutes before it struck the North Tower and nearly an hour and a half before another craft flew into the Pentagon. Standard policy is in place to deal with planes that do not respond properly to queries. Air controllers are expected to notify other aircraft in the vicinity as well as the parent airline if the flight is a commercial one; if the silent aircraft cannot be raised after a few minutes' time, controllers are expected to notify the Federal Aviation Administration (FAA) and the North American Aerospace Defense Command (NORAD), whose mission is to protect America's airspace (CR 17). This is ordinarily accomplished by launching fighter planes that rush to the position of the silent aircraft. The fighter pilots investigate, signaling if possible to the pilots who are under surveillance that they are to follow the fighters to a designated landing area. In case of noncompliance fighter pilots may be ordered to shoot down uncooperative aircraft. Apparently the shoot-down order is a presidential-level decision (Bamford, *Pretext* 16; Clarke 7). On September 11 interceptor planes were first launched at 8:52, almost forty minutes after air controllers were certain that flight 11 had been hijacked and some six minutes after it crashed. But no fighter jets made contact with any of the remaining suspicious craft, with the possible exception of United flight 93.

One must presume, as well, that the Secret Service has policy in place to protect the president and other national leaders during attacks on the nation. Why, then, was George W. Bush allowed to stick to his advertised schedule even though his Secret Service detail must have heard about the first attack shortly after it occurred? (CR 37; Griffin 57). Furthermore, as

Moore's film notoriously documents, Bush remained at the elementary school he was visiting throughout the second attack, thus endangering not only himself and his entourage but students, teachers, and school staff as well. He left about 9:34, nearly forty minutes after his escort learned of the first attack. More questions are raised by the fact that some facets of the White House account of Bush's movements on that day were subsequently shown to be false. The White House at first explained his failure to return immediately to Washington, D.C., for example, by claiming that there was a threat to Air Force One. The 9/11 Commission found no evidence that such a threat existed. Furthermore, had such a threat been made, the presidential plane should have been accompanied at all times by fighter jets, which were just minutes away when Bush was still in Florida. But escort planes did not accompany Air Force One until the president's plane took off from Barksdale air base in Louisiana, headed for yet another airbase in Nebraska.

Vice-president Richard Cheney was rushed to a secure location under the White House sometime between 9:00 and 10:00 that morning, along with National Security Agency (NSA) advisor Condoleezza Rice, other staff, and family members (Clarke 2; Paul Thompson 399). However, Secretary of Defense Donald Rumsfeld was still in his office at the Pentagon when that facility was hit some fifty minutes after the first crash. The evacuation of Capitol Hill began at 9:48, almost ten minutes after the crash at the Pentagon, although it is possible that Representative Dennis Hastert, who as Speaker of the House is next in line after Cheney to assume the presidency, was whisked away to a safe location some time earlier on the orders of Richard Clarke (Clarke 9; Paul Thompson 419).

The question remains, however: why weren't presumably standard defense policies followed on September 11, 2001? "Incompetence" is not an entirely satisfactory answer to such questions, although it is the simplest and most obvious, and this is the answer given by the 9/11 Commission (CR 339–60). On the other hand, revisionist Nafeez Mosaddeq Ahmed, who reviewed standard operating procedures for events like those of 9/11, as well as images of the events and testimony given by principals in interviews and news reports, concludes that there was "active obstruction of routine protective systems. . . . This appears to have been maintained through the orchestrated prolongation (for up to one and a half hours) of systematic negligence as the attacks occurred, on the part of elements of the FAA, NORAD, the Pentagon, the Secret Service, the White House and the President" (171). This explanation enters the realm of classic conspiracy theory, involving tens if not hundreds of people who supposedly stood down the air defense system. There is one difference between Ahmed's analysis and classic conspiracy theory, however, insofar as the perpetrators named here do not hide from view but are, in some cases, very public figures.

Proponents of both lines of argument forward empirical evidence and testimony to support their analyses. Unfortunately the events that transpired on September 11 demonstrate how little assistance is provided by facts and testimony in settling on a satisfactory explanation for events of such magnitude, particularly when the relevant physical evidence is missing or unavailable to most investigators. (Among revisionists the very lack of evidence is cause for suspicion.) Because of this handicap experts are often reduced to relying on the same materials (photographs and eyewitness testimony) that are available to amateur investigators.

Some of the more striking evidence involves the eerily graceful fall of the Twin Towers. The WTC towers were very strong, built to withstand storms and the buffeting of wind gusts across their girth and thirteen-hundred-foot height. They were reinforced by 47 steel core supports within and by 250 steel columns without (Griffin 13). In addition, the exterior columns were reinforced by strips of steel bolted together crosswise to form phalanges. Furthermore, the concrete floors were laid over interlocking steel trusses that were bolted to the exterior supports. All of this was done to insure redundancy in these very tall buildings so that if one structural feature were compromised, others would continue to support their weight. The Federal Emergency Management Agency's (FEMA) report on the buildings' collapse, which I take to be representative of the official account, states in its introduction that "the collapse of the towers astonished most observers, including knowledgeable engineers" (4).[7] The report claims that the impact of the aircraft, in addition to heat generated by the subsequent fires, was sufficient to cause the outer ring of steel struts to bend outward, thus allowing the concrete floors near the impact sites to collapse onto one another. However, FEMA's report is surrounded by careful qualifications explaining that its analysis is not "definitive" because investigators were hampered both by a lack of time and by lack of access to the debris (2, 1–14). Access to the debris was in fact limited, both while it was in place and during its transfer to another locale.

FEMA's is one of several theories that supports the official account of the towers' fall. On the PBS program NOVA Thomas Eager, an engineer at MIT, launched his theory that after the towers were damaged by the impact of the planes and once the fire became sufficiently hot to soften steel, the angle clips that held the impacted floors to the frame of the building began to "unzip" all around the buildings (http://www.pbs.org/nova/wgbh). Revisionists point out, however, that until September 11 no steel-reinforced building has ever been destroyed by fire (Hufschmid 34). They note that the hydrocarbon fires set by exploding jet fuel do not burn hot enough to cause steel to degrade unless the steel is subjected to such a fire for a long time—a possibility that seems belied by photographs taken of the towers prior to their collapse (http://www.911research.wtc7.net/talks/wtc/index.html). Revisionist Eric Hufschmid found a photograph that shows two women standing in the hole left in the North Tower by the plane's impact; were fires raging on that floor or in the immediate area it would of course have been impossible for human beings to remain in the vicinity (27). (The possibility is always open, however, that this photograph has been doctored.)

Engineers' assertions about the collapse of the buildings qualify as expert testimony, which ordinary citizens must take on faith unless they are willing to do the research necessary to verify them. Some portions of these arguments are supported by mathematical calculations that are beyond my ability to decipher, and I expect this is true for most other Americans as well (see the analyses at http://www.911-strike.com, for example). Such matters are important because revisionists make the startling claim that the Twin Towers, along with WTC building 7, were actually demolished by explosives appropriately placed throughout. They buttress this assertion by pointing out that the towers fell in the same way that buildings fall when their demolition has been carefully planned. Revisionists argue as well that large pieces of the upper portion of the South Tower, which, photographs show, broke off above the crash site and leaned outward prior to the fall of the rest of the tower, should have fallen relatively intact onto building 4 of the WTC rather than disintegrating into tiny bits (Hufschmid 43–44). They claim further that the energy generated by the pancaking collapse of the buildings was insufficient to account for the huge clouds of fine concrete dust that covered most of lower Manhattan after the towers fell; the concrete floors should not have been pulverized but should have broken into chunks if their rate of fall was governed only by gravity. Furthermore, both buildings collapsed very quickly, almost at the speed of free fall. Revisionists argue that in a nonaccelerated fall each floor of the buildings would have resisted the pressure from those above, if only momentarily, thus slowing the rate of collapse. In addition, nearby structures suffered damage from the blowout of debris during the fall. This blowout measured nearly three times the girth of a tower, by some estimates; it was too extensive and too powerful, revisionists claim, to have been generated by the weight of successively collapsing floors. And as we all saw on television, once the dust settled, no very large pieces of steel remained among the ruins of the towers. The shattered steel included the core supports, each of which measured thirty-six by fifteen inches; these supports were one hundred millimeters thick at the base of the buildings.

These speculations are complicated by the fact that there is no satisfactory explanation for the fall of WTC 7 on the afternoon of September 11. This building was not hit by an aircraft, and photographs show only small fires burning on several of its floors, which may have been started by blowout from the fall of the towers. Larry Silverstein, leaseholder of the building, told PBS that he asked the fire department to "pull it," which is engineering slang for demolition (Paul Thompson 467).[8] WTC 7 imploded moments after he made this request, suggesting to revisionists that explosives had been planted there prior to the day of the attacks (Hufschmid 82–84).

Revisionists marshal other evidence to support their claim about demolition, but this should suffice to show its nature. If forensic engineers could examine the debris that remained after the towers fell, they might be able to confirm either the official or the revisionist account or some other version. However, the debris was rapidly carted away under tight security, and most of it has now been destroyed or dispersed around the world. If any evidence ever surfaces that supports revisionist versions of the towers' fall, of course, the implication is that someone with expertise in demolition and relatively unlimited access to the towers planned the explosions to occur during the aftermath of the planes' collisions with the buildings, ostensibly to enhance the shock and drama of the event. This thesis implies in turn that the hijackers had at least one accomplice on the ground, and it implies as well that the accomplice(s) might have been well-known to staff and inhabitants of the tower complex. It is something of a leap from these assumptions to a charge of official complicity, but such leaps are regularly made by 9/11 conspiracy theorists.[9]

Perhaps the most vexed issue in 9/11 conspiracy writing is raised by events at the Pentagon.[10] Here again the available evidence consists mainly of photographs and eyewitness accounts, because the physical evidence—the remains of whatever hit the building—was apparently gathered up quickly and sequestered (http://www.911research.wtc7.net). The official account claims that the Pentagon was hit by American flight 77. Some revisionists accept this claim, while others argue that something else struck the building—a missile or a smaller aircraft, perhaps a military plane (Meyssan). Apparently the craft that hit the Pentagon, whatever it was, executed a 270-degree turn while spiraling downward some seven thousand feet before crashing into the west wall of the Pentagon very near to ground level.[11] Some revisionist authors argue that a barely trained pilot (Hani Hanjour, according to the official account) could not have executed either this maneuver or those necessary to fly a very large aircraft so fast and so low to the ground as is required by the official version (Hufschmid 104). Eyewitness accounts of this event are hopelessly contradictory, as we might expect during a traumatic event of this magnitude, but a preponderance of those who were nearby agree that a jetliner "dove toward the Pentagon at a shallow angle and exploded at or in front of the façade."[12]

Some empirical evidence is provided by photographs of the Pentagon crash site taken prior to firefighters' arrival on the scene (Hufschmid 99). Revisionists who do not accept that flight 77 struck the Pentagon make two points based on these photos: that insufficient debris lay on the lawn beneath the crash site to account for the disintegration of a large aircraft and that the hole in the exterior of the building is not large enough to accommodate a Boeing 757. The relative lack of debris is odd, but photographs from the crash site in Pennsylvania demonstrate that very little debris remains from even a large aircraft if it is flying fast enough when it hits the ground or a building. Photographs do show the ruins of an engine inside the Pentagon walls, and there is much controversy about whether or not these engine parts can have come from a 757. A smaller nearly round hole was punched into the third ring of the building, and those who accept the official account can assume from this evidence that the wings and one engine of the plane disintegrated on impact, while the fuselage and/or the other engine tunneled through three rings of the building. Of course none of this evidence discounts the possibility of a different craft or a missile striking the building. The Pentagon did little to bolster the official account when on March 7, 2002, it unofficially released several frames of a surveillance tape that purportedly shows an aircraft about to fly into the building (Hufschmid 97). Conspiracy enthusiasts have demonstrated, fairly convincingly, that these photographs have been doctored (http://www.con spiracyplanet.com). Furthermore, the release of these photographs several months after the event raised the suspicion that they were disseminated in order to discount the influence of Meyssan's books about the incident. Other surveillance cameras were operating near the crash site at the time of the crash, including one at a gas station across the street. This tape was confiscated by the FBI some thirty minutes after the crash and has not been released to date.

Obviously this revisionist claim begs a very large question: if flight 77 did not hit the Pentagon, where is it, and where are its passengers? I am not sure what revisionists gain by arguing that the Pentagon was hit by a missile or a military aircraft, other than casting suspicion on the official account and/or shoring up conspiratorial distrust of the military and the government. Surely the destruction of a very large commercial craft with passengers and crew on board better served the purported purpose of generating sufficient spectacle and shock to move the American people toward support of preemptive wars than would the firing of a missile on a military installation. For these reasons some revisionists have now abandoned the missile theory (Hoffman).

If the plot called for a fourth crash, into the White House or the Capitol, the attack truly was planned as a full-scale assault on the material symbols of American power. Had the takeoff of United flight 93 not been delayed by some forty minutes, and had its passengers hence not had time to learn of the other hijackings, this aircraft might have crashed in Washington, D.C., rather than in a field in rural Pennsylvania. This is a chilling thought, given that Capitol Hill was not fully evacuated until after the crash at the Pentagon. Proponents of the revisionist account suspect that United flight 93 was actually shot down over Pennsylvania (http://www.flight93crash.com). Griffin in fact considers the possibility that the flight was shot down precisely because its passengers threatened to regain control of the aircraft (50). Eyewitness accounts of this crash conflict. Some eyewitnesses attest that the plane was rocking back and forth as it neared the ground or that it was flying upside down. Both of these accounts could confirm the official version, which asserts that passengers rushed the cockpit to thwart the hijackers; the pilot might have rocked the wings in order to throw the rebellious passengers off their feet. Other witnesses on the ground claim that they heard an explosion before the plane descended into view. Witnesses claim as well that debris fell to the ground as far as eight miles from the crash site and into a lake that is two and a half miles from the site, suggesting that the plane was coming apart prior to the crash. A tape made from a phone conversation with a passenger apparently recorded the sound of an explosion and rushing wind. I say "apparently" because to date only investigators and the families of passengers and crew have been allowed to listen to tapes of phone calls made from the plane.

Yet other eyewitness accounts confirm the presence of additional aircraft in the vicinity of flight 93's crash site, even though commercial aircraft had been grounded all over the country by the time it fell to the ground. Several people swear they saw a small "white plane." These witnesses may have seen a C-130 that was ordered to the area by Vice-president Cheney, but it is doubtful that anyone would confuse this very large craft with an executive jet or a military fighter plane, which is what these witnesses say they saw. Interestingly enough, in December 2004 Secretary of Defense Donald Rumsfeld remarked in passing that flight 93 was "shot down over Pennsylvania."[13] (The secretary was later characterized as having misspoken.) If flight 93 was indeed shot down by either a missile or a military jet, this fact mitigates in part the charge of utter incompetence on the part of government and the military. On the other hand, it renders somewhat less powerful the heroic myth that has grown up around the rebellious passengers of flight 93, a myth that many Americans apparently find comforting (http://www.flight93memorialproject.org).

The 9/11 Commission placed some blame for the attacks on faulty intelligence or on mismanagement in the nation's intelligence agencies (CR 400–406). However, Richard Clarke, the chief intelligence officer at the White House, told the commission that intelligence agencies had both general and specific expectations about the planned attacks and that they informed the administration of this on several occasions.[14] Clarke's account was confirmed by the delayed declassification and release in February 2005 of a portion of the 9/11 Commission report that detailed fifty-two such reports made to the FAA between April and September of 2001.[15] Nor was this the first time the World Trade Center had been targeted by terrorists—a huge bomb demolished the lower floors and several subbasements in 1993. An Islamic militant named Ramzi Yousef was later tried and convicted for this act (Miller, Stone, and Mitchell). By 1990 Osama bin Laden had begun masterminding attacks on U.S. interests, and some authorities think that he was involved in the first attack on the WTC. Certainly, bin Laden is implicated in the attack on the U.S.S. *Cole* in 2000. Between 1998 and 2001 U.S. intelligence agencies had many warnings that he planned to make an attempt inside the country, using aircraft as weapons (Paul Thompson 20–54). In fact the association between bin Laden and an attack on the World Trade Center was so easy to make that when the head of the CIA, George Tenet, heard on the morning of September 11 that a plane had crashed into the North Tower, he blurted out bin Laden's name. If these accounts are accepted, it follows that blame might more usefully be directed toward the policy makers who interpret intelligence generated by the various agencies than toward intelligence sources themselves. Failure to prepare for attacks predicted by intelligence sources does not imply complicity. However, such failure does indicate a certain negligence of responsibility, negligence that authors of the official account were apparently unwilling to attribute to members of the Bush administration.

But I Was Actually There . . .

Do revisionist accounts of the events of September 11 deserve our attention? The postmodern skeptical tactic recommended by Quinby, of locating events in cultural time and place, uncovers the historical evidence reviewed above that suggests that bin Laden and his operatives had both the desire and the ability to carry out spectacular attacks on this country and its assets. But historical research also establishes that the American government regularly lies to its citizens and that military or intelligence communities have in the past plotted violence upon citizens in order to move them to support a given policy (Alterman; Bamford, *Body* 82–91). Nor does liberal skepticism provide much assistance to someone who is trying to decide whether revisionist accounts of the events of September 11 deserve consideration. As I hope I have demonstrated, the usual tests of authority and data are not always helpful in determining the worth of alternate accounts. And there are also logical difficulties involved in disproving a conspiracy. As revisionist Eric Hufschmid opines, when everybody is looking at the same evidence (or lack of it), the only way one reading can be thought better than another is if its authors find "a more convincing speculation" about what that evidence means (15). In other words, the burden of the argument moves past understanding into persuasion. In this view the chief difficulty with the revisionist account is its plausibility; it is hard to imagine that a conspiracy involving so many people could be successfully carried off. On the other hand, the number of conspirators required by the official account is not small, given the elaborate planning and enormous resources necessary to carry out the attacks. Some of the presumed hijackers lived in the United States prior to 2001, moving freely about the country—in some cases for years (CR 215–41). Mohamed Atta traveled about the world prior to the attacks, using major airports, even though he and others of the hijackers were on watch lists. The real difference in the plausibility of the two accounts, then, is that the official version names conspirators who are widely regarded as criminals (and worse) by Americans, while the revisionist account casts suspicion on officials of the federal government. In other words, the degree of plausibility accruing to each account depends on whether an audience is willing to accept the villains it conjectures.

Nevertheless, critics have resorted to liberal notions of truth and reason as means of discounting revisionist arguments. In his review of Meyssan's work James S. Robbins calls Meyssan an "imbecile" and a "half-wit."[16] He further links revisionist accounts of 9/11 to Holocaust denial, thus implicating Meyssan with anti-Semitic conspiracy theories. He asserts that "the answer to Meyssan and other such revisionists is the truth, particularly the primary sources, the body of knowledge compiled by those who experienced the events in question." Robbins is among those primary sources, having actually witnessed the crash at the Pentagon from the window of his office, which is about a mile and a half away. Interestingly he admits that he did not actually see flight 77 hit the building: "The sight of the 757 diving in at an unrecoverable angle is frozen in my memory, but at the time, I did not immediately comprehend what I was witnessing. There was a silvery flash, an explosion, and a dark, mushroom shaped cloud rose over the building." Robbins's insistence that his proximity to the event insures the truth of the official account is obviously not an instance of agency panic but is, rather, an iteration of the liberal canard that presence manifests truth, that the evidence of the senses is primary and always to be trusted. But Robbins's defense of the official narrative is understandable. To abandon that narrative is to open the possibility that subsequent events, such as the wars in Afghanistan and Iraq, were not just and necessary responses to a ferocious attack on America.

Jodi Dean argues that conspiracy theory is "an expression of pain, of the violation of a body politic" ("If Anything" 102). Certainly the revisionist argument I explore here represents a hypothetical violation of the civic imaginary called "the American people." Dean argues further that conspiracy writing "seizes a pleasure from the pain . . . an enjoyment at the site of a perceived diminishment of political and economic efficacy that substitutes a different sort of agency, one configured around linked screens, around watching and knowing" ("If Anything" 102). In cyberia, she writes, "'being informed' stands in for 'being engaged'" ("If Anything" 102). She may be right about this. Revisionists claim that inquiries into the events of September 11 to date have been politically compromised, and they call for a completely open investigation (Nafeez Mosaddeq Ahmed 299; Griffin 147–68). They argue that the Bush administration cannot afford to allow suspicions as weighty as those reviewed here to linger in citizens' minds.

My response to this proposal is that Bush's election in 2004 suggests, to the contrary, that his administration is suffering no negative consequences whatever as a result of its action or inaction on and prior to September 11. This plea for full disclosure feels to me like another expression of the liberal hope that if all relevant facts are available, understanding will take place (and justice will be done?). Barring the virtual impossibility of such an investigation being undertaken in the near term, I wonder what full disclosure could accomplish, given that it would necessarily expose either massive incompetence or a profound disregard for duty—not to mention the more repellant possibilities—on the part of both elected and appointed officials.

7

HOW BELIEFS CHANGE

In *The Trouble with Principle* Stanley Fish tells the story of a Klansman who rejected Klan ideology. The change occurred when the Klansman heard a leader of the group say that upon its assumption of power "defectives of a variety of kinds would be put into special colonies or otherwise dealt with. This . . . point was accompanied by a list of defectives, and among those named were persons with cleft palates. It so happened that the daughter of the once, and now instantly former, white supremacist was herself afflicted by that condition" (282). Fish points out that this moment could have taken another direction: "it would have been perfectly possible for the devoted father to have said to himself, 'Well, I really love Mary, but the cause is the cause and I guess she'll have to go'" (282). This story provides an interesting example wherein a believer was jolted out of belief by sudden awareness of a contradiction between an ideologic and a powerful emotion—his love for a daughter. We don't learn from Fish's version whether or not the former Klansman's "conversion on the spot" altered any of his other beliefs. Did the conflict between Klan ideology and his daughter's circumstance forge new articulations or disarticulations? Did the "instantly former" Klansman become aware, for example, that the Klan's ugly policies of exclusion apply to other people who fulfill its definition of non-Aryan imperfection? To give up Klan belief is to end a set of practices—attending meetings, reading literature, associating with like-minded members of the group—but forgoing belief in Klan ideology does not require a former believer to give up his family, his job, his religious beliefs, his lifestyle, or even his racism. If Klan belief and belonging mattered less to this former white supremacist than did his love for his daughter, that was the case because his subscription to that ideology was not tightly bound up with other beliefs and values he holds. Indeed, in this case the man who abandoned the Klan gained a lucrative new identity as "the author of a best-selling expose" (282).

Fish names a second source of conversion—submission to authority—in addition to the fortuitous collusion of circumstance. He writes: "each of us has . . . someone or some text—the Pope, the Bible, Elvis, Lionel Trilling, Nietzsche, Satchel Paige, the *Turner Diaries*—whose authority is assumed, to the extent that we will think at least twice before dismissing or not taking seriously his or her or its pronouncements" (*Trouble* 283). In this essay Fish names only these two openings for change, and if my reading is correct he presents would-be rhetors with a stultifying problem. The appearance of a persuasive moment—when circumstances or authority converge with a belief system in such a way as to offer convincing proof that a change in belief is appropriate or necessary—is difficult to anticipate. Fish is aware of this. With regard to authority, he notes that "any authority, no matter how longstanding its hold on your imagination, can be dislodged in an instant, although that instant cannot be willed, cannot be planned for, and need not ever occur" (*Trouble* 283). Fish cites William James to the effect that belief is prior to rationality and that it is to some extent inaccessible to consciousness (*Trouble* 284). I heartily agree with both of these points. I agree as well that there is no "independent reality" that can "present itself" to individuals in such a way that they change their minds about it or anything else (Fish, *Trouble* 283). But Fish's model is of little use to rhetoricians insofar as it effectively denies rhetorical efficacy.[1] In this view a rhetor who wants to change someone's belief must be content to wait for adherents to find exceptions to its truth claims in their life circumstances or must muster sufficient and appropriate dissenting sources of authority. These difficulties are compounded by the nature of belief, which mitigates against either of these events occurring. Ideology and affect can color readings of circumstance so that the "reality" they construct always already confirms their correctness. Christ's failure to reappear on earth has resulted in disappointment and disaffection for some apocalyptists, but others simply renew their efforts to determine the correct time of the return (Festinger, Riecken, and Schachter). And since dissenting rhetors are configured in apocalyptist discourse not as authorities but as enemies, their chances of challenging the status of biblical authority within that discourse are slim. Furthermore, rhetors must also cope with a number of postmodern caveats, the most important of which is that one's desires (given that one can determine what those are) can never be enacted perfectly in discourse. Much less can a rhetor successfully predict a persuasive outcome.

Despite this limited scenario, persuasion does occur, as successful advertising and political campaigns attest. People can be converted to religion, and they can also reject the religious beliefs in which they were raised. Accounts given by formerly fundamentalist Christians record no such moment of enlightenment such as that which occurred for Fish's Klansman. Here is Dan Barker, writing about his conversion away from fundamentalist religious belief: "It was like tearing my whole frame of reality to pieces, ripping to shreds the fabric of meaning and hope, betraying the values of existence. It hurt. And it hurt bad. It was like spitting on my mother, or like throwing one of my children out a window. It was sacrilege. All of my bases for thinking and values had to be restructured" (qtd. in Babinski 301). Barker says that he also had to discard the respect and reputation he enjoyed in the community of believers (Babinski 302). His account vividly demonstrates what is at stake for those who reject densely articulated belief systems: identity, family, community, values, and a way of construing reality itself. Others who have rejected such beliefs report that the process of change can take a long time, occurring over a span of years.[2]

Fundamentalist Christians are certainly not without argumentative resources: within limits introspection and argument are endemic to conservative Christianity. Believers are trained from childhood to defend their version of Christianity against others. And so it might be said that conservative Christians have a good deal of experience with argument, perhaps more than those Americans who do not feel a recurring necessity to defend their beliefs. Michael Warner notes of his childhood Pentecostalism that "religious culture gave me a passionate intellectual life of which universities are only a pale ivory shadow" ("Tongues" 40). A crucial difference is contained in that word *passionate*: fundamentalist religious belief is intimate, visceral; it resonates in the very bodies of believers.

Single-Mindedness and the Privilege of Isolation

Let's add a contextual qualification to Fish's model. Obviously an exception to any belief system may be articulated within that system only if and when it begins to circulate among believers. The process of rhetorical change can begin, then, with admission of a new or countering claim to a belief system. With the advent of technology enabling global communications, the really hard question to answer is not how exceptions and counterclaims can circulate, but how they can be heard within communities whose beliefs they challenge. Here is a relatively trivial example of the difficulty. On January 11, 2005, a forum on freerepublic.com was thrown into a veritable frenzy by the news that Mel Gibson, the director and producer of *The Passion of the Christ,* had expressed admiration for Michael Moore's *Fahrenheit 9/11.* Freepers, as contributors to this message board are called, suppose that Gibson is a devout Christian, and hence they could not believe that he would approve of Moore, who in their opinion is anti-American because he opposes the war in Iraq. Within this community the epithet "anti-American" also implies "non-" or "anti-Christian." The ideologic is in fact rife with articulations that are not commonplaces outside of freeper discourse: all Christians are patriots; opposition to war is not patriotic, is even anti-American; no Christian can admire the work of someone who is antiwar, and so on. A few contributors tried to overcome the discontinuity, cautioning patience until the report was confirmed or pointing out that the admiration might be aesthetic rather than political since both men are filmmakers. But most posters condemned Gibson and all his works on the spot, on the strength of an unconfirmed rumor. Thus does ideologic resist encounters with discontinuity. Freepers can hear contradictions, but they cannot accept them; they are more willing to abandon a hero than to disarticulate their belief system in order to accommodate new information. Freepers enjoy the privilege of ideological isolation within their online community; any poster who does not toe the ideological line is savagely threatened.

Given this realization, I will hazard that new or countering beliefs are more likely to be heard and considered by subalterns, those who are subjected to rather than subjects of a hegemonic discourse. That is to say, counterhegemonic beliefs may be taken up more readily among those who are not included in a dominant subjectivity, who are reckoned by and within it as different. Women are objectified by and within patriarchy; as Simone de Beauvoir famously observed, in that discourse women are "the other." In patriarchal cultures, then, women move within a hegemonic ordering that conjectures them in ways in which they do not always recognize themselves (girls or chicks, mothers, sex objects, whores, crones, witches). Depending on the relative force available for maintenance of a hegemony—its extent of dispersal, the success of practices and institutions that enforce it—even those who are objectified by it may nonetheless accept its strictures, as many women readily identify with patriarchal values. But events and practices can coalesce in such a way that disconnects can create openings in the apparently seamless articulation of hegemony. Such a disconnect or opening may make available realignments among lines of force in such a way that potential rhetors can articulate different conjectures and authorize different ways of connecting beliefs. Clearly something like this happened during the 1960s when white women discovered that African American women working in the civil rights movement designed interventions, led projects, and made important decisions, hence enjoying a degree of authority that was routinely denied women in the student movement, where they were expected to type, make coffee, and provide sexual services to movement men (Morgan 23; Echols 27). When such women compared the articulation of "woman's place" within each of the two movements, the differences enabled them to realize that depictions of women's relationships to men could, literally, be otherwise. With the opening of this discursive path they were able to articulate a dissenting set of beliefs. Men and women who were still inscribed as subjects of patriarchy quite literally could not grasp the claims made by second-wave feminists, although movement men were aware immediately that such claims threatened their hegemony. The appeal of second-wave feminism to disaffected women was not only that feminist criticism articulated the othered-ness of women within mainstream belief in such a way that women could discuss this experience, but that feminist theory attempted to articulate a discursive pathway wherein women could be depicted as subjects. Even though this last project has so far failed, its very articulation as a possibility has apparently been liberating for many women, although it has apparently been felt as oppressive by others.

If the double consciousness of subaltern groups is an "engine of change," to appropriate Fish's language (*Doing*), the implication is that people who are single-minded are less likely to change their beliefs. Single-mindedness is available to those who are situated in the *habitus* in such a way that they seldom hear or read arguments that carry sufficient force to change their beliefs. That is, single-mindedness is available to people who are either privileged and/or isolated from dissonance. Those who are configured by hegemony as subjects may enjoy the privilege of single-mindedness, and in Western culture that privilege has historically been reserved for white males of the propertied classes. In America the social movements of the 1960s challenged this privilege, but these challenges have created

doubt about access mainly in the minds of white men who are not eco-
nomically privileged (Wray and Newitz). That is to say, these movements
threatened men whose social privileges accrued chiefly from their race and
gender.

So we have elicited one contextual principle that can mitigate the
possibility of change—the single-mindedness that accrues to isolation or
privilege. At the very least this principle specifies Fish's claim about the
influence of circumstance on belief. If I am right about this, it follows that
those of us who want change should challenge privilege and isolation in
whatever ways we can find or invent.

Believers in Christian apocalyptism understand the importance
of isolation to the maintenance of single-mindedness. This is why they
home-school their children and why they see to it that adolescents social-
ize within strictly orthodox youth groups and camps. The belief system is
itself isolationist because of its depiction of believers as an elect who are
spiritually superior to nonbelievers. It is also nearly impervious to alternative articulations, given its legitimation by a divine authority, the dissem-
ination of whose word is carefully policed by professional proselytizers.
Their interpretations of that word can never be gainsaid by outsiders, who
are agents of evil. They can, however, be questioned by insiders who for
some reason experience the subaltern or double consciousness, when, for
example, their experience does not square with what they are being taught.
In his analysis of religious doubt Christian Smith reports that only a tiny
fraction of evangelicals doubt or defect from religious belief for purely intellectual reasons. These few "distrust their own religious beliefs because
cultural and religious pluralism erode[s] any sense of cognitive certainty"
or reject "the faith of their families because their traditional doctrines
came to seem unbelievable in a rational, naturalistic, pluralist, modern
world" (*American* 172). Doubt and defection are far more likely to occur
because of "suffering, tragedies, moral hypocrisy, ordinary life struggles
and troubles, offensive church actions, and relational network disruptions"
(*American* 172).

Bells and Whistles

Barbara Herrnstein Smith forwards a theory of belief that demands somewhat less patience from rhetors than does Fish's. She locates the sources of
disagreement precisely where liberal argumentation refuses to look. Differences in views, she writes, should be understood as "products of our and

their more or less different personal histories (familial, social, educational, and so on) and current positions in the relevant society. . . . People usually want to retain what they experience as their current goods—advantages, privileges, satisfactions, and so on—unless they are persuaded that other goods would be secure by their yielding some of them" (*Belief* 13). Like Mouffe, Smith implies that change can come about by rhetorical means only if a rhetor respects difference. This means, for example, that liberals gain little by trying to convert apocalyptists to liberal beliefs or policies by means of reason. Rather, a would-be rhetor should focus her persuasive efforts on the arousal of passion and desire. Smith writes that "we might alter the meaning of many of those people's experiences for them and introduce new sets of desires into their desires" if we can establish that the change we propose forwards "their interests and projects" (*Belief* 14). The argumentative case typically imagined in composition textbooks is an attempt by a rhetor to persuade hostile or uncaring others to accept a position in which the rhetor believes, usually by means of assembling data and testimony that support this position. But if Herrnstein Smith is correct, this is the wrong way to go about persuasion.

Herrnstein Smith's reflexive theory of belief also assumes continuous interaction between individual bodies and the *habitus*. She notes that an individual's beliefs are changed in the same way they are maintained: "Specifically, our individual tendencies to respond in certain ways to certain perceived cues are strengthened, weakened, or reconfigured by the differential consequences of the responses we actually make. That is, depending on the consequences (harmful or beneficial, as predicted or contrary to prediction, and so on) of the actions we perform by virtue of the beliefs that we have, certain of our beliefs (tendencies to perceive and behave in certain ways) will be strengthened, others will be weakened, and various sets of them will be reconfigured" (*Belief* 45). It may be well to recall at this point that "the environment" to which we react is also a construct, built up over time by emotion, cognition, and memory. We "change our minds" when encounters with the environment, as we perceive and understand it, convince us that it is in our best interests to do so. Humans' "best interest" may once have been survival, but that remains true only for those whose situation is desperate. "Best interests" may now include less immediate concerns such as belonging to a community or the achievement of status. Once one becomes a member of a desired community, the community itself offers little internal impetus for change; and in most cases the acquisition of status requires conformity, perhaps exemplary conformity, with community standards. Rhetorically speaking, insiders engage chiefly in epideictic discourse, either praising community values or devaluing the beliefs circulating in other communities. Deliberative rhetors, on the other hand, risk becoming outsiders to a community because they must, of necessity, advocate attention to discontinuity or difference. Whether they persuade or not depends upon the density with which the community's beliefs are articulated with one another and upon the degree to which the system resonates for believers.

Every party to a deliberative rhetorical exchange assumes the risk that his or her beliefs will be altered by the exchange if certain ethical conditions are met within the situation: everyone is accorded the respect due to participants; all parties grant that every other party is an adversary in Mouffe's sense. Of course these are precisely the conditions that fundamentalists (of all kinds) refuse to meet. In the present argumentative climate the burden of seeking change falls unfairly on liberals rather than on apocalyptists. This is so because postmoderns, liberals, and other skeptics can more easily abandon portions of their belief systems than can apocalyptists. A liberal's identity, family relations, friendships, and memberships in academic, religious, and civic communities are not necessarily threatened by a change in belief (to the extent that those beliefs are not bound up with fundamentalisms of any kind). If the ideology of clarity seems to be a truly formidable intellectual edifice, imperviously fortified against rhetorical assault, it also entails a serious rhetorical lack or limit: reluctance either to invent new premises that might attract people who for some reason cannot accept the entire ideology or to qualify existing premises. Because of this all-or-nothing quality, a finite number of people are available for conversion. That is to say, people who cannot accept the entire ideology are not among the potential converts. Academic scholars who study apocalyptist culture sometimes note that their own immersion in this culture did not result in their conversion. Vincent Crapanzano reports being shaken, but not persuaded, by a fundamentalist's attempt to convert him:

Several Fundamentalists tried to convert me with . . . military tactics. One was Bob Murray, a full-time evangelist in downtown Los Angeles. He had been a gang leader in one of the Los Angeles slums before "becoming a Christian." Listening to him, I began to see a parallel between the violence of his past and that of his present militancy. Finally I just fled. I had been interviewing him when he suddenly and quite rudely interrupted me. "Let me just ask you one question," he said. "Have you received the baptism of the Holy Spirit?" That was the beginning.

Systematically, relentlessly (mercilessly, I kept thinking to myself), he proceeded as best he could—and his best was good—to expose the errors in my thinking, to declare my view of the world an enormous, Godless defense, and to chip away at it, punctuating his attacks with biblical quotation, prayer, and the demand that we pray together. He tried to shame me into accepting any one of a number of his presuppositions, for then we would share a common ground that would lead, God willing, to my conversion. He caught me off guard and offered me no escape for more than four hours. (83)

Scholars who themselves profess religious belief are as likely to remark on the intellectual differences between Christian fundamentalism and other sorts of religious belief as are secular historians and social scientists (Frykholm 10; Harding, *Book* 33–60; Strozier 18–19). All of which is to say that anyone who is not a fundamentalist is willing to entertain difference, to live with it, so to speak. Such people are more versatile argumentatively; they are more comfortable inventing new arguments to fit changed circumstances; adapting to the beliefs of audiences; and resisting persuasion to beliefs that seem to them to be incoherent, misguided, or ethically repellant. That is why skeptics, postmodernists, liberals, and progressives must take up the argumentative burden imposed by the present cultural situation.

Some Proffers toward In(ter)vention

Fish insists, correctly, that a "theory of change" is not available because "engines of change" are thoroughly contextualized, firmly located with the beliefs and practices of specific communities (*Doing* 150, 153). If he means *theory* in a representational rather than a productive sense, I must agree. If theory is taken to be a generalization about performances, however, perhaps it is possible to name strategies and tactics that may be of use in some situations. Ancient rhetors developed hundreds of specific tactics for inventing appeals to desire, values, and *pathos,* and I will not rehearse them here.[3] But I will name a few rhetorical strategies that may be of use in contemporary civic arenas. The suggestions forwarded here run against the grain of liberal common sense about argument. But as I hope I have shown, the common sense is no longer effective.

What is requisite first of all is for rhetors to be heard, for attention to be paid. Story is, perhaps, the most efficient means of garnering attention. I use this term here in the ancient rhetorical sense, where it refers to some exemplary narrative, historical or fictional, that makes a point by illustration or comparison (Aristotle, *Rhetoric* II.20). Aristotle says that examples are effective because they serve as witnesses. Coincidently or not, *witnessing* is the term used by Christian fundamentalists to designate conversion attempts. The telling of exemplary stories is a common tactic during such attempts. Susan Harding recounts an afternoon spent with a persuasive preacher who witnessed to her chiefly by telling stories about the aimless and meaningless life he led before his own conversion. She writes: "Campbell was ostensibly describing himself here, but because he had put me in his narrative in his place, he was also describing me. Indeed, he was refashioning me" (*Book* 44). Wayne Booth, reminiscing about his childhood subscription to Mormonism, notices the abundance and power of stories—about family, about neighbors, about the founders of the religion—that tie believers to the belief system. He writes:

In our monthly testimony meetings, when someone wanted to express why the Church was the only true Church, the testimony was almost never in the form of doctrinal argument; it was always a story: "I believe that the Lord Jesus Christ and God the Father appeared to Joseph Smith in the Sacred Grove and gave unto him the power to translate the gold plates that are the Book of Mormon, which I know to be the true word of God." Or: "I thank our Father in Heaven for the miracle I experienced on January 30, 1910, when I was dying of a mysterious illness. The elders came and laid their hands upon my head and they gave unto me a blessing, and the illness was instantaneously lifted from me. At that moment I knew with a certainty I had never known before that . . ." Or: "Just before my fifteenth birthday, thirty years ago, in this very meeting house, Sister Ashby was taken with the spirit and spoke in tongues, and Sister Anderson was given the power to translate what the spirit had spoken." ("Rhetoric" 368)

For Booth experiences relayed in oft-told stories "were real for me, often realer than my memory of what had happened the day before" ("Rhetoric" 368). I think we overlook how often all of us use stories as means of persuasion. For example, we attempt to convince a colleague to persist or desist in some practice or behavior by telling her the story of another colleague who came to a good or bad end by behaving in a similar way.

Perhaps the most persuasive stories in a polity are its myths. Conservative Christian activists know this, and that's why they have written Calvinist Christianity into the story of the founding of the United States. Those of us who want to preserve a space for secular negotiation and discussion would do well to construct and tell exemplary stories about America's founding that serve those purposes. It is often said of liberal rhetors that they are policy wonks who lack "an emotionally compelling vision" (Hardisty 32). This is unfortunate because a liberal vision lies close to hand in the history of America's Constitution and its progressive revisions toward inclusion. In my opinion liberals ought to tell stories from that history, and tell them often. Those who are concerned about voting irregularities would do well to compose vivid historical conjectures about the days when literacy tests were the norm or when women were imprisoned and force-fed because they demonstrated against their exclusion from the franchise.

Conjecture is closely related to story, differing only in that it need not entail a narrative. Liberals often ask of conservative Christian activists: what do they want? A more useful first question for those who oppose the political agenda of the Christian Right might be: what do we want? Liberals and progressives ought to articulate their political desires and construct vivid conjectures that illustrate this desired future. Pierre Bourdieu argues that "specifically political action" is possible; this action "aims to produce and impose representations (mental, verbal, visual or theatrical) of the social world which may be capable of acting on this world" (*Language* 127). Subversive representations construct a "counterposing . . . paradoxical pre-vision, a utopia, a project or programme, to the ordinary vision which apprehends the social world as a natural world" (*Language* 128). This pre-vision, or pre-diction, "aims to bring about what it utters." It follows that liberal and leftist rhetors should not only tell audiences that they support universal health care; they should depict the world as it would exist with this policy in place, and they should depict it with all the *pathos* and compelling detail they can muster.

A rhetor who wants to alter beliefs has to arouse an affective response—to get attention. A rhetorical appeal to a belief may arouse or intensify an emotional response if it either confirms or denies some element of the targeted belief system. (When a rhetor invents and forwards a position that is new to a community, the novelty can arouse passion only if it counters some belief already in place or if the community in question gets excited about new ideas.) Confirmation may not be of much use in deliberative rhetoric, and it may in fact be impossible if there is no common ground between the rhetor and a hostile or indifferent audience. If confirmation is available, its use may arouse satisfaction in an audience, and it may enhance a rhetor's *ethos* as well. When a rhetor appeals to beliefs that are already in place in a community, her appeal will set off a chain of ideologic. Emotional response is likely to be warm when her appeal confirms community belief—that is, if she engages in the form of epideictic rhetoric known as encomium, or if, like Rush Limbaugh, she belittles or criticizes countering beliefs, thus reaffirming community wisdom. Her proposition will arouse confidence, benevolence, joy, perhaps even love. If on the other hand she champions a countering belief with sufficient force or frequency so as to be noticed by the community, her position will provoke anger and fear, perhaps even hatred. But her audience is paying attention.

Rhetors cannot afford to ignore the values held by those whose beliefs they wish to change. But liberals and progressives who want to convince others to accept their values first need to grasp that equality, freedom, tolerance, and the rest are also values. That is to say, the importance accorded to these values derives from their privileged position within an economy of belief, an economy that is demonstrably not shared by conservative Christians for whom the privilege granted in liberal thought to freedom of conscience, say, emphatically does not go without saying. Liberals and progressives have to admit, finally, that they too are pursuing a civic vision that values some character traits over others if they want to engage fruitfully in argumentative exchange. They also need to figure out how these values articulate with policy recommendations. When they advocate that civil unions or marriage be available to gays, for example, liberals and progressives need to make clear both to themselves and to opponents that they are in this case applying the value of equality before the law, a value that is at least implicit in the Constitution and that has achieved certain legal rights for other groups, rights that are now taken for granted in most quarters of America.

At least two routes are available in this regard, always recognizing that circumstances may render either of these inappropriate and hence ineffective. One option is to demonstrate the superiority of alternative values. This approach is very difficult, particularly when values are imbricated with a densely articulated and resonant ideology. Frankly it is hard to imagine a set of values that might successfully counter the importance of family, God, and nation to those who take them to be universal and nonnegotiable. However, these values are fairly narrowly defined within that belief system, and they can be rewritten. Family, for example, can be reconstructed to include groups of committed relatives or friends who share a home. And there are other values that many people hold, some of which are explicitly Christian and which may thus be persuasive to apocalyptists: loving one's neighbor; helping those who are hungry, ill, or infirm, and so on. Enlightenment values include the rule of law and advocacy of justice. Values such as these can be forwarded and exemplified as forcefully as possible.

A second route is to demonstrate the contingency of given values or sets of values by locating them in space and time, thus destabilizing the system of belief in which these same values are taken to be noncontingent. This is the route taken by postmodern skepticism, and, admittedly, this is not an easy task either. But it can be done. Legal theorist Didi Herman read hundreds of pages of *Christianity Today* in order to distill its authors' evaluation of homosexuality over a period of forty years (25). To no one's surprise she discovered that in this discourse homosexuality is treated as a sin (69). Within the economy of Christian thought this identification constructs homosexual practices as offenses against God. Knowing this, Herman put herself and her readers in a position to disarticulate this evaluation, to rearticulate homosexual practices within some other discursive economy where they can be valued differently. That is to say, Herman's intellectual work produced a path, opened a way, for invention. Rhetors have attempted to exploit the Christian language of love as a means of recontextualizing fundamentalist attitudes about homosexuals, but this strategy has been fairly effectively countered by a commonplace ("Love the sinner; hate the sin") that reiterates and reinforces the dominant reading. Nonetheless, love is a central value in Christianity. Taking this tack a rhetor might be able to demonstrate the hateful effects of defining homosexuality as sin. Rhetors could also deploy the economy of nature, arguing that since homosexual practices are not a choice they cannot be sinful (of course this approach risks essentialism). In all these instances the very deployment of a different vocabulary begins the work of recontextualization, thus demonstrating the contingency of the devaluation of homosexuality within conservative Christian discourse.

A final suggestion involves disarticulating a particular belief from the others with which it is articulated. This strategy lies closest to liberal reasoning; the difference is that it articulates beliefs or values from one ideology with those of another. Some exemplary questions: If abortion is murder, doesn't murder also occur when a woman is forced by the state to bear a child to term if doing so will end her life? Isn't capital punishment also murder by the state? Isn't war the murder of innocents just as abortion is claimed to be? To disarticulate ideologic requires discernment and skill, and the success of this strategy very much depends on the relations between rhetors and audiences because it requires time and patience from both parties.

I end with the hope that my readers will find, or open, many more paths of invention than I have been able to name here.

NOTES

Chapter 1. On (Not) Arguing about Religion and Politics

1. I am aware that this statement has a certain "well-duh" quality about it, particularly since the 2004 election. But Americans seem to have difficulty naming this antagonistic relation as a source of our refusal to argue with one another, in part because the connection of religion to politics is notoriously off-limits as a topic of conversation. Articulating the precise points of conflict between liberalism and Christian fundamentalism is complicated by the fact that liberalism has recently been reduced to a caricature that papers over the truly deep implication of American thought with Enlightenment liberalism. Moreover, while most Americans are Christians, and while many are aware of the general outlines of the apocalyptist account of the end of the world, the more arcane aspects of the apocalyptist theology that motivates conservative Christian activism, as well as its implications for American democracy, remain relatively well hidden from view.

I hope it is clear that this book is not about the so-called culture wars. I am trying, rather, to find ways to negotiate past the ideological differences that seem to be stifling civic conversation. Conflicts between religion and politics are not new in American history, and in some respects the current discursive situation is an instance of a pattern that dates at least to America's founding. See Morone.

2. For Laclau and Mouffe's discussion see *Hegemony* 134–45. I return to the notion of hegemony and its relation to ideology in chapter 3.

3. See Arblaster for a history of liberalism, and see chapters 2 and 6 of this book for discussions of liberal rhetorical theory. The bibliography on liberalism is enormous. Here I can only point to some of its best-known theorists: Jürgen Habermas, John Rawls, and (arguably) Richard Rorty. Liberalism has been found wanting by conservatives, of course, but it has also been challenged by communitarians (see Frazer and Lacey), feminists (Hirschmann; Pateman), and postmodernists (for example, Connolly, *Why I Am Not*).

4. The study, called the American Religious Identification Survey 2001, or ARIS, was conducted by the Graduate Center at CUNY. Jacoby discusses its results, available at http://www.religioustolerance.org.

5. The definitions of *fundamentalism* and *evangelicalism* are contested by historians of religion. See Ammerman, "North American"; Marsden; and Christian Smith, *American*. As I point out in the text, one may profess either fundamentalism or evangelicalism without accepting apocalyptism. But Nancy Ammerman claims that belief in biblical inerrancy and millennial dispensationalism is definitive of fundamentalist Christianity ("North American" 15–17). If she is correct, apocalyptism and fundamentalism coincide. However, I reiterate that some Christian fundamentalists may not be apocalyptists, and many people who accept apocalyptic narratives are not practicing Christians (Quinby, *Anti-Apocalypse;* Wojcik).

6. To be saved, one must have a personal experience of Christ (see chapter 4). I borrow the terms *apocalyptism* and *apocalyptist* from historian Norman Cohn in preference to the even more tongue-twisting *apocalypticism* and *apocalypticist*. Here *apocalyptism* is meant to refer to a specific kind of end-times belief—that is, millennialist dispensationalism—and so I reserve the term *apocalyptic* for references to secular visions of world-ending catastrophes, as well as those conjectured by non-Christian religious traditions (see chapter 4). See Cohn, *Cosmos* for the archaic and ancient histories of apocalyptic idealism. See Cohn, *Pursuit;* Kyle; and Damian Thompson for histories of apocalyptism during the Common Era. See Paul Boyer for an account of American apocalyptism. See Quinby, *Anti-Apocalypse;* and Wojcik for accounts of secular apocalyptic belief.

7. See http://www.washingtonpost.com, Nov. 8, 2004.

8. I define *super-patriotism* as a variety of American nationalism that brooks no dissent from national policy, particularly during periods of national crisis. That is to say, super-patriotism is a fundamentalist nationalism insofar as super-patriots are given to denigrating those who oppose their beliefs, as in the incident recounted at the beginning of this chapter. It is tempting to argue a stronger case, that super-patriotism interprets difference as antagonism; read this way it is an attempt to articulate a coherent and unassailable American identity, to police the boundaries of "us" so rigorously that citizens who dissent can be read as threats to American hegemony. This reading explains the association of protestors with Saddam Hussein, as well as accusations that liberals are "soft on terrorism." For a history of American patriotism see Cecilia O'Leary.

9. I am not promulgating a binarist argument in this book. I treat inclusivity and exclusivity as existing on a range of ethical possibilities, and I realize that there are situations in which exclusivity is to be preferred. Because evaluation is always located, in context, anything can become a value in relation to anything else. See Herrnstein Smith, *Contingencies;* and chapter 3 of this book. I do not want

my preference for an inclusive politics to be read as support for liberal pluralism, which is itself exclusive (see chapter 2).

10. On June 18, 2004, the blog "Orcinus" reprinted examples of hateful commentary circulating on the Web and in the mainstream media (http://www. dneiwert.blogspot.com). Orcinus is a liberal blog, and so its examples are from right-wing discourse. The style of argument reprinted below is not untypical of right-wing Web sites such as FreeRepublic.com. Among the more virulent comments collected on "Orcinus" were these:

> "I hate all you f*ing Democrats. You f*ng deserve to be die. Hopefully we can kill the f*ing bunch of you soon."

> "Fuckin Leftist traitors break the law and think they should get away with it?! FUCK YOU YA GODDAMN LEFTIST PUKES AND DON'T EVEN THINK OF FUCKING WITH FREE REPUBLIC MOTHERFUCKERS! WE WILL BEAT YOU DOWN IN THE STREETS NEXT FALL!!!!"

> "If I see you or any of your comrades from Dem Underground I will kick the living shit out of you you filthy faggotcunt traitor."

> "Do not identify yourself as leftist out on the street you piece of shit or you will be beaten unconscious you goddam enemy of america!!!!!"

Expurgated and more modulated versions of this animosity can be heard daily from the likes of Rush Limbaugh, Bill O'Reilly, and Michael Savage. The comments demonstrate the sexism and homophobia that circulate in some conservative circles. The frequency with which references to homosexuality ("faggotcunt," "suck Saddam's dick!") appear in scatological diatribes directed against the Left suggests to me that the men who use such language are threatened by loosening gender boundaries.

Leftists can also resort to potentially dangerous practices. On July 1, 2004, a comment was posted to "Eschaton," a popular left-wing blog, claiming that James Dobson's Focus on the Family had printed the home address of filmmaker Michael Moore in its newsletter (http://www.atrios.blogspot.com). I watched astonished as the phone number of Focus on the Family was posted to the thread and posters reported making repeated calls to its office, speed-dialing the number. Most recounted polite conversations with those who answered their calls. Eventually, though, someone posted Dobson's home address, thus performing exactly the same gesture deplored at the beginning of the thread.

11. That is to say, Christian fundamentalists do not accept the liberal-scientific principle of objectivity, which assumes that people can remain neutral toward information and events. See Moffett for an extended discussion of this feature of Christian fundamentalist belief.

12. Jürgen Habermas is of course the best-known contemporary theorist and defender of the public sphere. Its critics have pointed out that the liberal notion of

a public sphere to which all citizens have equal access is a fantasy. See, for example, Warner, *Publics*.

Chapter 2. Speaking of Rhetoric

1. Invention was the first of five canons of ancient rhetorics (the others are arrangement, style, memory, and delivery) because it was studied prior to the other canons, but it was also first in the sense of "primary." Classical rhetoricians (500–323 BCE) devoted more attention to invention than to any other canon, including style. Rhetoricians did not become preoccupied with style until the Hellenistic and Roman periods. For general histories of rhetoric in the West see Conley, *Rhetoric;* Kennedy, *Classical* and *Comparative;* and Vickers. For histories of Greek rhetoric see Enos, *Greek;* and Kennedy, *Art of Persuasion* and *Greek.* For histories of Roman rhetoric see Enos, *Roman;* and Kennedy, *Art of Rhetoric.* For an account of ancient Greek and Roman rhetorical theories see Poulakos and Poulakos.

2. For histories and discussions of ancient notions of stasis see Heath; Nadeau. For a discussion and demonstrations of the contemporary usefulness of stasis see Crowley and Hawhee.

3. An *enthymeme* is a rhetorical deductive argument. It differs from arguments in logic insofar as its premises need not be true; they need only be accepted by the relevant community. For Aristotle's formulation see *Rhetoric* I.ii.1357a; for scholarship on the *enthymeme* see Bitzer; Conley, "Enthymeme"; and Poster. For a bibliography of sources see Hood. I discuss *enthymemes* further in chapters 3 and 6.

4. There is an exception to this claim: Elaine Scarry argues that the point of extreme torture is to alter the victim's subjectivity and hence erase the possibility of resistance. Her analysis suggests, then, that extreme torture can achieve persuasion: under its influence victims actually acquire a different set of beliefs.

5. Feminists and others argue that submission to law works violence on those who find themselves in disagreement with it (for example, Brown; Cornell, *Heart;* Fish, *Imaginary;* Patricia Williams). There is ample evidence to suggest that laws discriminate on the basis of class, race, gender, sexuality, and other differences. For a meditation on this reality see chapter 2 of Connolly, *Ethos.* See Jensen for an analysis of violence done by ideology. In *The Will to Violence* Susanne Kappeler argues that the opposition subject/object, characteristic of Western culture, actually produces violence. But see, on the other hand, Judith Butler's argument that a distinction must be maintained between hurtful language and violent action, at least in law (*Excitable*).

6. See Cicero, *De Inventione* I.xv. See Quintilian's *Institutes* (XII.x) for thorough discussions of the influence of location and situation on choice of an appropriate rhetorical appeal.

7. Booth continues to struggle with the paradoxes thrown up by liberal rhetorical theory. In a more recent essay on Mormon fundamentalism, for example,

he puzzles through his inability to accept any longer the religious mythology to which he subscribed as a young man ("Rhetoric").

8. I make no other claim than compatibility for the relation of ancient rhetorics and postmodern thought. See Billig, *Arguing* for an attempt to reinvigorate social psychology by means of a reading of ancient rhetorical theory. Billig's agenda is not explicitly postmodern, however.

9. For a debate about the viability of reclaiming very old vocabularies for postmodern use see Schiappa, "Neo-Sophistic"; and Poulakos. Seen from Schiappa's position, my wrenching of concepts out of their specific historical situations for use in another is among the most offensive tactics in a *bricoleur*'s satchel. But see Jarratt for an elegant example of this approach. I am aware that danger inheres in the practice of yoking terminology borrowed from theorists working in disparate fields. A term such as *the symbolic,* for example, carries a specific theoretical resonance within Lacanian psychoanalysis such that it cannot easily be reconciled with Bourdieu's use of the term *habitus* within his own theoretical analytic. When I exploit the work of contemporary theorists, considering their relations with one another and with that of ancient rhetoricians, I try to remain cognizant of historical difference and of the political and ethical risks entailed in forgetting the politics of the spatial and temporal milieu in which each theoretical construct was invented.

10. John Leanos, an artist who teaches at my university, created a poster in homage to Pat Tillman—who played football for Arizona State and for the Arizona Cardinals before he was killed by friendly fire in Afghanistan. The poster was met with shrieks of outrage and torn down from its initial display in a public space. The artist himself received a series of hateful, obscene, and racist e-mails, including several death threats. In a talk given to colleagues and students Leanos explained that his effort was created out of respect for the dead man, drawing on the artistic tradition of *los muertes.* He pointed out that even though the Cardinals and the university circulate Tillman's image for profit, there have been no calls for censorship of this use. That is to say, some people and institutions can make some arguments at some times and in some places; others may not.

11. Stanley Fish is the rhetorical theorist par excellence of the finitude of available forces. See, for starters, "Going Down the Anti-Formalist Road," in which Fish characterizes the antifoundationalist "denial of independent constraints" as nonetheless existing in "a world where the brakes—in the form of the imperatives, urgencies, and prohibitions that come along with any point of view (and being in a point of view is not something one can avoid)—are always and already on" (*Doing* 12).

12. Altemeyer's findings suggest that relative openness to persuasion depends on psychological factors constructed by a life history. For the argument that strict or abusive child-rearing practices can produce authoritarian adults see Greven; and Milburn and Conrad.

Chapter 3. Belief and Passionate Commitment

1. See http://www.whitehouse.gov./news/releases/2001/09/20010913-7.html. Four years later Bush continues to associate bin Laden and his followers with evil; see http://www.whitehouse.gov./news/releases/2005/10/20051006-3.html.

2. As I argue in chapter 2, in liberal thought observations and perceptions are treated as evidence that is then manipulated by means of reason. Because it begins with empirical evidence, liberal reasoning is a skepticism. For a more detailed explanation of the nature of liberal skepticism see Popkin and Stroll; and chapter 6.

3. Raymond Williams provides a useful historical synopsis of uses of the term *ideology* in *Keywords*. Although the term's use was inaugurated by French *philosophes* during the Enlightenment, for rhetoricians the most useful scholarship on ideology emanates from Marx and neo-Marxist thinkers: Althusser, Gramsci, Williams, Hall, Jameson, and others. See McKerrow. Because Marx focused on the productive nature of discursive systems, he and his followers were able to develop quite useful ways of thinking about collective belief, as opposed to liberal thinkers who privilege the inventive potential of individuals and who must, therefore, look for the sources of invention and belief in the psyches of individuals.

4. For discussions of ancient thought about conjecture and demonstrations of its uses see chapters 1, 3, and 4 in Crowley and Hawhee.

5. Herrnstein Smith is not claiming that belief and action are the same thing, nor am I. Action reinforces belief, and the acquisition and maintenance of belief are enhanced by action. Nevertheless, there is a difference between believing that war protestors are misguided fools and opening fire on an antiwar demonstration. It is crucial that a distinction between speech and action be maintained in law, as Judith Butler powerfully demonstrates in *Excitable Speech*. I maintain a distinction—or better, a fold or mediation—between belief and action on similar grounds. Confusion arises when one associates bodily movements with belief or speech because of the continuing influence of the old body/mind dichotomy, which, when applied to belief and action, renders the latter "mindless." As we shall see, this distinction requires radical rethinking.

My citations of Herrnstein Smith (and Fish, for that matter) signal that my analyses of belief resonate with those made by neopragmatists. Pragmatism was influentially articulated by William James, following Pierce, during the early twentieth century. The subtitle of James's *Pragmatism* links it to "old ways of thinking." Contemporary students of neopragmatism also include Steven Mailloux and Cornel West.

6. The notion of identity became problematic within postmodern and postcolonial scholarship during the 1980s because it risked association with the liberal humanist self and because it authorized so-called identity politics. As its critics pointed out, identity politics attempted to extend the liberal notion of subjectivity to groups, thus frustrating the postmodern sense of difference as a reflexive

relation. See Fuss. I assume here that an identity is not the same as an individual. Identities are constructed by and within the *habitus,* and their constructions are always in flux as a result of their reflexive relationship to environments. Those who require the authority of science as backing for such a reading can look to the work of Antonio Damasio, who defines a "self" as "a perpetually recreated neurobiological state" (*Descartes'* 100). The perpetual re-creation occurs in reaction to or consort with successive encounters with environments.

7. See Damasio, *Descartes', Feeling,* and *Looking;* Frijda, Manstead, and Beam; and LeDoux, *Emotional* and *Synaptic.* Anthropologists have also weighed in on the role played by emotion in cognition and belief: see, for instance, Mithen; and Pascal Boyer.

8. Teresa Brennan reviews and discusses traditional uses of this terminology in *The Transmission of Affect* (3–9). See Sara Ahmed for a valuable study of rhetorical uses of emotions. Rei Terada notes that attempts to distinguish between emotions and passions frequently serve a desire to preserve the liberal subject (5). In the present theoretical milieu appeals to the body can still invite a charge of biological determinism. See Eve Sedgwick for a persuasive response to this charge (108–9). Damasio develops a reflexive theory of cognition, and of the self, that evades both biological and cultural determinism by effectively collapsing the nature/nurture distinction into a feedback loop (*Descartes'* 226–44). Books written for popular consumption about the hardwiring of belief should be read warily because they do lapse into determinism. Robert Wright's *The Moral Animal,* for example, makes tenuous and sometimes startlingly specific connections between emotional hardwiring and features of the *habitus,* such as gender roles, that are obviously constructions of history and culture.

9. Whether prior beliefs stem from experience or ideology is irrelevant because this model posits a reflexive, mutually constructive relationship between belief and experience. The notion of experience has a complex history in modern philosophical and rhetorical thought. For Locke and other modernist thinkers sensory perceptions constitute experience, which is in turn the gateway to reason. Hence experience is an important component in constructions of the liberal subject. Alongside Rei Terada, I argue that postmodern rejection of that subject does not require us to reject the notion of experience. Terada demonstrates that, for Derrida, experience moves much as textuality does—that is, experience is lived difference. It consists in perceptions and memories that are constructed by repetition-with-alterity (45). Experience includes emotion and affect. To say that we experience lived-in movements of difference is not to imply that anyone is necessarily a liberal subject. To the contrary, this definition of experience emphasizes bodily ways of knowing and believing of which modern thought is very suspicious.

10. My citation of Aristotle is not meant to essentialize emotional response. Neuroscientists and psychologists who study emotion agree that emotions are constructed and structured by bodies, environments, and the *habitus* in a constantly

reflexive interaction. Nothing in this model implies that emotional responses are free of cultural restraint. Aristotle's account of anger and other emotions is contingent but perhaps still useful, always allowing for the vast differentiating stretches of time and space that have intervened between the production of his texts and our readings of them.

11. People of my generation are aware that during this period student-faculty confrontations were often accompanied by the threat of force or the use of violence. Tellingly, given his liberal sympathies, Booth attributes the impasse to everyone's "loss of faith" in reasoning about values (*Modern* 7). In other words, he admits that "you gotta believe" in reason's efficacy before you will want to use it. In this early work his solution to the difficulty—a rhetoric of assent—does not differ very much from contemporary liberal proposals for the achievement of reciprocal understanding such as that offered by Guttman and Thompson.

12. This aspect of Lacan's theory is troubling because it establishes a formidable black hole at the center of human being. It is hard to rationalize activism, or much of anything else, from lack as a starting point. Deleuze and Guattari take Lacan to task on this point in *Anti-Oedipus* (25–35). They argue that his introduction of this "Great Other" into his theory reinscribes it in the very modes of thought from which Lacan tried to escape. In the spirit of *bricolage* I put Lacan's thought to use while refusing to adopt his positioning of absolute absence at the heart of desire.

13. Perhaps I should point out that when Zizek refers to "positive objects in reality" here he is not referring to Lacan's notion of the Real, although in strict Lacanian terms fantasies about objects such as strawberry cake can and do perform imitations or substitutions of desire for the unrealizable Real.

14. Of course the fantasies addressed by psychotherapy participate in the symbolic as well; psychotherapy is called for when an individual's imaginary cannot adjust satisfactorily to the demands of the symbolic.

Chapter 4. Apocalyptism

1. See, for example, a statement concerning the *Left Behind* novels issued by the Catholic bishops of Illinois and published in the *Catholic Post*, a newspaper serving the diocese of Peoria (http://www.cdop.org, accessed June 23, 2003). According to the bishops, a serious doctrinal difference is at issue: "Overall, these books reinforce an unhealthy and immature belief in a harshly judgmental God whose mercy we earn by good behavior." However, some Catholics now accept a fundamentalist take on apocalyptism (Paul Boyer 260–61; Dinges 120; Wojcik). Gary DeMar, a conservative Christian who is a reconstructionist and hence postmillennarian, has also expressed reservations about the theology advanced by the *Left Behind* series (Frykholm 176). Amy Frykholm's *Rapture Culture* is an informative study of responses to these novels by readers and journalists.

2. See Bawer for an impassioned discussion of the differing ethics of liberal and fundamentalist Christian belief and the theological effects of apocalyptism.

3. Prophecy interpreters are equally insensitive to the difference between Jewish religious practice and Jewish ethnicity. Much less do they distinguish between Jews and Israelis. Apocalyptists are conflicted about the important role played by "Jews" in end-time scenarios because many buy into the anti-Semitism that has tainted Christian belief, consciously or not, at least since the early Middle Ages (Armstrong; Cohn, *Warrant*). Strozier, for instance, cites a fundamentalist author who believes that the Nazis were agents of God insofar as they hastened the foundation of Israel by means of the Holocaust (197). As we shall see, anti-Semitism is woven into dispensationalism, which blames Jews for the failure of the Second Coming to occur soon after Christ's death. In order to hasten this event born-again Christians continually plot and fund schemes to rebuild the Temple, disregarding the fact that an important Islamic site of worship is also located on the Temple Mount. This meddling doubles the risk of violent confrontation as fundamentalists from three religions zealously monitor events occurring on that small piece of land. See Gorenberg.

4. Hence premillennialist belief in a "secret rapture" entails not one but two Second Comings (Stephen O'Leary 138). In a typical move LaHaye and Jenkins turn this apparent contradiction into an occasion for further interpretation: "Since we know there are no contradictions in the Word of God, our Lord must be telling us something here. Most scholars who take the Bible literally wherever possible believe He is talking about one 'coming' in two stages" (*Are We Living* 100).

5. All of the theological points made in this paragraph are taken from the second chapter of James Barr's *Fundamentalism*. I have not corrected Barr's sexist pronouns because nearly all fundamentalist theologians, pastors, and prophecy interpreters are men. Fundamentalist women are generally barred from creating doctrine, although they are crucial to the maintenance of churches and to conservative Christian political activism (Frykholm 98–99; Harding, *Book* 155). In her study of readers of *Left Behind* Ann Frykholm points out that female characters are stereotyped as either submissive helpmates (Chloe) or wanton whores (Hannah). Homosexual characters are caricatured as objects of derision and depicted as more susceptible to evil than are straights (the characterization of Guy Brod is a good example).

6. A woman who is divorced, for example, may find that her fellow churchgoers question the status of her eternal salvation because of her inability to succeed at marriage. In conservative Christian circles women are charged with keeping marriages together. If such unions dissolve they are thought to do so because wives could not keep their husbands' urges under control. See Ammerman, *Bible;* and Frykholm.

7. See http://www.CBN.com, Sept. 13, 2001.

8. See LaHaye's *The Merciful God of Prophecy, Revelation Unveiled,* and *The Rapture,* along with LaHaye and Jenkins's *Are We Living in the End Times?*

9. If true, this comment suggests that *Left Behind* has touched some of the unchurched, since no affiliated fundamentalist Christian would be ignorant of the many institutionally authorized tools that are available to assist those who want to read Revelation "correctly." Prominent among these tools is the *Scofield Reference Bible* (1909). For background on Scofield and his biblical commentary see Balmer, *Blessed* 52, 125 n. 27; Barr; Paul Boyer; and Marsden, *Fundamentalism.* A search for "end time" on the Internet uncovers a host of Web sites selling interpretations of the last events, along with brightly colored charts indicating the relation of these events to one another and to the bits of Scripture alleged to undergird the truth of the entire apocalyptist narrative.

10. Jenkins's name appears on title pages along with LaHaye's, but this sample is entirely typical of LaHaye's reduction of Schaeffer's more complex and nuanced histories. For comparative purposes see Schaeffer's *How Should We Then Live?*

11. Paul Boyer explains that during the Great Awakening America's "spiritual history" was explained apocalyptically by Jonathan Edwards and other preachers (72). Interestingly enough "God's prophetic plan" was expounded "in military and political terms," thus paving the way, spiritually, for revolution.

12. See Marsden, *Understanding* 165–68; Marsden, *Fundamentalism* 55–62; Strozier 185–87.

13. This renders it more similar to Catholicism and Judaism than any fundamentalist should like it to be. Harold Bloom recklessly argues that Christian fundamentalism's claim to inerrancy puts it in league with Islamic fundamentalism: "inerrancy for both groups is an unconscious metaphor for the repression of all individuality" (221).

14. See, for example, *Rapture* 33–34; *Are We Living* 101–2. LaHaye is coy about the precise moment at which the Rapture will occur because he knows that an errant prediction can put an end to a prophetic interpreter's credibility, as happened to William Miller in the nineteenth century (*Are We Living* 21–22). Nonetheless, he assures his readers that more prophetic signs are now being fulfilled than at any time in history and that he confidently expects the tribulation to begin within a generation (*Are We Living* 58–61).

15. See Paul Boyer 152–67; and Wojcik 149–58 for informative histories of this association in prophecy literature.

16. Stephen O'Leary reads apocalyptic mythology dramatistically, as enactments of both tragic and comic frames of reference (200–206).

17. I am aware that my argument begs the question at this point—if my avowedly postmodern definition of rhetoric is granted, apocalyptism is excluded by default from the category of "good rhetoric." Here I come up against the limits of my belief system. I have made a good-faith effort to represent apocalyptism and my

response to it, and at the moment I have no other option than to treat it as noncontingent until someone or something convinces me that I am wrong. I must also stay with my postmodern orientation until it no longer works for me or within the community with which I identify. Obviously I am aware of the contingency of my beliefs. So rather than attempting to certify them as truthful or noncontingent I retreat to ethical ground, where the principles of "love your neighbor" and "do no harm" are equally contingent but can be shared by mainstream Christians, liberals, and postmodernists alike. It is from this vantage point that I exclude apocalyptism from the category of "good" rhetoric. Perhaps I should remind readers at this point that the ethical claims I advance in this book concern ideologies rather than people. That is, I adumbrate a *rhetorical* ethic that applies to the invention of public discourse rather than to individuals.

Chapter 5. Ideas Do Have Consequences

1. Kirk and Weaver might now be usefully referred to as "paleoconservatives" to distinguish them from neoconservatives such as Irving Kristol and Paul Wolfowitz, were it not for the fact of Pat Buchanan's usurpation of that title (Hodgson 309–10). Unlike those of Weaver, who was an elitist, Buchanan's politics are populist (Crowley, "When Ideology"; Berlet and Lyons 338–40). His thinking combines the anticorporate aspect of traditionalist conservatism with the moral and social agenda of the Christian Right. Neoconservatism, on the other hand, is an economic and nationalist conservatism, although, as Kristol himself notes, some neoconservatives are also comfortable with the social agenda of the Christian Right (2). While traditionalism of the sort adumbrated by Weaver no longer dominates conservative thought, I posit that it still exerts pressure on neoconservatives insofar as it legitimates a habit of accepting hierarchy as natural and hence inevitable. In accepting this belief neoconservatism appeals to a first principle about the inevitable superiority of elites that resembles the appeal to divine authority made by the religious Right. And when this subscription to hierarchy is combined with the discourses of American nationalism and exceptionalism, it can legitimize rapacious foreign policy initiatives. See Frum and Perle for a particularly startling example of the neoconservative program. For histories and analyses of traditional conservatism see Dunn and Woodward; Nash. For histories of more recent conservatisms see Berlet and Lyons; Diamond, *Roads;* Durham; Hardisty; Hodgson; Edsall and Edsall; and Lind. For the connection between rightist politics and conservative religious belief see Capps; Conway and Spiegelman; Diamond, *Facing, Not by Politics,* and *Spiritual;* Herman; Lienesch; Oldfield; Martin; Melich; Watson; and Wilcox, *God's* and *Onward.*

2. Scholars disagree about how to define the Christian Right. For example, Wilcox characterizes it as "a social movement that attempts to mobilize evangeli-

cal Protestants and other orthodox Christians into conservative political action" (*Onward* 5). Herman, on the other hand, defines the movement in terms of its theology: premillennarianism and biblical inerrancy (12).

3. See Capps for an informative discussion of the effects of this decision at Bob Jones University. There is good reason to suspect that racism, or racialism, informs the work of some Christian political activists. Martin Lee discusses Pat Robertson's ties to the anti-Semitic Liberty Lobby and notes that ex-Klan member David Duke was endorsed by the head of the Louisiana Christian Coalition when he ran for governor of that state (358). While Lee is chiefly interested in the truly radical fringes of right-wing politics, he does remark on the "cross-fertilization of white supremacists and their somewhat less extreme (and far more numerous) religious Right cousins" (360). Other scholars have noticed this tie as well; see the relevant chapters in Berlet and Lyons; Diamond, *Roads;* and Martin, for example. Under Reed's direction the Coalition made overtures to African American Christians in an effort to overcome the taint of racism that tarnishes the movement (Watson 68). Given the long history of racist exclusion practiced by white fundamentalist churches in the South, a history that includes support for slavery and opposition to the civil rights movement of the 1960s, this gesture proved to be too little, too late. Nevertheless, the possibility remains open that African American fundamentalist Christians may discern sufficient ideological affinities with like-minded white Christians to establish political alliances.

4. The letter and list may be found at http://www.cc.org.

5. *Jerusalem Post,* Oct. 28, 1983, 3.

6. See http://www.SFGate.com, Aug. 28, 2004.

7. Those who subscribe to conspiracy theory might read this remark as evidence of Bush's complicity in those events. See chapter 6.

8. That this deductive chain is also informed by a patriarchal ideology that values women's lives less than those of yet-to-be-conceived children is not acknowledged by conservative Christian thinkers, who never question their presumption of male supremacy. For scholarly discussions of the implication of conservative Christian thought with patriarchy and masculinism see Bendroth; Brasher; DeBerg; and Griffith.

9. Michael Lienesch unravels this seeming contradiction by noting that for fundamentalist Christians capitalism is both a "moral enterprise" and a "religious endeavor" (109). In this belief system wealth accrues to those who work hard, and the poor have only themselves to blame for their straitened economic status. Because this set of beliefs dates to early American Calvinism, it is not hard to reconcile with traditionalism.

10. I borrow the term *super-rationality* from Jacqueline Rose's discussion of Thatcherism, and I use it here as though *super-rational* works in the same ways that *supernatural* does (*Why War* 59).

11. I generalize my account of conservative Christian social belief from several studies. Those not otherwise cited in this chapter include Berlant; Anna Marie Smith; Warner, "Tongues"; and Wray.

12. Perhaps this is a response to the more general softening of sexual proscription in the culture at large. The high divorce rate among evangelicals may have something to do with this as well. According to research undertaken by the Barna group, a Christian market research company, "Christians are more likely to experience divorce than non-Christians" (Barna Research Online, http://www.barna. org, Dec. 21, 1999). The divorce rate for "nondenominational protestants" was 34 percent, while 27 percent of born-again marriages ended in divorce. The divorce rate among atheists and agnostics was 21 percent.

13. Greven argues that the use of corporal punishment is not authorized in the Bible but stems, rather, from the historical legacy of early American religious belief (52). He connects corporal punishment of children to aggression and violence and suggests that widespread use of this practice may account for the violent character of American culture (196, 203). See also Milburn and Conrad.

14. See Associated Press, Feb. 24, 2004.

15. A footnote to this assertion quotes a passage from a book published by Regnery, a conservative press. Its author, Balint Vazsonyi, is quoted as follows: "All [Greek philosophy, Roman law, the French Enlightenment] were noted, all [Luther, Calvin, Zwingli] played a part, all entered the thought process of America's founders. But the sole book that originated beyond the English Channel, and which they retained in its entirety, was the Bible" (239 n. 8). Clearly this citation does not authorize the much more specific assertion that LaHaye and Noebel make in the text.

16. Despite Article 6, until 1997 the South Carolina state constitution declared that "no person shall be eligible for the office of governor who denies the existence of the Supreme Being" (Silverman 198). In 1990 Herb Silverman, a professor of mathematics and self-professed atheist, ran (unsuccessfully) for governor in order to test the legality of this clause in the state's constitution. He then applied to become a notary public, and he won this right in 1997, when the state supreme court decided that South Carolina's constitution violated Article 6 (Silverman 202).

17. The inflection of American patriotism with Christian symbols and rituals was amply evident in the aftermath of September 11. The House of Representatives voted unanimously that signs reading "God Bless America" were to be posted in public schools (O'Leary and Platt 173). A makeshift monument near the crash scene of flight 93 in Pennsylvania featured wooden angels painted red, white, and blue, and visitors posted signs urging God to bless the heroes who had attempted to disrupt the hijacking. Kintz notes that the addition of "an American God" to nationalism can produce "a patriotism that uses love of country as a weapon" (*Between* 276).

18. The argument about John can be turned into an enthymeme whose relations are valid, as follows: Human behavior is predictable for the most part. For the most part, people who party hard on weekends are late for work on Monday. John partied hard on Sunday, so (the rule of human behavior predicts that) he will be late for work on Monday.

19. Here the connecting premise has to be something like "Bush's presidency is a sign from God because Bush works in accord with God's plan." It may even be "because Bush agrees with me" or "because I believe this to be so." Tautologies like these seem inescapable when the truth of the major premise depends on the presumption of a super-rational deity.

20. Transcript of *This Week,* http://www.ABCnews.com, Nov. 7, 2004.

21. *National Review Online,* http://www.nationalreview.com, Aug. 2, 2001.

22. *New York Times,* Dec. 19, 2004.

Chapter 6. The Truth *Is* Out There

1. The Christian Right is not entirely responsible for this state of affairs of course. Lying and distortion are staples of political discourse. See Bok. See Alterman for studies of presidential lies.

2. The Waxman Report, from which this information is taken, is a study of the curricula of seventeen abstinence-only sex education programs done at the behest of Congressman Henry Waxman. During the week the report was released the American Heritage Foundation released a response charging that Waxman's study was in turn "riddled with errors and inaccuracies" (Webmemo 615, http://www. heritage.org, Dec. 2, 2004).

3. *New York Times Magazine,* Oct. 17, 2004, 51.

4. The quality of testimony is generally certified by the proximity and capability of witnesses. Expert testimony depends on credentials and specialized experience, although conspiracy theorists can go to great lengths to discount expert testimony that contradicts their major premise. The Federal Emergency Management Agency's claim that the towers of the World Trade Center pancaked, for example, is roundly dissed in the conspiracy literature about 9/11. See Hufschmid; Russell.

5. A case in point is the recent abandonment of the "no-757-at-the Pentagon" theory first put forward by Thierry Meyssen. September 11 conspiracy theorists have begun to realize that this claim is so difficult to establish, and so counterintuitive, that it harms their overall argument. See Hoffman.

6. All times given in this chapter are Eastern Standard Time. Times are taken from Paul Thompson and/or *The 9/11 Commission Report,* hereafter cited in the text as "CR." Before I begin my review of 9/11 accounts, I want to echo Dean's reply to Shermer. That is to say, I believe that 9/11 conspiracists believe what they write. And if they don't believe it, they have some motive for promoting interpretations in which they have no faith, a motive that is inaccessible to me and about which

I do not wish to guess. Much less am I concerned here with discerning the truth of the events of 9/11 or of the explanatory accounts that have been constructed concerning them, as though either is possible. As a citizen I care very much about who is responsible for these events, and I fervently hope the perpetrators will one day be brought to justice. But as I argue earlier, truth and reality (whatever that is) are not necessarily connected to either the circulation of belief or the staging of desire.

7. The FEMA report is number 403, entitled "World Trade Center Building Performance Study." It is available at http://www.fema.gov/library/wtcstudy.shtm.

8. Hufschmid thinks that WTC building 7 was the object of the entire exercise (90). This building housed the offices of several banks, but it was also occupied by entities of the federal government, including the CIA. Furthermore, it contained a shelter designed to protect the mayor of New York City during just such an attack as occurred on 9/11.

9. In a startling example Daniel Hopsicker's *Welcome to Terrorland* assembles evidence of CIA involvement with Mohamed Atta and others of the 9/11 hijackers. Hopsicker explores Atta's movements in Florida prior to September 11, and if his research can be trusted, Atta was a slick dresser and something of a party animal. At the very least these findings call into question the assumption that Atta was a fundamentalist Islamist.

10. For example, Chip Berlet's review of Griffin's book for Political Research Associates is typical of the combative tone of such discussions. See http://www. publiceye.org/conspire/conspiracism-911.html. Griffin's response is posted there as well.

11. See http://www.washingtonpost.com, Oct. 12, 2001.

12. See http://www.911research.wtc7.net/pentagon/evidence/index.html. The sites http://www.Killtown.911review.org and http://www.911-strike.com have useful compendia of eyewitness accounts of this event, as well as the crash of flight 93 in Pennsylvania.

13. See http://www.wnd.com, Dec. 27. 2004.

14. I happened to read Tom Clancy's *Debt of Honor* (1994) shortly after I finished writing a draft of this book. The novel concludes with a 747 being flown into the Capitol. It is hard to believe that America's intelligence community had not likewise imagined such a scenario prior to 9/11.

15. See http://www.nytimes.com, Feb. 10, 2005.

16. See http://www.nationalreview.com/robbins/robbins040902.asp, Apr. 9, 2002.

Chapter 7. How Beliefs Change

1. In an essay entitled "Beliefs about Belief" Fish again designates experience and authority as the available persuasive alternatives (*Trouble* 279–84). If I am

reading right, here he participates in a liberal tradition of argument wherein "facts" and "testimony" are treated as the most effective sources of persuasion (Crowley, *Methodical* 1990). Fish might object to this characterization of his position because his take on belief is professedly antifoundational; that is, it is grounded on no general principle, including liberal reason. And Fish does depart from liberalism to the extent that he locates belief in ideology rather than in the psychology of individuals. In an earlier essay called "Change" he argues that change occurs when "interpretive communities" change their interpretive practices; awareness that change has occurred can dawn only after it has happened (*Doing* 140–60). A bumper-sticker theory of change, this: "Change Happens." Barbara Herrnstein Smith dryly remarks that Fish "does not develop an altogether satisfactory alternative account of the dynamics of belief" (*Belief* 166 n. 11). Fish's thinking about belief seems to depend on the limited sort of antifoundationalism I outline in the first chapter of this book. For example, he suggests in "Faith before Reason" that individuals develop a relatively closed system of First Beliefs from which all others depend (*Trouble* 263–75). Also see Olson 78–84.

2. See the accounts in Babinski, and see Christian Smith's meditation on religious doubt (*American*).

3. See Corbett and Connors; Corbett and Eberly; Crowley and Hawhee; and Hauser. Billig, *Arguing;* and Minnich contain critiques of standard argumentative practices that can double as useful catalogues of inventional strategies. George Lakoff has lately become a rhetorician of the special topics of politics: for advice on how to argue with conservatives see his *Don't Think of an Elephant* and *Moral Politics.*

WORKS CITED

Ahmed, Nafeez Mosaddeq. *The War on Freedom: How and Why America Was Attacked September 11, 2001.* Joshua Tree, CA: Tree of Life, 2002.

Ahmed, Sara. *The Cultural Politics of Emotion.* New York: Routledge, 2004.

Alcorn, Marshall. *Changing the Subject in English Class: Discourse and the Constructions of Desire.* Carbondale: Southern Illinois UP, 2002.

Altemeyer, Bob. *The Authoritarian Specter.* Cambridge: Harvard UP, 1996.

Alterman, Eric. *When Presidents Lie: A History of Official Deception and Its Consequences.* New York: Viking Penguin, 2004.

American Religious Identification Survey. New York: Graduate Center, City University of New York, 2001.

Ammerman, Nancy. *Bible Believers: Fundamentalists in the Modern World.* New Brunswick: Rutgers UP, 1987.

———. "North American Protestant Fundamentalism." In *Fundamentalisms Observed.* Ed. Martin Marty and R. Scott Appleby. Vol. 1 of The Fundamentalism Project. Chicago: Chicago UP, 1991.

Arblaster, Anthony. *The Rise and Decline of Western Liberalism.* Oxford: Basil Blackwell, 1984.

Arendt, Hannah. *The Human Condition: A Study of the Central Dilemmas Facing Modern Man.* New York: Doubleday, 1959.

Aristotle. *On Rhetoric: A Theory of Civic Discourse.* Trans. George Kennedy. New York: Oxford UP, 1991.

———. *The Politics.* Trans. T. A. Sinclair. Baltimore: Penguin, 1962.

Armstrong, Karen. *Holy War: The Crusades and Their Impact on Today's World.* New York: Anchor, 1998.

Atwill, Janet. *Rhetoric Reclaimed: Aristotle and the Liberal Arts Tradition.* Ithaca: Cornell UP, 1998.

Babinski, Edward, ed. *Leaving the Fold: Testimonials of Former Fundamentalists.* Amherst, NJ: Prometheus, 1995.

Baldwin, Charles Sears. *Medieval Rhetoric and Poetic Interpreted from Representative Works.* New York: Macmillan, 1928.

Balmer, Randall. *Blessed Assurance: A History of Evangelicalism in America.* Boston: Beacon, 1999.

———. *Mine Eyes Have Seen the Glory: A Journey into the Evangelical Subculture in America.* New York: Oxford UP, 1989.

Bamford, James. *Body of Secrets: Anatomy of the Ultra-Secret National Security Agency.* New York: Anchor, 2002.

———. *A Pretext for War: 9/11, Iraq, and the Abuse of America's Intelligence Agencies.* New York: Anchor, 2005.

Barker, Daniel. "Losing Faith in Faith." In *Leaving the Fold: Testimonials of Former Fundamentalists.* Ed. Edward Babinski. Amherst, NJ: Prometheus, 1995.

Barkun, Michael. *A Culture of Conspiracy: Apocalyptic Visions in Contemporary America.* Berkeley: California UP, 2003.

———. *Religion and the Racist Right: The Origins of the Christian Identity Movement.* Rev. ed. Chapel Hill: North Carolina UP, 1997.

Barr, James. *Fundamentalism.* Philadelphia: Westminster, 1977.

Barron, Bruce. *Heaven on Earth? The Social and Political Agendas of Dominion Theology.* Grand Rapids: Zondervan, 1992.

Barthes, Roland. *Mythologies.* New York: Hill and Wang, 1972.

Bawer, Bruce. *Stealing Jesus: How Fundamentalism Betrays Christianity.* New York: Crown, 1997.

Bendroth, Margaret. *Fundamentalism and Gender, 1875 to the Present.* New Haven: Yale UP, 1993.

Bennett, David. *The Party of Fear: The American Far Right from Nativism to the Militia Movement.* Rev. ed. New York: Vintage, 1995.

Berlant, Lauren. *The Queen of America Goes to Washington City: Essays on Sex and Citizenship.* Durham: Duke UP, 1997.

Berlet, Chip. "Dubious Claims about the 9/11 Attacks." *Political Research Associates,* http://www.publiceye.org/conspire/Post911/dubious_claims.html.

Berlet, Chip, and Matthew Lyons. *Right-Wing Populism in America: Too Close for Comfort.* New York: Guilford, 2000.

Bevilacqua, Vincent. "Vico, Rhetorical Humanism, and the Study Methods of Our Time." *Philosophy and Rhetoric* 18 (1985): 70–83.

Biesecker, Barbara. "Michel Foucault and the Question of Rhetoric." *Philosophy and Rhetoric* 25 (1992): 351–64.

Billig, Michael. *Arguing and Thinking: A Rhetorical Approach to Social Psychology.* 2d ed. Cambridge: Cambridge UP, 1996.

———. *Ideology and Opinions: Studies in Rhetorical Psychology.* London: Sage, 1991.

Bitzer, Lloyd. "Aristotle's Enthymeme Revisited." *Quarterly Journal of Speech* 45 (1959): 399–408.

Bivins, Jason. *The Fracture of Good Order: Christian Anti-Liberalism and the Challenge to American Politics.* Chapel Hill: North Carolina UP, 2003.

Blair, Hugh. *Lectures on Rhetoric and Belles Lettres*. 2 vols. Ed. Harold F. Harding. Carbondale: Southern Illinois UP, 1965.

Bloom, Harold. *The American Religion: The Emergence of the Post-Christian Nation*. New York: Simon and Schuster, 1992.

Blumenthal, Sidney. "Smiting the Infidels." *Salon,* http://www.salon.com, April 20, 2004.

Bok, Sissela. *Lying: Moral Choice in Public and Private Life*. New York: Vintage, 1989.

Boone, Kathleen. *The Bible Tells Them So: The Discourse of Protestant Fundamentalism*. Albany: SUNY UP, 1989.

Booth, Wayne. *The Company We Keep: An Ethics of Fiction*. Berkeley: California UP, 1988.

———. *Critical Understanding: The Powers and Limits of Understanding*. Chicago: Chicago UP, 1979.

———. *Modern Dogma and the Rhetoric of Assent*. Chicago: Chicago UP, 1974.

———. "The Rhetoric of Fundamentalist Conversion Narratives." In *Fundamentalism Comprehended*. Ed. Martin Marty and R. Scott Appleby. Vol. 4 of The Fundamentalist Project. Chicago: Chicago UP, 1995.

Bourdieu, Pierre. *Distinction: A Social Critique of the Judgement of Taste*. Trans. Richard Nice. Cambridge: Harvard UP, 1984.

———. *Language and Symbolic Power*. Trans. Gino Raymond and Matthew Adamson. Cambridge: Harvard UP, 1991.

———. *The Logic of Practice*. Trans. Richard Nice. Palo Alto: Stanford UP, 1990.

———. *Outline of a Theory of Practice*. Trans. Richard Nice. Cambridge: Cambridge UP, 1977.

———. *Pascalian Meditations*. Trans. Richard Nice. Palo Alto: Stanford UP, 2000.

Boyer, Pascal. *Religion Explained: The Evolutionary Origins of Religious Thought*. New York: Basic Books, 2001.

Boyer, Paul. *When Time Shall Be No More: Prophecy Belief in American Culture*. Cambridge: Harvard UP, 1992.

Bracher, Mark. *Lacan, Discourse, and Social Change: A Psychoanalytic Cultural Criticism*. Ithaca: Cornell UP, 1993.

Brasher, Brenda. *Godly Women: Fundamentalism and Female Power*. New Brunswick: Rutgers UP, 1998.

Brennan, Teresa. *The Transmission of Affect*. Ithaca: Cornell UP, 2004.

Briody, Dan. *The Iron Triangle: Inside the Secret World of the Carlyle Group*. Hoboken, NJ: John Wiley and Sons, 2003.

Brown, Wendy. *States of Injury: Power and Freedom in Late Modernity*. Princeton: Princeton UP, 1995.

Burke, Kenneth. *A Rhetoric of Motives*. Berkeley: California UP, 1969.

"Bush Signs Ban on Late-Term Abortion." CNN.com, http://www.cnn.com/2003/ALLPOLITICS/11/05/abortion.ap, November 6, 2003.

Butler, Judith. *Excitable Speech: A Politics of the Performative*. New York: Routledge, 1997.

————. *Gender Trouble: Feminism and the Subversion of Identity.* New York: Routledge, 1990.

————. *Subjects of Desire: Hegelian Reflections in Twentieth-Century France.* New York: Columbia UP, 1987.

Campbell, George. *The Philosophy of Rhetoric.* Ed. Lloyd Bitzer. Carbondale: Southern Illinois UP, 1963.

Campbell, Karlyn Kohrs. *Man Cannot Speak for Her: Key Texts of the Early Feminists.* New York: Praeger, 1989.

Capps, Walter. *The New Religious Right: Piety, Patriotism, and Politics.* Columbia: South Carolina UP, 1990.

Carpenter, Joel. *Revive Us Again: The Reawakening of American Fundamentalism.* New York: Oxford UP, 1997.

Castells, Manuel. *The Power of Identity.* London: Blackwell, 1997.

Cicero, Marcus Tullius. *De Inventione, De Optimo Genere, and Oratorum Topica.* Trans. H. M. Hubbell. Cambridge: Harvard UP, 1968.

————. *De Oratore.* Trans. E. W. Sutton and H. Rackham. Cambridge: Harvard UP, 1976.

Clarke, Richard. *Against All Enemies: Inside America's War on Terror.* New York: Free Press, 2004.

Clarkson, Frederick. *Eternal Hostility: The Struggle between Theocracy and Democracy.* Monroe, ME: Common Courage, 1997.

Clore, Gerald, and Karen Gasper. "Feeling Is Believing: Some Affective Influences on Belief." In *Emotions and Beliefs: How Feelings Influence Thoughts.* Ed. Nico Frijda, Antony Manstead, and Sacha Beam. Cambridge: Cambridge UP, 2000.

Cloud, Dana. "The Triumph of Consolatory Ritual over Deliberation since 9/11." In *Rhetorical Democracy: Discursive Practices of Civic Engagement.* Ed. Gerard Hauser and Amy Grim. Mahwah, NJ: Erlbaum, 2004.

Cohn, Norman. *Cosmos, Chaos, and the World to Come: The Ancient Roots of Apocalyptic Faith.* New Haven: Yale UP, 2001.

————. *The Pursuit of the Millennium.* Fairlawn, NJ: Essential Books, 1970.

————. *Warrant for Genocide: The Myth of the Jewish World-Conspiracy and the Protocols of the Elders of Zion.* Chico, CA: Scholars Press, 1981.

Condit, Celeste. *Decoding Abortion Rhetoric: Communicating Social Change.* Urbana: Illinois UP, 1990.

Condit, Celeste, and John Lucaites. *Crafting Equality: America's Anglo-African Word.* Chicago: Chicago UP, 1993.

Conley, Thomas M. "The Enthymeme in Perspective." *Quarterly Journal of Speech* 70 (1984): 168–87.

————. *Rhetoric in the European Tradition.* Chicago: Chicago UP, 1990.

Connolly, William E. *The Ethos of Pluralization.* Minneapolis: Minnesota UP, 1995.

————. *Why I Am Not a Secularist.* Minneapolis: Minnesota UP, 1999.

Conway, Flo, and Jim Spiegelman. *Holy Terror: The Fundamentalist War on America's Freedoms in Religion, Politics and Our Private Lives.* Garden City, NJ: Doubleday, 1982.

Corbett, Edward P. J., and Robert Connors. *Classical Rhetoric for the Modern Student*. 4th ed. New York: Oxford UP, 1998.

Corbett, Edward P. J., and Rosa A. Eberly. *The Elements of Reasoning*. 2d ed. Boston: Allyn and Bacon, 2000.

Cornell, Drucilla. *At the Heart of Freedom: Feminism, Sex, and Equality*. Princeton: Princeton UP, 1998.

———. *The Imaginary Domain: Abortion, Pornography and Sexual Harassment*. New York: Routledge, 1995.

Cox, Harvey. "The Warring Visions of the Christian Right." *Atlantic Monthly*, November 1995, 59–69.

Crapanzano, Vincent. *Serving the Word: Literalism in America from the Pulpit to the Bench*. New York: New Press, 2000.

Crothers, Lane. *Rage on the Right: The American Militia Movement from Ruby Ridge to Homeland Security*. Lanham, MD: Rowan and Littlefield, 2003.

Crowley, Sharon. *The Methodical Memory*. Carbondale: Southern Illinois UP, 1990.

———. "When Ideology Contaminates Theory: The Case of the Man from Weaverville." *Rhetoric Review* 20 (Spring 2001): 66–91.

Crowley, Sharon, and Debra Hawhee. *Ancient Rhetorics for Contemporary Students*. 3d ed. New York: Longman Pearson, 2003.

Damasio, Anthony. *Descartes' Error: Emotion, Reason, and the Human Brain*. New York: Harper Collins, 1994.

———. *The Feeling of What Happens: Body and Emotion in the Making of Consciousness*. San Diego: Harcourt, 1999.

———. *Looking for Spinoza: Joy, Sorrow, and the Feeling Brain*. Orlando: Harcourt, 2003.

Dean, Jodi. *Aliens in America: Conspiracy Cultures from Outer Space to Cyberspace*. Ithaca: Cornell UP, 1988.

———. "If Anything is Possible." In *Conspiracy Nation: The Politics of Paranoia in Postwar America*. Ed. Peter Knight. New York: New York UP, 2002.

DeBerg, Betty. *Ungodly Women: Gender and the First Wave of American Fundamentalism*. Minneapolis: Fortress, 1990.

Deleuze, Gilles, and Felix Guattari. *Anti-Oedipus: Schizophrenia and Capitalism*. Minneapolis: Minnesota UP, 1983.

De Luca, Kevin. *Image Politics: The New Rhetoric of Environmental Activism*. New York: Guilford, 1999.

Denzler, Brenda. *The Lure of the Edge: Scientific Passions, Religious Beliefs, and the Pursuit of UFOs*. Berkeley: California UP, 2001.

Derrida, Jacques. *Acts of Religion*. Ed. Gil Anidjar. New York: Routledge, 2002.

———. *Limited Inc*. Ed. Gerald Graff. Evanston: Northwestern UP, 1990.

———. *Of Grammatology*. Ed. Gayatri Spivak. Baltimore: Johns Hopkins UP, 1976.

———. *Writing and Difference*. Trans. Alan Bass. Chicago: Chicago UP, 1978.

de Toqueville, Alexis. *Democracy in America*. Trans. George Lawrence. 2 vols. New York: Harper and Row, 1969.

Detwiler, Fritz. *Standing on the Premises of God: The Christian Right's Fight to Redefine America's Schools.* New York: New York UP, 1999.

Diamond, Sara. *Facing the Wrath: Confronting the Right in Dangerous Times.* Monroe, ME: Common Courage, 1996.

———. *Not by Politics Alone: The Enduring Influence of the Christian Right.* New York: Guilford, 1998.

———. *Roads to Dominion: Right-Wing Movements and Political Power in the United States.* New York: Guilford, 1995.

———. *Spiritual Warfare: The Politics of the Christian Right.* Boston: South End, 1989.

Didion, Joan. *Fixed Ideas: America since 9/11.* New York: New York Review of Books, 2003.

Dinges, William. "Roman Catholic Traditionalism and Activist Conservatism in the United States." In *Fundamentalisms Observed.* Ed. Martin Marty and R. Scott Appleby. Vol. 1 of The Fundamentalist Project. Chicago: Chicago UP, 1991.

Dubois, Page. *Torture and Truth.* New York: Routledge, 1991.

Dunn, Charles W., and J. David Woodward. *American Conservatism from Burke to Bush: An Introduction.* Lanham, MD: Madison, 1991.

Durham, Martin. *The Christian Right, the Far Right, and the Boundaries of American Conservatism.* Manchester: Manchester UP, 2000.

Echols, Alice. *Daring to Be Bad: Radical Feminism in America 1967–1975.* Minneapolis: Minnesota UP, 1989.

Edsall, Thomas, and Mary Edsall. *Chain Reaction: The Impact of Race Rights and Taxes on American Politics.* New York: Norton, 1991.

Engel, Pascal, ed. *Believing and Accepting.* Dordrecht: Kluwer, 2000.

Enos, Richard Leo. *Greek Rhetoric before Aristotle.* Prospect Heights, IL: Waveland, 1993.

———. "The Hellenic Rhapsode." *Western Journal of Speech Communication* 41 (1978): 134–43.

———. *Roman Rhetoric: Revolution and the Greek Influence.* Prospect Heights, IL: Waveland, 1995.

Ezekiel, Raphael S. *The Racist Mind: Portraits of American Neo-Nazis and Klansmen.* New York: Penguin, 1995.

Fausto-Sterling, Anne. *Sexing the Body: Gender Politics and the Construction of Sexuality.* New York: Basic Books, 2000.

Fenster, Mark. *Conspiracy Theories: Secrecy and Power in American Culture.* Minneapolis: Minnesota UP, 1999.

Festinger, Leon, Henry Riecken, and Stanley Schachter. "Unfulfilled Prophecies and Disappointed Messiahs." In *Expecting Armageddon: Essential Readings in Failed Prophecy.* Ed. Jon R. Stone. New York: Routledge, 2000.

Fish, Stanley. *Doing What Comes Naturally: Change, Rhetoric, and the Practice of Theory in Literary and Legal Studies.* Durham: Duke UP, 1992.

———. *The Trouble with Principle.* Cambridge: Harvard UP, 1999.

FitzGerald, Frances. *Way Out There in the Blue: Reagan, Star Wars, and the End of the Cold War.* New York: Simon and Schuster, 2000.

Foucault, Michel. *The Archeology of Knowledge and the Discourse on Language.* Trans. A. M. Sheridan Smith. New York: Harper and Row, 1972.

———. "Governmentality." In *The Foucault Effect: Studies in Governmentality.* Ed. Graham Burchell, Colin Gordon, and Peter Miller. London: Harvester, 1991.

———. *The Order of Things: An Archeology of the Human Sciences.* New York: Vintage, 1970.

———. *Technologies of the Self: A Seminar with Michel Foucault.* Ed. Luther H. Martin, Huck Gutman, and Patrick Hutton. Amherst: Massachusetts UP, 1988.

Franklin, H. Bruce. *MIA: Or Mythmaking in America.* New York: Lawrence Hill, 1992.

———. *Vietnam and Other American Fantasies.* Amherst: Massachusetts UP, 2000.

Franks, Thomas. *What's the Matter with Kansas? How Conservatives Won the Heart of America.* New York: Henry Holt, 2004.

Frazer, Nancy, and Nicola Lacey. *The Politics of Community: A Feminist Critique of the Liberal-Communitarian Debate.* Toronto: Toronto UP, 1993.

Freud, Sigmund. *The Ego and the Id.* Trans. Joan Riviere. Ed. James Strachey. New York: Norton, 1960.

Frijda, Nico, Antony Manstead, and Sacha Beam, eds. *Emotions and Beliefs: How Feelings Influence Thoughts.* Cambridge: Cambridge UP, 2000.

Frum, David, and Richard Perle. *An End to Evil: How to Win the War on Terror.* New York: Random House, 2004.

Frykholm, Amy. *Rapture Culture: Left Behind in Evangelical America.* New York: Oxford UP, 2004.

Fuller, Robert. *Naming the Antichrist: The History of an American Obsession.* New York: Oxford UP, 1995.

Fuss, Diana. *Identification Papers.* New York: Routledge, 1995.

Gates, David, David Jefferson, and Anne Underwood. "Prophets of Pop." *Newsweek,* May 24, 2004.

Gibson, James William. *Warrior Dreams: Violence and Manhood in Post-Vietnam America.* New York: Hill and Wang, 1994.

Girard, Rene. "Generative Scapegoating." In *Violent Origins: Walter Burkert, Rene Girard, and Jonathan Z. Smith on Ritual Killing and Cultural Formation.* Ed. Robert Hamerton-Kelly. Palo Alto: Stanford UP, 1987.

Goldberg, Robert Alan. *Enemies Within: The Culture of Conspiracy in Modern America.* New Haven: Yale UP, 2001.

Gorenberg, Gershom. *The End of Days: Fundamentalism and the Struggle for the Temple Mount.* New York: Oxford UP, 2000.

Gorgias. "Encomium of Helen." In *The Older Sophists.* Ed. Rosamond Kent Sprague. Columbia: South Carolina UP, 1972.

Gorney, Cynthia. *Articles of Faith: A Frontline History of the Abortion Wars.* New York: Simon and Schuster, 1998.

Green, John C. "Evangelical Protestants and Civic Engagement: An Overview." In *A Public Faith: Evangelicals and Public Engagement.* Ed. Michael Cromartie. Lanham, MD: Rowan and Littlefield, 2003.

Greven, Philip. *Spare the Child: The Religious Roots of Punishment and the Psychological Effects of Physical Abuse.* New York: Knopf, 1991.

Griffin, David Ray. *The New Pearl Harbor: Disturbing Questions about the Bush Administration and 9/11.* Northampton, MA: Olive Branch, 2004.

Griffith, R. Marie. *God's Daughters: Evangelical Women and the Power of Submission.* Berkeley: California UP, 1997.

Gronfers, Martti. "Could Osama bin Laden Have Been a Woman? Masculinity and 9/11." In *Beyond September 11: An Anthology of Dissent.* Ed. Phil Scraton. London: Pluto, 2002.

Grossberg, Lawrence. *We Gotta Get Out of This Place: Popular Conservatism and Postmodern Culture.* New York: Routledge, 1992.

Guttmann, Amy, and Dennis Thompson. *Democracy and Disagreement.* Cambridge: Harvard UP, 1996.

Hall, Stuart. *Stuart Hall: Critical Dialogues in Cultural Studies.* Ed. David Morley and Kuan-Hsing Chen. New York: Routledge, 1996.

Harding, Susan. *The Book of Jerry Falwell: Fundamentalist Language and Politics.* Princeton: Princeton UP, 2000.

———. "Imagining the Last Days: The Politics of Apocalyptic Language." In *Accounting for Fundamentalisms.* Ed. Martin Mary and R. Scott Appleby. Vol. 4 of The Fundamentalist Project. Chicago: Chicago UP, 1991.

Hardisty, Jean. *Mobilizing Resentment: Conservative Resurgence from the John Birch Society to the Promise Keepers.* Boston: Beacon, 1999.

Hauser, Gerald. *Introduction to Rhetorical Theory.* 2d ed. Prospect Heights, IL: Waveland Press, 2002.

Hawhee, Debra. "Kairotic Encounters." In *Perspectives on Rhetorical Invention.* Ed. Janet M. Atwill and Janice M. Lauer. Vol. 39 of Tennessee Studies in Literature. Knoxville: Tennessee UP, 2000.

Heath, Malcolm. *Hermogenes on Issues: Strategies of Argument in Later Greek Rhetoric.* Oxford: Oxford UP, 1995.

Herman, Didi. *The Antigay Agenda: Orthodox Vision and the Christian Right.* Chicago: Chicago UP, 1997.

Herrnstein Smith, Barbara. *Belief and Resistance: Dynamics of Contemporary Intellectual Controversy.* Cambridge: Harvard UP, 1997.

———. *Contingencies of Value: Alternative Perspectives for Critical Theory.* Cambridge: Harvard UP, 1988.

Hirschmann, Nancy. *Rethinking Obligation: A Feminist Method for Political Theory.* Ithaca: Cornell UP, 1992.

Hobbes, Thomas. *Leviathan.* Ed. C. B. MacPherson. New York: Penguin, 1982.

Hodgson, Godfrey. *The World Turned Right Side Up: A History of the Conservative Ascendency in America.* Boston: Houghton Mifflin, 1996.

Hoffman, Jim. "The Pentagon No-757-Crash Theory: Booby Trap for 9/11 Skeptics." http://www.911research.wtc7.net/essays/pentagontrap.html, posted November 12, 2004; accessed July 11, 2005.

Hofstadter, Richard. *The Paranoid Style in American Politics and Other Essays.* New York: Knopf, 1965.

Hood, Michael. "The Enthymeme: A Brief Bibliography of Modern Sources." *Rhetoric Society Quarterly* 14 (1984): 159–62.

Hopsicker, Daniel. *Welcome to Terrorland: Mohamed Atta and the 9-11 Cover-up in Florida.* Eugene, OR: Madcow, 2004.

Hublin, Jean-Jacques, Fred Spoor, Marc Braun, F. Zonnenveld, and Silvana Condemi. "A Late Neanderthal Associated with Upper Palaeolitic Artefacts." *Nature,* May 16, 1996, 224–26.

Hufschmid, Eric. *Painful Question: An Analysis of the September 11th Attack.* Goleta, CA: Endpoint Software, 2002.

Hunter, James Davison. *Before the Shooting Begins: Searching for Democracy in America's Culture War.* New York: Free Press, 1994.

Isocrates. "Against the Sophists." In *Isocrates.* Trans. George Norlin. Vol. 2. Cambridge: Harvard UP, 1982.

———. "Antidosis." In *Isocrates.* Trans. George Norlin. Vol. 2. Cambridge: Harvard UP, 1982.

Jacoby, Susan. *Freethinkers: A History of American Secularism.* New York: Henry Holt, 2004.

Jagger, Allison. "Love and Knowledge: Emotion in Feminist Epistemology." In *Women, Knowledge, and Reality: Explorations in Feminist Philosophy.* Ed. Ann Garry and Marilyn Pearsall. Boston: Unwin Hyman, 1989.

James, William. *Pragmatism.* Mineola, NY: Dover Books, 1995.

Jarratt, Susan. *Rereading the Sophists: Classical Rhetoric Refigured.* Carbondale: Southern Illinois UP, 1991.

Jensen, Derrick. *The Culture of Make Believe.* New York: Context, 2002.

Kappeler, Susanne. *The Pornography of Representation.* Cambridge: Polity, 1986.

Kennedy, George. *The Art of Persuasion in Greece.* Princeton: Princeton UP, 1963.

———. *The Art of Rhetoric in the Roman World.* Princeton: Princeton UP, 1972.

———. *Classical Rhetoric and Its Christian and Secular Tradition from Ancient to Modern Times.* Chapel Hill: South Carolina UP, 1980.

———. *Comparative Rhetoric: An Historical and Cross-Cultural Introduction.* New York: Oxford UP, 1998.

———. *Greek Rhetoric under Christian Emperors.* Princeton: Princeton UP, 1983.

Kimball, Charles. *When Religion Becomes Evil: Five Warning Signs.* New York: Harper Collins, 2003.

Kintz, Linda. *Between Jesus and the Market: The Emotions That Matter in Right-Wing America.* Durham: Duke UP, 1997.

———. "Clarity, Mothers, and the Mass-Mediated National Soul: A Defense of Ambiguity." In *Media, Culture and the Religious Right.* Ed. Linda Kintz and Julia Lesage. Minneapolis: Minnesota UP, 1998.

———. "Culture and the Religious Right." In *Media, Culture and the Religious Right.* Ed. Linda Kintz and Julia Lesage. Minneapolis: Minnesota UP, 1998.

Knight, Peter. *Conspiracy Culture: From Kennedy to the X-Files.* London: Routledge, 2000.

Kramnick, Isaac, and R. Laurence Moore. *The Godless Constitution: The Case against Religious Correctness*. New York: Norton, 1997.

Kristol, Irving. "The Neoconservative Persuasion: What It Was, and What It Is." *Weekly Standard*, http://www.weeklystandard.com, April 20, 2003.

Kuhn, Thomas. *The Structure of Scientific Revolutions*. 3d ed. Chicago: Chicago UP, 1996.

Kyle, Richard. *Awaiting the Millennium: A History of End-Time Thinking*. Leicester, UK: Inter-Varsity, 1998.

Lacan, Jacques. *Ecrits: A Selection*. Trans. Alan Sheridan. New York: Norton, 1977.

———. *The Psychoses 1955–1956 (Seminar of Jacques Lacan, 3)*. Trans. Jacques-Alain Miller and Russell Grigg. New York: Norton, 1997.

Laclau, Ernesto. *Emancipations*. London: Verso, 1996.

———. *New Reflections on the Revolution of Our Time*. London: Verso, 1990.

Laclau, Ernesto, and Chantal Mouffe. *Hegemony and Socialist Strategy: Towards a Radical Democratic Politics*. London: Verso, 2001.

LaHaye, Tim. *The Battle for the Mind*. Old Tappen, NJ: Ravell, 1980.

———. *The Merciful God of Prophecy: His Living Plan for You in the End Times*. New York: Warner Books, 2002.

———. *The Rapture: Who Will Face the Tribulation?* Eugene, OR: Harvest House, 2002.

———. *Revelation Unveiled*. Grand Rapids: Zondervan, 1999.

———. *The Unhappy Gays*. Wheaton, IL: Tyndale House, 1978.

LaHaye, Tim, and Jerry B. Jenkins. *Are We Living in the End Times? Current Events Foretold in Scripture . . . and What They Mean*. Wheaton, IL: Tyndale, 1999.

———. *Left Behind: A Novel of the Earth's Last Days*. Wheaton, IL: Tyndale, 1995.

LaHaye, Tim, and Beverly LaHaye. *A Nation without a Conscience*. Wheaton IL: Tyndale, 1994.

LaHaye, Tim, and David Noebel. *Mind Siege: The Battle for Truth*. Nashville: Thomas Nelson, 2000.

Lakoff, George. *Don't Think of an Elephant! Know Your Values and Frame the Debate*. White River Junction, VT: Chelsea Green, 2004.

———. *Moral Politics: What Conservatives Know That Liberals Don't*. Chicago: Chicago UP, 1996.

Land, Jeff. "Sitting in Limbaugh: Bombast in Broadcasting." In *Media, Culture, and the Religious Right*. Ed. Linda Kintz and Julia LeSage. Minneapolis: Minnesota UP, 1998.

Lazarus, Edward. *Closed Chambers: The Rise, Fall, and Future of the Modern Supreme Court*. New York: Penguin, 1999.

LeDoux, Joseph. *The Emotional Brain: The Mysterious Underpinnings of Emotional Life*. New York: Simon and Schuster, 1996.

———. *The Synaptic Self: How Our Brains Become Who We Are*. New York: Penguin, 2002.

Lee, Martin. *The Beast Reawakens*. Boston: Little, Brown, 1997.

Levitas, Daniel. *The Terrorist Next Door: The Militia Movement and the Radical Right*. New York: St. Martin's, 2002.

Liddell, H. G. *An Intermediate Greek-English Lexicon Founded upon the Seventh Edition of Liddell and Scott's Greek-English Lexicon*. Oxford: Oxford UP, 1997.

Lienesch, Michael. *Redeeming America: Piety and Politics in the New Christian Right*. Chapel Hill: North Carolina UP, 1993.

Lifton, Robert Jay. *Superpower Syndrome: America's Apocalyptic Confrontation with the World*. New York: Thunder's Mouth/Nation, 2003.

Lincoln, Abraham. "Speech at Cooper's Union." In *The Collected Works of Abraham Lincoln*. Ed. Roy Basler. Vol. 5. New Brunswick: Rutgers UP, 1953.

Lincoln, Bruce. *Holy Terrors: Thinking about Religion after September 11*. Chicago: Chicago UP, 2003.

Lind, Michael. *Up from Conservatism: Why the Right Is Wrong for America*. New York: Simon and Schuster, 1996.

Liu, Yameng. "Invention and Inventiveness: A Postmodern Redaction." In *Perspectives on Rhetorical Invention*. Ed. Janet M. Atwill and Janice M. Lauer. Vol. 39 of Tennessee Studies in Literature. Knoxville: Tennessee UP, 2002.

Locke, John. *An Essay Concerning Human Understanding*. New York: Oxford UP, 1979.

Lyotard, Jean-Francois. *The Differend: Phrases in Dispute*. Trans. Georges van den Abbeele. Minneapolis: Minnesota UP, 1988.

Lyotard, Jean-Francois, and Jean-Loup Thebaud. *Just Gaming*. Trans. Wlad Godzich. Minneapolis: Minnesota UP, 1999.

Marcus, George, W. Russell Neuman, and Michael MacKuen. *Affective Intelligence and Political Judgment*. Chicago: Chicago UP, 2000.

Margolis, Howard. *Patterns, Thinking and Cognition: A Theory of Judgment*. Chicago: Chicago UP, 1987.

Marrou, Henri. *A History of Education in Antiquity*. Trans. George Lamb. New York: Sheed and Ward, 1956.

Marsden, George. *Fundamentalism and American Culture: The Shaping of Twentieth-Century Evangelicalism 1879-1925*. New York: Oxford UP, 1980.

———. *Understanding Fundamentalism and Evangelicalism*. Grand Rapids: Eerdmans, 1991.

Martin, William. *With God on Our Side: The Rise of the Religious Right in America*. New York: Broadway, 1996.

Mason, Carol. *Killing for Life: The Apocalyptic Narrative of Pro-Life Politics*. Ithaca: Cornell UP, 2002.

Massumi, Brian. *Parables for the Virtual: Movement, Affect, Sensation*. Durham: Duke UP, 2002.

McKerrow, Ray. "Marxism and a Rhetorical Conception of Ideology." *Quarterly Journal of Speech* 69 (1983): 192–205.

Melich, Tanya. *The Republican War against Women: An Insider's Report from behind the Lines*. Rev. ed. New York: Bantam, 1998.

Melley, Timothy. *Empire of Conspiracy: The Culture of Paranoia in Postwar America*. Ithaca: Cornell UP, 2000.

Meyssan, Thierry. *9/11: The Big Lie.* London: Carnot, 2002.

———. *Pentagate.* London: Carnot, 2002.

Milburn, Michael, and Shere Conrad. *The Politics of Denial.* Cambridge: MIT UP, 1996.

Miller, John, Michael Stone, and Chris Mitchell. *The Cell: Inside the 9/11 Plot, and Why the FBI and CIA Failed to Stop It.* New York: Hyperion, 2002.

Minnich, Elizabeth. *Transforming Knowledge.* Philadelphia: Temple UP, 1990.

Mithen, Steven. *The Prehistory of the Mind: The Cognitive Origins of Art, Religion, and Science.* London: Thames and Hudson, 1996.

Moffett, James. *Storm in the Mountains: A Case Study of Censorship, Conflict, and Consciousness.* Carbondale: Southern Illinois UP, 1988.

Mojtabai, A. G. *Blessed Assurance: At Home with the Bomb in Amarillo, Texas.* New York: Houghton Mifflin, 1986.

Morgan, Robin. "The Women's Revolution." Introduction to *Sisterhood Is Powerful: An Anthology of Writings from the Women's Liberation Movement.* Ed. Robin Morgan. New York: Vintage, 1970.

Morison, Samuel Eliot, ed. *Three Centuries of Harvard College: 1636–1936.* Cambridge: Harvard UP, 1936.

Morone, James A. *Hellfire Nation: The Politics of Sin in American History.* New Haven: Yale UP, 2003.

Mouffe, Chantal. *The Democratic Paradox.* London: Verso, 2000.

———. *The Return of the Political.* London: Verso, 1993.

Nadeau, Ray. "Classical Systems of Stases in Greek: Hermagoras to Hermogenes." *Greek, Roman and Byzantine Studies* 2 (1959): 53–71.

Nash, George. *The Conservative Intellectual Movement in America since 1945.* New York: Basic Books, 1976.

The National Commission on Terrorist Attacks upon the United States. *The 9/11 Commission Report.* New York: Norton, 2004.

Neel, Jasper. *Aristotle's Voice: Rhetoric, Theory, and Writing in America.* Carbondale: Southern Illinois UP, 1994.

Nietzsche, Friedrich. *The Genealogy of Morals.* Trans. Francis Golffing. New York: Anchor, 1956.

Noll, Mark. *The Scandal of the Evangelical Mind.* Grand Rapids: Eerdmans, 1994.

Oldfield, Duane. *The Right and the Righteous: The Christian Right Confronts the Republican Party.* Lanham, MD: Rowman and Littlefield, 1996.

O'Leary, Cecilia. *To Die For: The Paradox of American Patriotism.* Princeton: Princeton UP, 1999.

O'Leary, Cecilia, and Tony Platt. "Pledging Allegiance: The Revival of Prescriptive Patriotism." In *Beyond September 11: An Anthology of Dissent.* Ed. Phil Scraton. London: Pluto, 2002.

O'Leary, Stephen. *Arguing the Apocalypse: A Theory of Millennial Rhetoric.* New York: Oxford UP, 1994.

Olson, Gary. *Justifying Belief: Stanley Fish and the Work of Rhetoric.* Albany: SUNY UP, 2002.

Pateman, Carol. *The Sexual Contract.* Palo Alto: Stanford UP, 1988.

Peters, F. E. *Greek Philosophical Terms: A Historical Lexicon.* New York: New York UP, 1967.

Phillips, Kevin. *American Dynasty: Aristocracy, Fortune, and the Politics of Deceit in the House of Bush.* New York: Viking, 2004.

Philostratus. *Lives of the Professors.* Trans. Wilmer C. Wright. Cambridge: Harvard UP, 1921.

Pipes, Daniel. *Conspiracy: How the Paranoid Style Flourishes and Where It Comes From.* New York: Free Press, 1997.

Pippin, Tina. *Death and Desire: The Rhetoric of Gender in the Apocalypse of John.* Louisville: John Knox, 1992.

Plato. "Phaedrus." In *Plato: The Collected Dialogues.* Ed. Edith Hamilton and Huntington Cairns. Princeton: Princeton UP, 1961.

Popkin, Richard, and Avrum Stroll. *Skeptical Philosophy for Everyone.* Amherst: Prometheus, 2002.

Poster, Carol. "A Historicist Reconceptualization of the Enthymeme." *Rhetoric Society Quarterly* 22 (1992): 1–24.

Poulakos, John. "Interpreting Sophistical Rhetoric: A Response to Schiappa." *Philosophy and Rhetoric* 23 (1990): 218–28.

Poulakos, John, and Takis Poulakos. *Classical Rhetorical Theory.* Boston: Houghton-Mifflin, 1999.

Quinby, Lee. *Anti-Apocalypse: Exercises in Genealogical Criticism.* Minneapolis: Minnesota UP, 1994.

———. *Millennial Seduction: A Skeptic Confronts Apocalyptic Culture.* Ithaca: Cornell UP, 1999.

Quintilian, Marcus Fabrius. *The Institutes of Oratory.* Trans. H. E. Butler. 4 vols. Cambridge: Harvard UP, 1958.

Reiter, Jerry. *Live from the Gates of Hell: An Insider's Look at the Anti-Abortion Movement.* Amherst, NY: Prometheus Books, 2000.

Rhetorica ad Herrennium. Trans. Harry Caplan. Cambridge: Harvard UP, 1954.

Richards, I. A. *The Philosophy of Rhetoric.* Oxford: Oxford UP, 1936.

———. *Practical Criticism.* Somerset, NJ: Transaction, 2004.

Robbins, James. "9–11 Denial." *National Review Online,* http://www.nationalreview.com/robbins/robbins040902.asp, April 9, 2002.

Robertson, Pat. *The New World Order.* Nashville: Thomas Nelson, 1992.

Robins, Robert, and Jerrold Post. *Political Paranoia: The Psychopolitics of Hatred.* New Haven: Yale UP, 1997.

Rooney, Ellen. *Seductive Reasoning: Pluralism as the Problematic of Contemporary Literary Theory.* Ithaca: Cornell UP, 1989.

Rose, Jacqueline. *States of Fantasy.* New York: Oxford UP, 1996.

———. *Why War? Psychoanalysis, Politics, and the Return to Melanie Klein.* London: Blackwell, 1993.

Rossiter, Clinton, ed. *The Federalist Papers.* New York: Penguin, 1961.

Ruppert, Mark. *Crossing the Rubicon: The Decline of the American Empire at the End of the Age of Oil*. Gabriola Island, Canada: New Society, 2004.

Rushdoony, Rousas John. *The Institutes of Biblical Law*. Nutley, NJ: Craig Press, 1973.

Russell, Jerry. "Explosive Demolition? A Response to Bazant and Zhou." http://www.911-strike.com/demolition-pro-con.htm, posted March 28, 2002; last updated February 14, 2003; accessed July 15, 2005.

Sanchez, Raul. *The Function of Theory in Composition Studies*. Albany: SUNY UP, 2005.

Scarry, Elaine. *The Body in Pain: The Making and Unmaking of the World*. Oxford: Oxford UP, 1985.

Schaeffer, Francis. *How Should We Then Live? The Rise and Decline of Western Thought and Culture*. Westchester, IL: Crossway Books, 1976.

Schiappa, Edward. "Did Plato Coin 'Rhetorike'?" *American Journal of Philology* 111 (1990): 457–70.

———. "Neo-Sophistic Rhetorical Criticism or the Historical Reconstruction of Sophistic Doctrines?" *Philosophy and Rhetoric* 23 (1990): 192–217.

Schlafly, Phyllis. *The Power of the Christian Woman*. Cincinnati: Standard, 1981.

Sedgwick, Eve. *Touching Feeling: Affect, Pedagogy, Performativity*. Durham: Duke UP, 2003.

Sextus Empiricus. *Against the Schoolmasters*. Trans. R. G. Bury. Cambridge: Harvard UP, 1949.

Shakespeare, William. "Julius Caesar." In *The Complete Pelican Shakespeare*. 2d ed. Ed. Stephen Orgel. New York: Penguin, 2002.

Shermer, Michael. *Why People Believe Weird Things: Pseudoscience, Superstitions, and Other Confusions of Our Time*. Rev. ed. New York: Henry Holt, 2002.

Silverman, Herb. "Inerrancy Turned Political." In *The Fundamentals of Extremism: The Christian Right in America*. Ed. Kimberly Blaker. New Boston, MI: New Boston, 2003.

Slotkin, Richard. *The Fatal Environment: The Myth of the Frontier in the Age of Industrialization, 1800–1890*. New York: Atheneum, 1985.

———. *Gunfighter Nation: The Myth of the Frontier in Twentieth-Century America*. New York: Atheneum, 1992.

Smith, Anna Marie. *New Right Discourse on Race and Sexuality: Britain 1968–1990*. Cambridge: Cambridge UP, 1990.

Smith, Christian. *American Evangelicalism: Embattled and Thriving*. Chicago: Chicago UP, 1998.

———. *Christian America? What Evangelicals Really Want*. Berkeley: California UP, 2002.

Solomon, Robert, and Kathleen Higgins. *What Nietzsche Really Said*. New York: Schocken, 2000.

Spivak, Gayatri Chakravorty. *Outside in the Teaching Machine*. New York: Routledge, 1993.

Stewart, Charles J. "The Master Conspiracy of the John Birch Society: From Communism to the New World Order." *Western Journal of Communication* 66 (2002): 424–77.

Strozier, Charles. *Apocalypse: On the Psychology of Fundamentalism in America.* Boston: Beacon, 1994.

Tacitus, Cornelius. *The Annals of Imperial Rome.* Trans. Michael Grant. New York: Barnes and Noble, 1971.

Takaki, Ronald. *A Different Mirror: A History of Multicultural America.* Boston: Little, Brown, 1993.

Terada, Rei. *Feeling in Theory: Emotion after the Death of the Subject.* Cambridge: Harvard UP, 2001.

Therborn, Geron. *The Ideology of Power and the Power of Ideology.* London: Verso, 1980.

Thompson, Damian. *The End of Time: Faith and Fear in the Shadow of the Millennium.* London: Sinclair-Stevenson, 1996.

Thompson, Paul. *The Terror Timeline.* New York: Harper Collins, 2004.

Torfing, Jacob. *New Theories of Discourse: Laclau, Mouffe, and Zizek.* London: Blackwell, 1999.

Unger, Craig. *House of Bush, House of Saud: The Secret Relationship between the World's Two Most Powerful Dynasties.* New York: Scribner, 2004.

Untersteiner, Mario. *The Sophists.* Trans. Kathleen Freeman. New York: Philosophical Library, 1954.

Vickers, Brian. *In Defence of Rhetoric.* Oxford: Oxford UP, 1988.

Walker, Alice, and Pratibha Parmar. *Warrior Marks: Female Genital Mutilation and the Sexual Blinding of Women.* San Diego: Harcourt Brace, 1993.

Walsh, Jim. "Killer of Sikh Sentenced to Death." *Arizona Republic,* http://www.azcentral.com, October 10, 2003.

Walvoord, John. *Armageddon, Oil, and the Middle East Crisis.* Grand Rapids: Zondervan, 1990.

Warner, Michael. *Publics and Counterpublics.* New York: Zone, 2002.

———. "Tongues United: Memoirs of a Pentecostal Boyhood." In *The Material Queer: A LesBiGay Cultural Studies Reader.* Ed. Donald Morton. Boulder: Westview, 1996.

Warren, Howard. *A History of the Association Psychology.* New York: Scribners, 1921.

Watson, Justin. *The Christian Coalition: Dreams of Restoration, Demands for Recognition.* New York: St. Martin's, 1997.

Waxman, Henry. "The Content of Federally-Funded Abstinence-Only Education Programs" (The Waxman Report). http://www.democrats.reform.house.gov, December 2004.

Weaver, Richard. *Ideas Have Consequences.* Chicago: Chicago UP, 1948.

Weber, Samuel. *Institutions and Interpretation.* Minneapolis: Minnesota UP, 1987.

Weber, Timothy. *Living in the Shadow of the Second Coming: American Premillennialism 1875–1925.* New York: Oxford UP, 1979.

Whately, Richard. *The Elements of Rhetoric.* Ed. Douglas Ehninger. Carbondale: Southern Illinois UP, 1963.

Whyte, Dave. "Business as Usual? Corporate Moralism and the 'War Against Terrorism.'" In *Beyond September 11: An Anthology of Dissent*. Ed. Phil Scraton. London: Pluto, 2002.

Wilcox, Clyde. *God's Warriors: The Christian Right in Twentieth-Century America*. Baltimore: Johns Hopkins UP, 1992.

———. *Onward Christian Soldiers: The Religious Right in American Politics*. 2d ed. Boulder: Westview, 2000.

Williams, Patricia J. *The Alchemy of Race and Rights*. Cambridge: Harvard UP, 1991.

Williams, Raymond. *Keywords: A Vocabulary of Culture and Society*. Rev. ed. London: Oxford UP, 1983.

Wills, Garry. *Reagan's America: Innocents at Home*. New York: Penguin, 2000.

Wojcik, Daniel. *The End of the World as We Know It: Faith, Fatalism, and Apocalyptism in America*. New York: New York UP, 1997.

World Trade Center Building Performance Study. FEMA Report #403. http://www.fema.gov/library/wtcstudy.shtm.

Worsham, Lynn. "Emotion and Pedagogic Violence." *Discourse* 15.2 (1992–93): 119–48.

Wray, Matt. "White Trash Religion." In *White Trash: Race and Class in America*. Ed. Matt Wray and Annalee Newitz. New York: Routledge, 1997.

Wray, Matt, and Annalee Newitz, eds. *White Trash: Race and Class in America*. New York: Routledge, 1997.

Wright, Robert. *The Moral Animal: Why We Are the Way We Are: The New Science of Evolutionary Psychology*. New York: Vintage, 1994.

Zinn, Howard. *Declarations of Independence: Cross-Examining American Ideology*. New York: Harper Collins, 1990.

Zizek, Slavoj. *The Plague of Fantasies*. London: Verso, 1997.

———. *The Sublime Object of Ideology*. London: Verso, 1989.

INDEX

abortion, 28–29, 33–34, 94–95, 148, 158, 168
Act of Marriage, The (LaHaye and
    LaHaye), 148
Adams, John, 153
Adams, Samuel, 153
Aderholt, Robert, 158
affect, definition of, 82
African American Christian fundamen-
    talists, 214n3
agency panic, 174–75
Ahmed, Nafeez Mosaddeq, 179–80
alien abductions, 168–69
Althusser, Louis, 45
ambiguity, fear of, 147, 149
American Coalition for Traditional
    Values, 116
American Family Association, 135
Ammerman, Nancy, 8–9, 103
ancient rhetorical theory: adaptation of,
    46–47, 207n9; and man-measure doc-
    trine, 48; postmodernism and, 45–46;
    shortcomings of, 46; subject in, 50–51
anger, definition of, 86
antagonism, as essential to politics, 19–22
Antichrist, 126–28, 173
antifoundationalism, 13
anti-Semitism, 173–74
apocalypticism, 102–32; abortion and, 158;
    adaptability of, 107; appeal of, 126–30;
    approaches to, ix–x; articulation of, 61;

believers in, 103–5; in Bush administration, 142, 143, 158–59; communal aspect
of, 128–29; conspiracy theory vs.,
172–73; contingency of, 165; definition
of, 7, 204n6; democracy threatened by,
115, 131–32, 164; dispensationalism in, 61,
108–11, 114, 120, 131, 204nn5–6; disregard
for secular in, 110–11; ethics of, 130 32,
212–13n17; exclusionist character of, 131;
as fantasy, 128–29; fundamentalism
and, 204n5; historical interpretation in,
114–15, 118–20, 159–60; historical perspective on, 106–7; ideological function
of, 9; influence of, 104; international
politics and, 124–28; isolationism in,
194; liberalism vs., 10, 163; as myth,
127–28, persecution complex in, 129;
political views associated with, 7–10,
106, 111, 114–15, 125–28, 131–33; in popular culture, 126–27; principles of, 106;
in Reagan administration, 140; revenge
and, 129–30; September 11, 2001, and,
143, 158–59; vs. skepticism, 166–67, 169;
time in, 108–11, 114, 120; unbelievers as
viewed in, 115–16, 119, 129–32; violent
implications of, 105. *See also* prophecy
interpretation
Arblaster, Anthony, 5, 36, 90
Are We Living in the End Times? (LaHaye
    and Jenkins), 109